LOST BETWEEN THE STONES AND THE SEA

A JOURNEY OF DISCOVERY IN IRELAND

CHRIS BRAUER

DANDELION WINE PUBLISHING

ISBN 978-1-7773497-4-5

Cover photo by Jan Miko

An té a bhíonn siúlach, bíonn scéalach.

He who travels has stories to tell.

*As a language, Irish (*Gaeilge*) is unique to Ireland and is, therefore, of crucial importance to the identity of her people, her culture and to world heritage. Spoken for over two thousand years, Irish is one of the oldest living languages in Europe. Its history includes a protracted campaign of repression starting with the twelfth-century Anglo-Norman invasion. Therefore, I have included the original Irish (or Irish spelling) as often as possible. This may make the reading of* Lost Between the Stones and the Sea *a tad jarring at times – but I think it's a fair trade.* Sláinte*!*

CONTENTS

1. A Good Gentle Fella 1
2. A Savage Beauty 12
3. A Binding Agreement 23
4. A Thin Place 29
5. An Awkward Start 45
6. A Hint of Sweetness in the Air 50
7. A Glorious Crescendo 64
8. A Sublime Enigma 74
9. An Inexplicable Pull 81
10. A Thousand Sunrises and a Thousand Sunsets 89
11. A Pint or Two 102
12. A Good Day for the Mountain 114
13. A Cup of Tea 128
14. An Archeological Treasure Trove 136
15. A Pure Part of the Abyss 156
16. A Grand Day Out 171
17. A Curious Sight Indeed 184
18. A Stillness Here 193
19. A Wonderful Place to be an Introvert 205
20. An Adventurer's Best Choice 217
21. A Mangy Boulder 230
22. A Pleasant Hour on the Water 245
23. A Strong and Vibrant Culture 252
24. A Brutal, Bleak Existence 265
25. A Crucial Ingredient to Creativity 278
26. A Place of Otherness 287

Afterword 303
About the Author 307

CHAPTER 1

A GOOD GENTLE FELLA

"Have you been on a horse before?" the lady on the phone asked. Her West Kerry brogue was soft and musical, and I had to strain to understand. She slurred her vowels and it took a moment for my brain to catch up.

"Yes, I have," I answered. "A few times. But the last one didn't go so well."

There was no response.

"Almost ended up over a fence and into the dirt," I continued. "So I wouldn't call myself a seasoned rider."

There was the faint sound of a pencil scraping across the page. "I shall put you down as beginner then," she finally replied. "Got a horse that would be just grand for you this afternoon, about half-three or so. He's a good, gentle fella. Getting on in years, y'know, but friendly and doesn't rear. Use him for me first-timers. Think he'd be perfect for you."

"That sounds great," I said. "Looking forward to it."

I had requested an hour's ride but thought it best to

make the most of the opportunity. "Will an hour be enough?" I asked. "Can I book in for a longer ride?"

"An hour will be enough, especially if you haven't ridden in a while. Two or three hours may seem like a good idea now, but it can seem like a *very* long time indeed if you start to get sore. This way you'll be able to walk tomorrow."

"Right," I agreed. "An hour it is."

"Do you need directions? Do you know where we're at?"

The brochure had faded from too much sun through the windows of the breakfast room, but the simple map on the back was still legible. "Looks like you're just past the roundabout on the west side of town. At the Ventry Estate?"

"That's right, enough. Look for the sign, drive down a small bit and you'll see the stables. You won't miss it, at all."

I thanked her and handed the phone to Pat Neligan who, with his wife Anne, run Dúinín House, a charming B&B up the hill from the town centre of Dingle.

"So you're to be on a horse this afternoon, then? Ah, that's wonderful. It'll be grand, altogether."

"I'm sure it will."

Pat was the reason I had chosen to stay at Dúinín House. On his website, he described himself as a retired teacher, historian, and speaker of the Irish language. If anyone could direct me to the lesser-known archeological sites hidden away in farmers' fields or along the coastline of western Ireland, it would be this man.

I had been on the peninsula for a few days before spying the plastic stand by the window and the brochure for horse riding. Pat said he didn't know much about it but added, "The Ventry Estate – where the stables are located – is certainly worth a look."

He headed into the kitchen for the phone, and I agreed

to an hour's ride. Then stared down at my breakfast, picking away at the black pudding.

Pat couldn't help himself and laughed as he placed his hand on my shoulder. We had only met less than a week ago, but he took delight in hearing my stories every morning. Stories that involved me getting lost while driving along narrow country roads or walking in thick fog; climbing Mount Brandon with only bread, cheese and water and then fleeing down when a storm threatened to blow me off the summit. Several stories of random encounters with local livestock. Along the Saints' Path, there was little else but deep mud and sheep poop. And then I got lost in Ventry, only to be chased away by wild ponies. Now I wondered what awkward situations might arise on the back of a horse.

"Can't wait to hear how the day unfolds," he said. The sun caught his wispy white hair, combed down on either side of his balding head, as he looked out the window and then back at me. He grinned. His dark eyes, beaked nose and thin smile makes him look as if he is perpetually up to something. "I'm sure it'll all work out, so. Anyway, I'll leave you to finish your breakfast."

"Thank you."

A traditional Irish breakfast (totalling twelve-hundred calories) was meant for a full day's heavy work on the farm. While this is necessary for those tilling the fields or tending to sheep, it seems like a lot for today's health conscious and often sedentary culture. But that didn't stop me from eating like a king every morning.

After a bowl of yogurt and a glass of orange juice – neither of which is traditional – there was a basket of baked goods, a large pot of strong tea, and a huge plate that included rashers, sausages, black pudding, white pudding, eggs, and fried tomatoes. (This was actually a lighter version, without the fried bread or mushrooms.)

As I was thinking about punching another hole in my belt, Anne wished me good morning. She's a little shorter than Pat and is in good shape for a woman in her sixties. A ruddy complexion, golden blonde hair that swoops across her forehead. Dressed in her exercise clothes. "On me way to do the Pilates," she said.

"Ah... that's good," I replied.

I was continually surprised about what had penetrated rural Irish culture and what had yet to take root. There wasn't a decent cappuccino to be had, but Anne was off to her Pilates class. "Twice a week," she said. "It's grand."

The town of Dingle revealed itself through the large windows of the breakfast room as the sun broke through the fog and I finished the last of my tea. There is a softness to mornings on the west coast – as if, one by one, thin layers of blankets and bed sheets are cast off to reveal hills and homes and winding streets. I was content to watch the long grasses dance in the wind and listen to newborn lambs bleat from the adjacent property but, with layers of wool at the ready, it was time to get on with my day. Wanted to find a couple beaches and some early Christian settlements before my horse ride.

As the debate raged on about which sweater to wear on this crisp Atlantic morning, I wondered why I was paying to ride a horse. It seemed like a touristy thing to do, and horses are not something I naturally gravitate towards. Perfectly content to drive into nearby villages or poke around little shops before a cup of tea and a couple scones with homemade jam, but part of the reason I was in Ireland was to try new things and push myself outside my comfort zone. Horse riding (even for an hour) sure fell into that category.

DINGLE LIES within the *Gaeltacht* (where the government recognizes the traditional language as the predominant vernacular), so the street signs are all in Irish and I had to sound them out with great rapidity while driving around the traffic circle. Following signs to *Ceann Trá* (Ventry), over the short stone bridge, past the Dingle Distillery, up the hill, past the gas station and the graveyard where modern stone slabs and Celtic crosses stand side-by-side, the R559 is framed in by rough bush, occasionally broken up by low stone garden fences, driveways and unnamed lesser roads.

Most properties feature modern houses – some of which are advertised as B&Bs – but the old stone buildings (often capped with red tin roofs) are still in use, either for storage or merely as a reminder of the past. Though rough bush and thick tangled trees frame the properties, the lawns are manicured and the houses are kept in beautiful condition.

Further out of town, the bushes and hedges are replaced by overgrown trees that hang over and shade the road. The skeletal shadows become thicker and thicker until the dense woods of Burnham (*An Bóthar Buí*) blocks out most of the sun. Driving past ivy-covered tree trunks, I realized the route on the brochure gave little indication as to where the riding centre might be.

Where the light no longer penetrates the thick forest and the tops of the trees bend over the road, a small white sign, half covered in greenery, points the way to Coláiste Íde Stables. There are no signs for the Burham Riding Centre, and I had no idea if the stables and the riding centre were one and the same. Nevertheless, along the narrow country lane, past a collection of stone cottages, I followed signs into the Ventry Estate.

The lane eventually becomes a driveway, and I made my way through a couple open gates to a small parking lot. Stopped the car and looked around. Old dry-stone walls and a couple smaller gates break up the thick greenery, but I still couldn't see any signs for the riding centre.

Silence enveloped the thick woodland and three-hundred-year-old masonry. There were no signs of life save for myself. It was as if I had left the modern world behind – all the sights and sounds of people moving from one place to another without direction – and had arrived in a place weighed heavy by memory. It was a realm occupied solely by the spirits – centuries of soft cries, muffled laughter, stolen kisses and prayers in the night.

Though I had spent time alone, wandering along the ocean's edge towards unknown destinations or sitting among ancient stonework where rituals and burials were performed, I was still unaccustomed to the absence of noise. It felt uneasy, as if I had made a wrong turn somewhere in a complex labyrinth and wasn't sure how to continue – wasn't sure if I should be weaving myself further into the maze or try to work my way home.

Took a deep breath, closed my eyes, calmed myself down, found comfort in the silence, and walked the perimeter of the parking lot. 'I am not here to be comfortable,' I reminded myself. 'I am here for something else entirely.'

In the distance, high above me, a single bird called out. It was difficult to determine from which direction it came. Retraced my steps, wondering if perhaps this was a sign from the spirit realm. Would this winged creature help guide me out of the darkness and into the light? Would it show me how to be present in the moment, so that I may learn to live in harmony? Was this my moment of enlightenment?

And then, through the greenery, I spied stone steps that lead to a tall building.

The faint sound of wind blowing through the tops of trees made me pause as I circled through the undergrowth. There were only five minutes remaining before my ride was to begin and all my senses were heightened. Cautiously, I made my way up each step – stopping ever so often to listen for any hint of movement.

Weaving through all sorts of sharp branches and thorny thicket, hoping not to draw attention to myself, I came across a low window. Inside were stern-looking men and women in formal dress peering at computers or madly scribbling away on notepads. Some sort of official insignia hung on the wall. Slinking past, I could hear the beating of my heart above the muted wind. Another window, and one man looking outside as he rubbed his neatly trimmed beard. He must have been deep in thought, and didn't see me as I willed myself invisible.

Then a loud ringing jolted me out of my skin. It echoed across the land and my brain hurt. It was somehow familiar and yet terribly jarring. It was a school bell. Coláiste Íde, I later discovered, is an all-girls' Irish-speaking boarding school.

Classroom doors flew open and a flood of teenage girls in mauve-coloured uniforms thundered down the hallways. Sneaking about in the bushes and peering into windows suddenly took on a different tone. Explaining myself to a gaggle of girls and their headmaster – or possibly the local *gardaí* – was not something I felt a burning desire to experience while exploring this fine country. Springing out of the undergrowth as quickly and quietly as could be, I bolted down the stone steps and back to the parking lot. The mystical bird was nowhere to be found. She was probably far away. Laughing at me.

Soon after, a car pulled in next to mine. A woman in riding breeches stepped out.

"Excuse me," I said, trying to sound calm.

"Ah... yeah?" She rushed around, piling all sorts of things into her arms.

"I'm looking for the Burnham Riding Centre. I'm supposed to meet someone at 3:30pm."

"Well, that would be me. But I'm running a bit behind."

"Anything I can do to help?"

"School just let out," she replied in way of an answer. "Just getting everything together. One of me students is on her way."

Ireland beyond the big cities is a place where not much seems to move with any sense of urgency, but this woman was frantically pulling all sorts of ropes and leather bits and horse-riding attire out of the car and piling them into her arms. She muttered something under her breath, kicked the door closed, and marched towards the white gates stained by rain and moss. Following behind, I finally spied the sign for the Burnham Riding Centre.

The original stonework is blackened by years of wet. The roof is covered by moss, but the paving stones are kept clean. The stables are tidy and organized.

As the horses were being prepped, I noticed that they were not the majestic mighty animals that I was used to back home, but more pony sized. And I had no trouble picking out which one was mine. It was elderly and half-blind. Wouldn't be able to go beyond a slow trot if its life depended on it. Still, I approached cautiously. “Anything you need me to do?” I asked.

“You need to grab a helmet in the tack room, just there,” the woman said and pointed me towards a dark room full of cobwebs.

The thick cracked windows allowed a minimal amount of light to illuminate the whitewashed room. Ivy and years of outdoor grime blocked out most of the sun and, with my arms ahead of me, I knocked down the cobwebs. Towards the back is a collection of guest helmets. Tried on half a dozen but they all wobbled on my head. After tucking the least wobbly option under my arm, I walked back outside and signed the bottom of the waiver left on an old wooden chair outside the tack room. The woman was strapping on the halters and leads, and checking the animals’ feet before a quick brush-down.

Then she turned to me. “This will be your horse,” she said. “His name is Jack. He’s an Irish cob.” She turned back to the majestic animal and gave it a scratch on the side of his face. “Good fella, ain’t ya?” Half-expected the horse to answer back.

His feathered white hocks were stained, his chestnut neck showed patches of grey, and his beard was yellowed as if he had been smoking a pipe for many years. His eyes were still alert, and I gently scratched his face before slipping my left foot into the stirrup. While short in stature, Jack was a wider breed of horse, and I gave myself a significant heave up and over to compensate. Almost ended up on the other side and onto the cold hard ground, but quickly rebalanced myself and was ready to go.

“How’s it going over there?”

“Yeah, fine. All good,” I answered.

The smell of the old horse, oiled leather, and the freshness that permeates Ireland filled my nose. Jack shifted underneath me and the saddle creaked and groaned.

There was some commotion behind me, and I twisted in my saddle. A teenage girl was quickly getting suited up after flinging her heavy backpack on the old wooden chair.

"My name's Deirdre," said the woman who finally seemed to relax. "And that's Saoirse. She goes to the school just there."

"I'm Chris," I said. "From Canada."

"Ah, good. Canada. Lovely country, I hear. Never been, meself. Are you ready to get on the trail, then?"

"I think I am, yeah."

"Comfy?"

"Comfy enough."

"We'll just give Saoirse a minute or two, and then we'll be off."

I nodded in response, feeling Jack breathe underneath me. Settled into the saddle, found my feet were not far from the ground, and didn't feel as nervous as I had been throughout the day.

"Jack doesn't like being at the front – he doesn't like to lead for some reason – and he doesn't like to be at the back either so you'll be in the middle, if you don't mind."

"Sounds good," I said.

The trail through Burnham Woods is wide and sunlight poured in between the trees. Sheltered from the wind, Jack seemed content to do what he had been doing most of his life. At a slow, safe pace I watched the world go by and took deep meditative breaths – sometimes focusing on the golden beams that wash the world in an amber glow, and other times on the shadows where the wild things are.

"They say that these woods and the nearby lagoon are quite unique," said Deirdre when a few clouds blew in and muted the sunlight. “There’s a lot of unusual, exotic species from all over the world here.”

“How did that come to be?” I asked.

“Not sure, really. Something to do with a management scheme to reclaim the area.”

I was expecting Deirdre to comment further, but for the next twenty minutes the only sounds were of horses and the gentle wind. Only a series of small gates interrupted the rhythm of our ride.

Though my head still knocked inside my loose-fitting helmet, and I still felt like an oversized man on a small elderly horse, Jack’s gentle rhythm lulled me into quiet contemplation.

CHAPTER 2

A SAVAGE BEAUTY

A few months earlier, I had been standing at my living room window in small-town southeastern British Columbia and warming myself up with a thimble of whiskey after walking alone through the nearby wetlands. It had snowed recently and, though the highways were clear, the country roads were still slushy and miserable. It would be another couple months before it was safe to run. Rather than opt for a sterile half-hour on a treadmill at the local gym, I laced up my hiking boots and explored a seldom used path that follows the underground gas line.

After edging my car off the road, there was nothing but the silent grip of winter. The snow weighed heavy on the branches and the muted sun behind heavy clouds robbed the world of contrast.

Mine was the only car and I searched for any movement from curious woodland animals. There was nothing scurrying in the underbrush or birds perched on high branches, but the silence wasn't uncomfortable or frightening. In the absence that allows the mind to wander, I continued my private adventure and escaped momentarily from the artificial world of concrete and steel.

Snow crunched underfoot. I stopped briefly where I had once spied an ermine that playfully poked his head from various holes in a fallen log, but there was no sign of him. Further on, where tall birch and poplar trees replace open fields, is a worn wooden bench and I brushed the snow off before sitting down. I had walked the trail a dozen times over the past couple years, but only at that moment did it occur to me what I had been searching for. It was a sacred space – a private sanctuary for creative incubation – but most of all I was hoping to find a place where I belonged. Where I could feel connected. A part of a whole.

It was something I had battled with before. At the age of twelve, I spent lunch hours walking the perimeter of the schoolyard alone – preferring to observe my classmates from a distance rather than engage in meaningless play. My teacher introduced me to the short stories of Ray Bradbury and I sat in quiet corners while journeying to the era of dinosaurs and 1920s Illinois. Desolate lighthouses, African veldts, and Martian landscapes.

It was the same in junior high. But loneliness isn't much fun and, by the following year, I made several attempts to fit in somewhere. Aware of my antisocial tendencies, my parents encouraged me to find my people. So I hung out with head-bangers who wore Metallica t-shirts, but the music wasn't to my taste. Hung out with nerds but couldn't fathom spending my nights playing Dungeons & Dragons. The preppies were nauseating, the drama students were far too extroverted, the jocks walked around like orangutans, and the skaters were emotionally distant.

I was desperate to get my driver's license during my

final year of high school so I could escape the drudgery of the suburbs and head downtown to peruse bookstores and eat hot dogs from street vendors, or disappear for an hour into the nearby park and ramble up woodland trails. My classmates would return with paper bags full of squished burgers from fast-food outlets and I would return with dirty feet from hiking alone in sandals. My mother tried to convince me that university would be different.

It was. For a while. Discussing the poetry of Leonard Cohen, attending Tibetan film festivals, and joining the fencing club helped, but eventually I became bored and restless. My marks slipped year by year. Weekends were spent strapping on a pack and hitchhiking the Gulf Islands to escape the tedium of research papers and exams. My antisocial tendencies were soon replaced by misanthropic tendencies, and I considered quitting school to pursue the vagabond life. These romantic notions were squelched, however, after several nights in open fields – waking up cold and wet.

As a young teacher, there was little time to worry about not fitting in with my colleagues. This suited me just fine. I had no interest in spending time with those that took themselves too seriously, or were soured by negativity, or were more interested in discussing the latest episode of some inane American teenage drama than debating the tough questions around educational reform (as my father often did around the dinner table).

Wasn't sure why I felt this way. Social anxiety had nothing to do with it. Nor did a fear of what others might think of me. It wasn't an issue of owning my uniqueness. Most days, I was perfectly content with who I was and what I was accomplishing in life. Content to remain an observer – wandering alone with a small journal and pen, and jotting down bits of whatever floated around in my head. At a certain point, I just accepted that I would always feel like an outsider.

After spending time in Mexico, Malaysia and Germany, it was easy to see that we are far more alike than different. And I began to cast off my misanthropic tendencies in favour of being mildly anti-social.

With my wife and two sons, I lived for almost three years in a small town on the southern shores of the Arabian Peninsula. The Omani people are warm and welcoming and, in many ways, I felt more fulfilled professionally than back in Canada. But, again, this was not my culture. I could no more be an Omani than a Martian.

Time away from my home and native land allowed me to see its history and culture in a different light, but I still felt the same about my place in it.

I had no right to feel out of sorts in small-town Canada. It's beautiful and safe, and there's a lovely used bookstore that serves a mean cappuccino. But as I watched the sun set behind the mountains, I couldn't help feeling that something was still off. That I didn't belong. Try as I might, I couldn't get excited about another mediocre restaurant, or sub-par cover band, or end-of-season sale on big black trucks.

Tourists from all over the world come to trek through the untamed wilderness of British Columbia. They find solace in the jagged coastline, thick rainforests, and Rocky Mountains. They romanticize the Indigenous peoples that have lived here for more than ten thousand years, or the early explorers that came looking for the Northwest Passage. But this never excited me, and I felt adrift. While Canadian history is rife with colourful characters and stories of survival, I never felt a part of the narrative.

Several people do feel a strong spiritual connection to the nearby mountains and lakes and forests. The animals and the wind, and the whispers that filter through the cedars – guiding them in times of personal strife.

Though I do feel a sense of peace when sitting alone on a weathered bench in the silence of winter, there is no strong connection to the land or the history or the mythology.

Later that evening, as I looked out my living room window, I wondered if there was a place or a culture or a mythology that I could connect with on a deeper level.

'Where is my place?' I asked myself. 'Where do I belong? Who are my people?'

Doubt and negativity shadowed my thoughts, but I couldn't blindly accept that a sense of belonging was a fruitless pursuit. Plus, I was too curious to give up.

Instead of trying to find the silver lining in the toque-sporting snow-shovelling marijuana-smoking Tropic of Hockey, I finished my whiskey, propped open my laptop, and decided to book a ticket to some far and distant land.

Hadn't travelled on my own for a long time, and was a little nervous about the prospect. But I knew it was a necessity. While travelling with my family fills me with all sorts of warm fuzzies, a voyage of self-discovery must be done alone.

Dozens of travel memoirs and old maps littered my writing desk. I toyed with climbing Machu Picchu or staying at a Hindu ashram in northern India. One night I had a dream about driving a bright red 1968 Austin Mini with a goat herder and a belly dancer around eastern Turkey. But none of these adventures excited me.

My time alone wandering the streets of Hong Kong and disappearing into the dense rainforests of the Pacific Northwest as a young man was life altering, but I no longer had a burning desire to hitchhike, sleep in ditches, or survive for days on bulk granola. I wanted to travel somewhere that embraced quiet contemplation but also celebrated life in song. Somewhere teeming with magic and mystery, but also had food I would recognize and a few of the creature comforts I had become accustomed to. Peru, India and Turkey would have to wait.

I had been to Ireland once before, a few years earlier, when my wife surprised me with airline tickets. We rented a car and drove around the southern half of the country, visiting as many places as we could in eight days. My fascination with the country grew every hour we were there, and after returning home I delved into Irish history, art, mythology, folklore, music, and soda bread recipes. My Irish bookshelf soon grew from a couple dozen to over a hundred.

There were so many countries I had yet to travel to, and it felt like cheating to return somewhere familiar, but Ireland was calling me to its rugged shores and there was no other option but to answer.

When I casually mentioned to acquaintances at the grocery store about my interest in the culture, and was soon departing for the Emerald Isle on my own, the inevitable question was why. I made some reference to the country's long human history and the mysterious markings on standing stones, but this was only so I could get home and start dinner. The real reason was still unknown to me.

My unexplained attraction to Ireland isn't unique. People from all over feel some mysterious pull towards the Land of Saints and Scholars. The joke is that the world is divided into two kinds of people: those that have been to Ireland, and those that dream of one day doing so. Before leaving, I searched the Internet but there were only silly clichés. 'Ireland is a place where dreamers may find their wings,' wrote one blogger. 'It is a place where faeries whisper on the wind, and songs of days gone past still stir the soul.' Pages and pages of poorly constructed paragraphs about the rolling hills and stone fences, about waterfalls and rainstorms, and what someone called 'the wonderfulness of creation'. Bulleted top-something lists that included archeological sites and graveyards, castles and pubs, music and art, and the gift of the gab.

All these things are valid, but they aren't enough. Not for me. A country can hardly be defined by the brief history outlined in introductions at the beginning of guidebooks. There has to be more than clichés and tourist hotspots. While I wanted to see and experience all the top-this and top-that, and buy a t-shirt or two, I also wanted to feel a deep connection to the essence of the land and its people. I ached to discover whether I could quiet the mind long enough to listen to the very breath of Ireland, and whether that breath would comfort me and let me know me that I belonged.

And so I had come on my own quest. A journey of discover in Ireland.

"You alright there?" asked Deirdre as we made our way through the final gate.

"Oh, yeah," I answered back. "Just enjoying the scenery."

"We'll be heading up Ballymacadoyle Hill in a minute."

"Okay." Having returned to the present, I inquired about the property. "Could you tell me a bit more about where we are – about the estate?"

"I only know a bit about the area, really. Lord Ventry's family came to Dingle in 1666, and he had Burnham House built in 1750. The estate is surrounded by a hundred and four acres, which includes the fifty acres of woodland. It now houses Coláiste Íde – the all-girls' school – with about one hundred forty students. That started in 1927."

We passed the elegant Georgian home, painted a soft yellow and bathed in afternoon sunlight. The reflection of deep blues at high tide cut through the bramble, and the open fields of Ballymacadoyle Hill (*Baile Mhic an Daill*) came as a welcome relief. The bush-line that separates the grazing patches led us onwards. The incline isn't steep, and we continued at the same pace as before.

"Go on, Saoirse," said Deirdre, "Go ahead at a trot, now. We'll continue along and meet you at the viewpoint."

At that, Saoirse gave her horse a quick kick and was off. Part of me wanted to do the same, but I remembered my last experience with a horse and decided against it.

"Would you like a photo of yourself?" asked Deirdre as we took a break on top of the hill and gazed out towards Slea Head and the Blasket Islands.

"Yeah, sure... why not?"

Checked the viewer screen, and looked as ridiculous as I imagined. But this moment wasn't about loose fitting helmets or elderly horses. It was about finding a natural rhythm, and allowing the pressures and demands of linear time to fade away. It was about being aware of the raw unadulterated beauty around me, and how to best appreciate it.

None of us were in a rush to get back and we looked out towards Dingle Harbour as the grasses, in a myriad of green, danced in the wind. Jack shifted and the saddle creaked, and I thought on the lost souls that found solace as they stood on the far reaches of Europe – looking out at the eternal blues of ocean and sky. The dark shadows of Burnham Wood only hinted at a thousand secrets whispered across time, and I wondered whose bare shoulders had felt the pale warmth of the spring sun after the rains. Thought about the story of Oisín – skilled warrior and poet – who journeys to the fabled Land of the Youth after following a beautiful maiden on horseback, and I remembered a quote from Yeats.

Faeries, come take me out of this dull world,
for I would ride with you upon the wind,
run on the top of the disheveled tide,
and dance upon the mountains like a flame.

We made our way back down as a late-afternoon wind blew off the water. The sunlight, now battling cloud cover again, became focused golden beams and reflected off the Irish Sea. It lit up the nearby hills and stone fences that make the pastures a patchwork quilt.

At the bottom of Ballymacadoyle Hill, we settled back into formation with Saoirse at the front and Deirdre bringing up the rear. The woods help block the wind, but I could still feel the temperature dropping. As we passed the estate house Deirdre asked, "Do you have Irish heritage?"

"No," I answered. "I don't think so – none that I know of, anyway. I've just been interested in Ireland for a while."

"There's been a lot of people over the last few years, come to dig up records and such about their family. They want to discover their roots and find their ancestral home and whatnot, and I thought maybe you were here to do that."

"No," I said. "I'm not here for any of that. Just visiting."

We rode the rest of the way through the woods in quiet. I soaked in the simple beauty of being on a horse and, after the ride was over, thanked Deirdre and Saoirse for a memorable afternoon before heading back into town.

On the short drive back to Dingle, I thought more about my desire to wander around rural Ireland. About all the dog-eared books and grocery-store receipts to keep my place, and how I finally came to see the country as a land of contrasts where history and myth seamlessly interlace with each other. Perhaps this was the key to why the country and culture were so appealing to me. Maybe if I walked through the unforgiving mist and stood at the border between our world and the Otherworld, or roamed and rambled along the shoreline and up into the mountains before tucking myself into warm pubs at the end of the day – listening to traditional music that celebrates all aspects of life as the resident dog naps by the fireplace – I could confirm my theory.

Maybe if I sat on cold stone during quiet mornings, when the cosmos gently unfurl and all the colours are muted, and contemplate how the early people survived through so many hardships and yet found ways to create beautiful works of art, I could find the answer as to what drew me to its warm embrace.

Prominent nationalist Thomas Davis once remarked, "It is not blood that makes you Irish but a willingness to be part of the Irish Nation." If that's the case, then maybe my willingness was enough to propel me forward in my quest. The more time I spent with my head buried in dusty tomes or driving aimlessly along country roads or stumbling onto lesser-known archeological sites, the more I felt a burning desire to continue down the shamrock-laden rabbit hole. I wanted to share in the long heritage of storytelling, and hear the mournful cry of uilleann pipes while sipping whiskey, and stand alone inside the beehive huts during Atlantic storms. Wanted to witness the eternal battles above, listen to the waters below, and imagine what grand feasts await those who are invited into the realm of the faeries.

Maybe, like those in late medieval Norman Ireland, I was becoming 'more Irish than the Irish themselves' and what drew me to the country couldn't easily be defined.

After spending time in Connemara, Oscar Wilde described the area as 'a savage beauty'. He may have been describing the contrast of dark, brooding mountains and sun-kissed white-sand shores, rolling verdant hills and endless low stone walls, ruined abbeys and elegant Georgian architecture, or tiny cottages and mighty castles, but I think this is too literal an interpretation. I believe the famed writer realized, as I did, that the entire country is more than a collection of visual contrasts. It goes far deeper.

My hope was that, with a bit of time on my own, I would not only witness the visual contrasts but also begin to understand all that cannot be seen. Perhaps I would also find a sacred space that felt like my own. A connection to the mountains and lakes and forests. Perhaps the animals, and the wind, and the whispers that blow over the patchwork hills would guide me. Perhaps I might finally find a place in this world that feels like home.

CHAPTER 3
A BINDING AGREEMENT

Woke up early on my first morning in Ireland. Jet lag had made it a restless night and, when there was just enough light to see shapes in the room, I looked over to the bedside table but there was no clock. No phone or device of any kind. Outside was the hint of dawn through the thick fog, and my initial thoughts were of crawling back into bed until my wife woke up. Instead, I got dressed in a thick Aran sweater, snuck out the door, along the hallway, and down the stairs.

Closed the main door to the house with a gentle click and walked along the path of small white stones that weave through the dewy grass. There was only my shallow breathing and the crunch of gravel underfoot. The fog muffled any other sound as I squinted through the dim light towards the narrow country lane below. A weathered bench faces out towards the hills and I sat down, warming my hands with my breath. No idea what time it was or why I had left the comfort of my room to sit in the cold.

An orange tabby cat suddenly appeared and jumped onto my lap. She nestled herself in to keep warm and I buried my frozen fingers into her fur. Though I was worried what my wife might think if she awoke to find me missing, the cat had no intention of letting me leave as the world revealed itself in soft blurs. She began to purr, and this indicated a binding agreement: the cat would keep me company and, rather than fret about silly things, I would focus only on this singular moment – this rare opportunity to witness magic in its purest form as the border between two worlds slowly closed for another day.

The fog slowly lifted, exposing old stone fences and taller skeletal trees. Hints of greenery blended softly with subtle shades of blue and purple as night crept into day. I could feel nothing of the physical, save for a strange sense of embrace – as if all the elements of the natural world were comforting me. It was as if some force was holding me – wrapping its arms around me – after a long absence of touch. It refused to let go, and my instinct was to twist in an attempt to break free. I wanted to distance myself from it. But I also recognized my need for surrender – to collapse into its arms and feel intense emotions once again. It was an unfamiliar and uncomfortable feeling, and it seemed to expose a vulnerability I wasn't prepared to share. The cat shifted slightly to let me know that, while its eyes may be closed, it was fully aware of my resistance and that I wasn't fulfilling my end of the bargain.

"Give me a minute," I said. "This isn't easy."

Though I had been raised in a loving family, where both my mother and father showed affection on a regular basis, I was not someone who felt comfortable with prolonged physical contact. My parents joked that healthy human beings need a minimum of eight hugs a day, but I argued otherwise. Upon entering the teaching profession, the male teachers especially were repeatedly warned not to touch students in any way – even a tap on the shoulder – for fear that it would be misconstrued by either the pupils or their parents. "Don't put yourself at risk," said one professor. "The only safe place for your hands is in your pockets."

In all my years of teaching, I didn't call a student to attention by tapping their shoulder or comfort a student by giving them a hug – even if they were being bullied or had lost a family member – for fear of what rumours might end my career. Never giving thought as to how this would affect me on a psychological level, or whether this would later affect my relationship with my own family. But, as the first beams of sun washed the world in light and reflected off the nearby Neolithic site, I gave myself permission to be open and vulnerable.

Dropped my shoulders, took meditative breaths, and focused on nothing but the slow movement of time. There was no need to be anywhere else. Nothing to gain from living in the past or in the future. I needed to focus on the gift of the present – the voices that can only be heard when one is truly open to receiving guidance.

The idea that humans are intimately connected to the earth has persisted throughout time and across cultures, and yet today – especially in the Western world – we have largely forgotten this. As I gently rubbed the cat's cheeks and felt its therapeutic vibrations, I knew there was only one choice: to trust that the magical and mystical elements would embrace me and guide me.

Maybe I would learn, little by little, to accept intimacy. Maybe I could stop mumbling about my desire to be emotionally vacant and connect not just with the land and the stories and the spirits, but also connect with individuals. Replace the voice that consistently whispers, 'No one will notice if you leave the party and slip into the night' with one that reassures me that I am worthy of both physical and emotional connection.

Or perhaps this was all just a ridiculous notion. Perhaps this was asking too much of an orange tabby cat, or an ancient site blanketed in fog, or a country as a whole. Would wandering alone along the ocean's edge or up a mountain or into the occasional pub help me unravel some deep-seeded need for belonging, or would I end up back on a plane across the Atlantic just as lost as when I first arrived?

The cat wedged itself further into the folds of my wool sweater, and I felt myself release. "Okay, little one. If only for a moment, I will let down my guard. I will allow myself to be guided."

The landscape finally fell into focus. "How many others throughout the millennia have experienced similar awakenings," I asked the cat as she stirred. "What had those early inhabitants felt on mornings such as this one? What did they whisper while they gathered to perform their sacred rites?"

But these were questions for later. The tabby jumped off my lap, stretched, and went in search of birds and mice. She had completed her end of the bargain as I had completed mine.

The muted sounds of farmhands echoed from the back of the property. It was time to head inside and see if my wife was awake.

Paula was still in bed but her eyes were open. She blinked a few times before asking, "Have you been up long?"

"Just for a bit," I lied. "Are you ready for some breakfast?"

Soon after, we sat at a table for two and our hostess

arrived with a pot of tea. A small sugar bowl and matching creamer were already on the table.

"Full Irish, is it, for the both of you?"

"Yes, please," I answered. We had no idea how much food that meant. We do now.

"And how did you sleep?" she asked.

"Off and on," I answered. "But the room is wonderful and there's a great view. It's so quiet."

Irene was the epitome of Irish hospitality and, as she laid her hands gently on our shoulders, she said, "I'll be back with a bit of breakfast. You'll feel much better after a cup of tea." She disappeared into the kitchen, and we thought about our arrival the afternoon before.

We had never stayed at a bed and breakfast prior to this one – it seemed too intimate – and our first instinct had been to find a hotel. But many B&Bs are large farmhouses with several rooms and ensuite bathrooms, and best of all was the promise of local tips and tricks to make our stay more memorable. I booked our first night at the closest one to the Brú na Bóinne Visitors' Centre.

"You're very welcome," said Irene as she answered the door. "You'll be wanting a cup of tea, of course. But first I'll show you to your room."

The eighteenth-century farmhouse was warm and inviting. Paula and I took our shoes off in the foyer.

"Ah, you must be Canadian," said Irene.

"Yeah," I said. "How do you know?"

"Because you both took off your shoes. Canadians take off their shoes. Americans don't. I don't mind either way, unless you've been mucking about on the farm. This is a working farm, y'know. We've got some chickens in the back there, and we sell the eggs. I try to remind the boys to take off their boots before they step inside, but it's a constant battle. God knows I try."

"How many chickens do you have?" I asked.

"Oh, not that many," she answered. "About three hundred, I'd say."

We followed Irene upstairs and to our room. An hour later, we had a quiet dinner in a nearby village and then got an early night.

As we were finishing up our breakfast, and were flipping through a guidebook, Irene pulled up a chair and sat with us. "You'll be off to see the site, then, this morning?"

"We are," I replied. "Do we need to book a tour, or can we just show up?"

"You can go any time you'd like, but I'll ring them up and see if they can fit you in first thing. Are you interested in seeing Knowth as well as Newgrange? I'd do both if I were you. That is, if you have the time."

"We don't have a set schedule," I said. "We're just playing it by ear."

"Then you best make time for Knowth. The site contains more than a third of all megalithic art in Western Europe."

"Is that right?"

"T'is, indeed," said Irene. "It'd be a pity to come all this way and not see it."

"Then please book us in for both."

Irene disappeared into the kitchen only to return a few minutes later. "You're all set. You're expected for the 9:30am tour of Newgrange and then Knowth after that. A good half-day there, but the day is lovely. The sun is out. It's warm. You'll have a grand time, I'm sure."

CHAPTER 4
A THIN PLACE

We walked under the vine-covered latticework, past the small trickling streams, and arrived just as the doors to the Brú na Bóinne Visitors' Centre were opening. Once inside, we were given our bus schedule in the form of a sticker that we dutifully slapped on our chests.

"You have about thirty minutes before your bus leaves," said the man behind the desk. "Best to give yourself ten minutes or so to walk over the bridge and up the hill to where it'll pick you up. It doesn't give you much time to see the displays, but you're free to spend as much time as you'd like afterwards."

Since spying Newgrange earlier that morning, I had been eager to walk inside the five-thousand-year-old passage tomb. But the bus wasn't going to leave any earlier than scheduled just because I was impatient.

We wove through a partial full-scale replica of the chambers at Newgrange *(Sí an Bhrú)* and Knowth (*Cnóbha*), as well as exhibits of the Neolithic homes, dress, food, tools and weapons, and spent a few minutes reading up on the history of Ireland's early people.

Although no hard evidence has been discovered to confirm the theory, it's assumed that ice age travellers followed their hunt over the land bridge from the United Kingdom. As the ice carved up the country around 14,000 BCE, the land bridge to Ireland melted away, blocking off any further plant or animal species that may have made their way over. Recent carbon dating of a bear bone has shown that Ireland was occupied in 10,500 BCE, and these early Paleolithic people hunted, possibly cooked, and survived in any way they could.

Numbering only a few thousand, the hunter-gatherers of the later Mesolithic period did leave significant evidence. They survived on a diet of seafood, birds, wild boar and hazelnuts, and hunted with spears, arrows and harpoons. They lived in seasonal shelters of stretched animal skins over wooden frames.

The Neolithic people arrived from France and Spain around 6000 BCE. Using stone axes, they cleared land to create permanent farms for their domestic sheep and goats. Around 4300 BCE, cattle arrived in Northern Ireland and the red deer was introduced from Britain. The Neolithic people also started to cultivate cereal: mainly wheat and barley. As they cleared land for agriculture, erosion and overgrazing soon caused much of the land to stagnate, acidify, and eventually evolve into peat bogs.

Cultivation sparked a major turning point in Irish history. Open spaces were now cleared, people largely stayed within the same area, and less effort was needed to find food. The earliest farmers lived as family units in rectangular structures and made simple farming tools of wood and stone. They also made woven baskets and wide-mouthed, round-bottomed pottery.

It is the burial practices of the Neolithic people, however, that are the most fascinating. In the south of the country, people were buried in pits with important items to take back to the afterlife. Later, two or three individuals were buried together in small stone chambers. The surrounding stones were carved with elaborate designs. Large and small stone basins have been found with human ashes, as well as carved mace heads, beads, and other pieces of art.

The most striking characteristic of the Neolithic people in Ireland was the appearance of megalithic monuments: court tombs, passage tombs, portal tombs and wedge tombs. While the passage tombs constitute the smallest group in terms of numbers, they are the most impressive in terms of size and importance. The most famous of these is at Newgrange, now a UNESCO site and the oldest astronomically aligned monument in the world – older than Stonehenge and the pyramids at Giza.

Imagine having the ability to travel through space and time. Breathing a sigh of relief as a beam of light cuts through the darkness inside the newly built passage tomb of Newgrange. Witnessing the dawn of a new year on England's Salisbury Plain when Stonehenge was first constructed. Standing among the ancient Egyptians at the Temple of Karnak when the sun rises between the portals of the Great Gate of Nectanebo and bathes the sanctuary of Amun-Re in light. Imagine looking towards the heavens with the ancient Mayans as a shaft of sunlight filters through the hole at a temple in Tulum – creating a star-burst effect – or tracking the seasons with the Ancestral

Puebloan people at Chaco Canyon, New Mexico when a wedge-shaped beam strikes the Sun Dagger petroglyph.

Paula nudged me back into the present. "We need to go if we're going to catch our bus."

"You're right," I muttered. "I was just..."

"I know," said Paula. "You were somewhere else."

After weaving through the small crowd that had gathered by the café and gift shop, we exited out the back door.

As we crossed the bridge, I stopped to watch the waters of the River Boyne (*An Bhóinn*) make their way towards the Irish Sea. Was there enough time to flip through a couple guidebooks and read about the history and myths associated with the river – the Battle of the Boyne in 1690, or the tale of Finn McCool (*Fionn mac Cumhail*) capturing Fiontán, the Salmon of Knowledge (*An Bradán Feasa*)?

Paula turned around and not-so-gently reminded me that our ride was due to leave in three minutes.

We arrived as the end of the queue was boarding the bus. As we found our seats, everyone shuffled through their packs and dug out cameras in case anything interesting happened during the ten-minute ride. Most were wearing light rain jackets, even though it was sunny and warm.

"*Dia dhuit*, everyone," said the young woman standing at the front of the bus. "That means 'hello' in Irish."

Everyone on the bus nodded.

"Welcome to Brú na Bóinne," she continued with a tourist-friendly smile. "And what a lovely day it is for it. The name Brú na Bóinne means the 'palace' or the 'mansion' of the Boyne. It refers to the area within the bend in the river and it's home to one of the world's most important prehistoric sites. It looks like you've all found a seat, so we'll head out soon."

It was a syrupy start to the morning but I met my wife's

gaze as she took my hand and, with that simple gesture, knew that she shared in my enthusiasm. Though she may not have fully understood the impact of that first morning, she knew that something stirred inside me. Something had awakened. I don't get excited easily, but sitting among a crowd of tourists on a brightly painted bus as we motored through quiet country lanes was causing my heart to race.

While I couldn't explain at that moment why exactly the Neolithic site meant so much to me, and still hadn't told her about my time with the cat and the fog, she was patient and knew that I would explain myself later.

We wound along, past fields of intense green and small modern-day stone cottages. One man tending his garden stood up and waved, and half the passengers waved back.

The bus parked next to a tall hedgerow, and the young woman from the bus herded us together before wishing us a good day. She passed us on to another young woman standing at the gate. We were then led along a gravel walkway and over the knoll.

The sun shone brightly off the quartz stones imbedded within the outer wall and everything seemed carefully placed for optimal viewing. The lawn was freshly mowed and even the sheep in the next field looked staged. Nothing looked five thousand years old.

"I'm going to pass you on to Seán, your tour guide," said the second young woman as she gathered everyone together, "and he'll soon take you inside Newgrange – but first he's going to go over a bit of the history. And it's a lovely day for it, so."

Looking the part of a retired archeologist with his grey beard and tweed sports coat (complete with tan leather elbow patches), Seán took his place at the top of the wooden steps that lead over the kerbstones and inside the passage tomb. Already a few tourists were snapping photos as he cleared his throat.

"You may be wondering," he began, "about the outer walls of Newgrange. For those of you that have had a chance to see the early photographs taken before the reconstruction, you will know that the outside looked very different not that long ago. Even though the inside was perfectly intact, the passage was covered by earth that had slipped over time.

"When Irish identity was suppressed during the occupation of the English, Newgrange was almost forgotten. But in 1699, the landowner at the time decided to use what he thought was a pile of stones for a new road on the property. He subsequently discovered a cave. This was, in fact, the entrance to Newgrange. You can see that entrance behind me."

The morning sun beat down. Seán was getting warmer and warmer in his wool jacket.

"Archaeologist Michaél J. O'Kelly led the extensive excavation (and subsequent restoration of the exterior) in the early 1960s, and spent over a decade working on the site. Keep in mind that the appearance of the outside of Newgrange is one person's interpretation of how it might have appeared. This reconstruction is controversial still today. The dispute centres around the quartzite stones and cobbles fixed into a near-vertical steel-reinforced concrete wall surrounding the entrance of the mound. If you visit Knowth later today, you will notice that the quartzite stones are laid out as a type of apron around the site instead."

Seán reached inside his pocket for his keys. "I'd like to speak a little further about the stone in front of you before we take a peek inside, but first I'll give you a few minutes while I unlock the gate."

Though I usually prefer to explore sites on my own, rather than get passed on from one cheerful tour guide to the next, I was content to wait my turn and blend into the crowd. Newgrange in the harsh light of day is not as romantic as when sitting on a weathered bench at dawn with a magical cat, but this was the only way I could gain access.

The mound at Newgrange was originally drum-shaped. It had a flat top and steep sides. Over the years, the sides fell forward, giving the mound a more rounded, natural looking shape. It is now about twelve meters high and about eighty meters across. The base of the mound is held in place by ninety-seven huge kerbstones. When the loose stones of the mound collapsed, the kerb stayed in place, holding the original shape of the monument against the pressure of the collapsing materials. The quartz and granite of the original façade lay at the bottom of the collapsed material and, as Seán explained, Professor O'Kelly decided to restore the front part of the mound to what he thought was its original appearance.

While we waited for Seán to call us together, some tourists took photographs while others walked around without direction. It wasn't difficult to determine who were the Irish among us; they had their eyes closed and were facing the sun like flowers in early spring – soaking in as much Vitamin D as possible before the rains came.

Seán continued. "The most famous symbol of early pre-Celtic Ireland is the triple spiral, or triskele, and it features prominently on the entrance stone (or kerbstone K1). As you can see in front of you, the stone essentially blocks the front entrance to Newgrange."

Enough was enough. Though I promised myself that I wouldn't hide behind the lens of a camera while gallivanting around Ireland, I snapped photos from various angles like everyone else. There was no way anyone could resist.

"In looking at the kerbstone, we see all sorts of shapes and patterns – diamonds, waves and swirls," said Seán. "It is regarded as one of the finest achievements of European prehistoric art, but we don't know what any of it really means. We can only guess. Some see ocean waves, mountains and clouds. Maybe the early people were mirroring the land they lived on – as above, so below. Others believe the priests designed it after a drug-induced hallucination. One popular theory is that it represents the passing of time. The swirls especially could be linked to the Winter Solstice and perhaps they represent the movement from our world to the worlds beyond."

Seán then divided us into two smaller groups; the inside of the passage tomb can only hold a small number of people. While the first half of the group disappeared into the dark passage, the second half were given some time to further explore the outside of the mound. Paula and I headed around the back to inspect the Neolithic art.

The only other stone to rival the entrance stone is known as Kerbstone 52 (K52), located at the back of the mound and diagonally opposite. It too features spiral ornamentation and vertical parallel lines. The three spirals to the left comprise two larger clockwise designs and one smaller more tightly wound anti-clockwise spiral, supposedly representing the summer and winter suns. To the right of the stone, are three particularly notable symbols, each consisting of three circles surrounded by double lines roughly elliptical in shape.

Archeological investigations were carried out to establish if there was a second passage behind this stone, but these proved inconclusive. However, an earlier mound was discovered, proving that this area was of ritual significance even before the great mound and chamber at Newgrange had been constructed.

Without the distraction of other tourists vying for the perfect vantage point, I took a moment to ponder the ancient carvings and reflect on their possible meaning. There is no prevailing theory as to what the symbols on this stone refer to. Perhaps they represent something concrete, or maybe they were a tool to help guide the ancient people to a higher level of consciousness. Forgetting all that I had read about the various interpretations of Neolithic art, I speculated without limitation. Perhaps the left half of Kerbstone 52 is the physical world (as it seems calmer and gentler to the eye), and the right side are the internal workings of the mind or even the soul (as it seems more chaotic).

The duality of the kerbstone caused me to think further on the duality of life – how the physical and nonphysical can either mirror each other or be in complete opposite. Standing before the ancient monument, I wondered how this physical chamber could mirror the internal chamber of the individual. 'What does mine even look like?' I wondered. 'Is it a place of comfort, or a place where melancholy (or even hopelessness) festers in the dark?'

At first, I only knew what it doesn't look like. Nothing like a well-lit airplane hanger with organized tools and engine grease. Not a model home with brand new beige love-seats. Not a sports bar with big screen televisions. If I'm honest with myself, it looks cavernous. Not open or inviting. There might places of subtle beauty where the sun pours in from above and one can rest their weary bones, but also rough corners and jagged edges that tear flesh and draw blood if one is not careful. Pockets of warmth that comfort the lonely, but also places where the lonely dare not go.

And what would fill this cavernous space? Books, probably. And some jazz on vinyl. Both organized alphabetically. Also suitcases – antique suitcases stacked precariously on top of each other – full of emotions locked tight with brass buckles that I have no interest in unfastening. Almost convinced myself that they don't exist, but they continue to accumulate and take up more and more space.

Issues of belonging, openness and vulnerability are better left ignored. Okay for others; not for yours truly. But maybe Ireland would be the catalyst for dealing with these demons that I have kept at bay.

My hope is that ultimately, like the kerbstone, there would be a sense of balance in my internal chamber – that for every dark corner there is also a beam of light, and for every suitcase there is an orange tabby cat snoozing on a weathered bench.

As the sun continued its path across the sky, and reflected off the quartzite stones, a quiet voice from deep inside the cavern asked, 'What now? While you visualize your internal chamber, and come to terms with its duality, what can you do today to help heal yourself and become a source of light in a world consumed by shadow?'

'Maybe,' answered another voice, 'the secret is to invite others – whether in the physical realm or the spiritual realm – to enter this space. At first you could just invite beauty. Allow the elements of the natural world to soften the hard edges, drive the cold winter away, or hold your hand as you stumble towards the light. And then, perhaps, those that cannot be seen – those that reside in a world just beyond our own. They could enter, say a good morning, and plug in a few lamps. But not florescent lamps. Those are horrible. Maybe, instead, they could bring Himalayan salt lamps. That would be fine.

'Maybe they could share stories and listen to a little jazz. But not free jazz. At least, not right away. And then, finally, you could invite others inside the chamber to teach you all the ways in which to be a lighthouse keeper – guiding others to safety when all seems lost. The opening is only large enough to let in a few brave souls, but maybe in time you could make it wider and more inviting. Maybe these new arrivals could help you unlock the brass buckles. But not all of them. At least, not right away.'

Paula touched my shoulder to bring me back, and we circumnavigated the mound as the first half of the group emerged into the light.

Though we had explored the partial full-scale replica of the chamber, I wasn't sure how I would react once inside. Neither of us said a word as we filed up the wooden steps and into the dark. These steps are a modern construct; those residing in the Neolithic Age had to climb over. The meter-high stone would have been a considerable barrier and may have also represented a psychological barrier to those that held Newgrange sacred.

Illuminated by modern lighting, the tight passage slopes gently upwards and is lined on each side with large standing stones. We crouched so as not to whack our heads, awkwardly shuffling forward. About halfway there is a slight bend to the right. The passage is less than twenty meters long, though it felt longer, and we finally gathered at the central chamber.

In the cold embrace of the earthen structure, we waited for Seán's lecture to continue. No one in the group said anything. It is a tight space, and we stood shoulder-to-shoulder, but it wasn't claustrophobic. Instead, I felt uplifted – as if suspended from the confines of time. Calm and unafraid. Part of the universal existence.

Those that write about sacred sites in Ireland – like Newgrange – often use the term 'a thin place'. They are locales where the distance between heaven and earth collapses, and one is able to catch a glimpse of the divine or the transcendent. The curtain between the living world and the eternal, spiritual world is almost nonexistent. Some visitors to these thin places claim to experience an odd sensation that somehow the past, present and future meet. Travel to thin places does not necessarily lead to a spiritual awakening, but often one is jolted out of old ways of seeing the world. "Heaven and earth are only three feet apart," the Celtic saying goes, "but in thin places that distance is even shorter."

Was this the reason a quiet voice had echoed from deep inside? Had I been guided to a higher level of consciousness by lingering alone at dawn with a strange cat? I couldn't begin to fathom how to best answer these questions.

Instead, my mind refocused as the lecture continued.

"You will see that the interior arrangement of the structure is three recesses, giving the chamber a cruciform shape," said Seán. "The chamber itself has needed very little conservation and no restoration. There are stone basins in each of the recesses and it is believed that these basins held the ashes of the cremated. You may have already noticed further carvings here inside, and if you look above us you can see the chamber roof. It is what they call a corbelled roof, meaning that it is dome-shaped and made with large, interlaced slabs of rock."

In the cool surroundings, Seán adjusted his coat and

pulled on his shirt cuffs. He seemed more at ease inside the passage tomb than out in the sunshine.

"The stone basin in the back recess is broken and the story goes that in 1795 a man from Connacht had a dream that there was gold buried there," said Seán. "There wasn't."

The group snickered but, as the lecture continued, I had empathy for the man from Connacht. Like him, I too felt that there had to be more to the inside of this mysterious place than a cold dark passage, ancient stone basins, and strange carvings. Though I had no desire to sneak inside during the dead of night to search for a secret stash of jewels, I could understand why this place continues to spark the imagination and take root in the subconscious.

"As I'm sure many of you know by now, Newgrange is the oldest manmade structure to incorporate the rising sun on the winter solstice," said Seán. "Designed and built around 3200 BCE, it also features a light box above the entrance. Even today, just before 9:00am – on the days surrounding the shortest day of the year – the sun rises over the nearby hills and, four minutes later, a shaft of golden sun illuminates the inner chamber. The early people of Ireland likely built this site to celebrate the defeat of darkness. It would serve to mark the dawn of another year.

"When it was originally built, the light would have struck the back of the cruciform chamber but, due to changes in the earth's axis over the millennia, it now stops two metres short. This event lasts seventeen minutes before the sun rises too high for the light to enter the chamber and everything is plunged into darkness again for another year.

"Now if you will all move slightly to one side – I know it's a small space – I'd like to mimic the morning light on the winter solstice as it would have appeared five thousand years ago. Modern lighting isn't quite the same, but it's all we have. That is unless, of course, you win the annual lottery and are lucky enough to see it yourself."

The lights were turned off and we were plunged into darkness until a thin beam of gold cut through the black. Though it was artificial, the simplicity of it caught me by surprise. It must have had the same effect on all those that shared the chamber. Like myself, no one dared to disturb the silence with a word or even a breath.

The affect that Newgrange had was palpable. Both lost in thought, Paula and I boarded the bus with the other tourists who were also less animated than an hour before.

Our next stop was the nearby site of Knowth.

A more complex structure than Newgrange, Knowth has two passageways and remained a centre of considerable importance until the end of the Middle Ages. It was built around the same time as its counterpart but, unlike Newgrange, the site continued to be used by various cultures and for different purposes over several thousands of years. Though Newgrange is more famous and nearby Dowth (*Dubhadh*) is likely to be older, Knowth has a collection of more than four hundred engraved stones and some finely carved artifacts dating from five thousand two hundred years ago. The main mound is surrounded by at least eighteen small structures, many of which have (or had) engraved slabs that probably predate the mound. The Stone Age people would have gathered at Knowth twice a year for the equinox celebrations: after the crops were sown, and before they were harvested.

The people of the Early Bronze Age (about 2000 BCE) buried the cremated remains of their dead at the site, but active occupation of Knowth appears to have then lapsed for about two thousand years. Around the time of Christ, it was again used as a place of burial. But, following this period, Knowth never regained its function as a sacred site. From then on, through the Early Christian period and on into the Middle Ages, Knowth was used as a fortified dwelling.

Experts in Neolithic art have commented that there is a different feel to the carvings at each of the monuments. The art at Newgrange has been described as formal and stylized, while that of Dowth is seen as unsophisticated by comparison. The carvings at Knowth have more flair, are bolder and more confident.

Back at the visitors' centre, Paula and I headed into the café and split a scone with clotted cream and jam. We shimmied for space around the displays we had missed earlier in the day and then poked around the gift shop, where shelves are stocked full of t-shirts, dishtowels, magnets, pocket watches, wall hangings and guidebooks. After ten minutes, I amassed a considerable amount of tourist tat.

"Please remember we have limited space to carry much of anything home," said Paula. "Are you sure you want to load up on stuff now – on our first day?"

I looked down at the goods precariously piled in my arms. "Oh, I'm sure."

It is for good reason that Brú na Bóinne is the most visited archaeological site in all of Ireland. There is something visceral that connects so many on such a personal level – whether it's a spiritual connection or just a fascination with the ancient past. The darkness comforts and soothes, and to be able to stand inside a sacred place that appears in so many stories and myths, built at the dawn of Irish identity, is almost overwhelming.

I was prepared for an Ireland that didn't live up to my

romantic expectations – a country overrun with tourists taking selfies in front of stone circles, clogging up pubs for overpriced pints in Temple Bar, and handing over fistfuls of money for anything with the word 'Celtic' on the packaging. I was not prepared to be mysteriously drawn outside on a cold dark morning and held hostage by the resident cat until I had a moment of epiphany. Not prepared to confront my issue with intimacy, or reflect on my internal chamber, or slip into a sense of shared universal existence, or feel a part of human history that spans back several thousands of years. Even though Brú na Bóinne was full of tourists with cameras and rain jackets, I was in no way disappointed. Instead, I was struck by an overwhelming sense of place and felt the beginning of a connection to a mythology that was not my own.

As we mapped out the rest of our afternoon, I was more excited than ever. While we were like any other tourist with our rental car and guidebooks, and only had a week in which to explore, I knew one day I would be back. Wasn't sure when or with whom, but I knew that this was the beginning of something important.

CHAPTER 5
AN AWKWARD START

Three years later, I arrived at Newgrange for the second time. After revisiting the Neolithic art, and witnessing the defeat of darkness by artificial light in the five-thousand-year-old passage tomb, I knocked back a cup of tea and climbed into the rental car with my gift shop purchases.

As much as I appreciate travelling with my wife, I knew I had to return to Ireland without her. A true quest must be taken alone.

Bid my family adieu, flew across the great expanse of Canada and the cold Atlantic, and then drove north from Dublin (*Baile Átha Cliath*). But, as is always the case when I travel solo, my journey had its fair share of missteps.

Love travelling. Not great at it. While I love *being* there, I'm terrible at *getting* there.

It started with what was probably good advice from my travel agent. "Small airports have a tendency to cancel their flights without much notice," she began. "You should leave enough time to drive to Calgary if you have to. Just in case. You never know."

She booked me a ticket for the earliest flight of the day and, a month later, this fearless adventurer arrived at the nearest airport an hour before take-off. The flight departed on time and, after thirty-five minutes in the air, I arrived in Calgary. Then eight hours of hanging around. Drank coffee, ate cold Mexi-fries at Taco Time, and watched several episodes of *Father Ted* (an unhinged Anglo-Irish sitcom – or, perhaps more accurately, an Irish sitcom paid for with British money) on my laptop, and still had four-and-a-half hours to kill.

Finally, the man behind the counter looked at my itinerary, shrugged his shoulders, and told me I would have to collect my bags in Heathrow. "You'll have to collect your luggage in London, and then check in again before you board your flight to Dublin."

"Okay," I said. Didn't bother to ask why.

By the time my flight for Heathrow was boarding, I had been up for almost twelve hours. Already tired of travelling and hadn't yet left Canada.

Most of the flight went by without incident. However, with only half an hour before touching down, I vomited. Feeling fine, hanging out, and then wham-o. This hadn't given me much time to find a sick bag, wedged between the in-flight magazines, so some of it landed on my jeans.

After exiting the plane, with jeans smelling like stale vomit, I went to collect my luggage. Staggered to the appropriate turnstile, picked up my bags, and then headed over to the British Airways check-in counter. Handed over my ticket and the young lady behind the counter punched in my information. After a few minutes, she typed something more before making a disapproving noise that meant she had no idea what to do next. "You don't seem to be booked with British

Airways," she said. "You need to go to the Aer Lingus counter."

Couldn't recall any mention of Aer Lingus before, but I thanked the lady and went in search of the airport map. The Aer Lingus counter is all the way across the Heathrow airport, in a completely different terminal.

Headed back across the first terminal, waited for the underground train for ten minutes, travelled by underground train for twenty minutes, and then spent ten minutes crossing the other terminal before queuing up at the Aer Lingus check-in counter.

The young woman there welcomed me with a smile and punched in my information. After a bit, she typed something more into the computer before making a disapproving noise that meant she had no idea what to do next. "You don't seem to be booked with Aer Lingus," she said. "You need to go to the British Airways counter."

"But I was just there," I uttered, "and they told me to come here. Now you want me to go back and try again?"

"Yes," she answered.

After almost forty-five minutes, I queued up again at the British Airways check-in counter. Lost and bewildered, I then noticed the general information desk where a uniformed man stared into the abyss of airline travellers.

Explained that I had just spent almost two hours crossing terminals and travelling by underground train, and didn't know what to do next.

"Let's have a look, then, shall we?"

Handed over my ticket, and he punched in my information. After a few minutes, he typed something more before making a disapproving noise.

Finally, there was a moment of clarity. "Huh," he said. "That's interesting. I think that I solved the problem. But it's not good news, I'm afraid. Here's the thing: you arrived from Calgary and landed here in Heathrow. But it seems your next flight – your flight to Dublin – leaves from Gatwick. Not Heathrow. Gatwick is all the way across the city and there's no way you'll make it in time. Did you use a travel agent? Because this is a serious mistake."

Tried not to panic. "Is it possible," I began, "to book a flight from here to Dublin, without having to go to Gatwick?"

"I will check." He typed away. And then typed some more.

"It is, yes," he finally answered. "But it will cost you £115."

"Damn," I replied. Didn't know what else to do but hand over £115. It felt like a hostage situation. "When is the flight?"

"Three hours from now."

"Do it."

"Are you sure?" he asked.

"Yes," I said. "But I'm firing my travel agent."

Many hours later, having flown across the Irish Sea and hoping the stink from my vomit-stained jeans had dissipated, I found a beautiful raven-haired woman behind the car rental counter in the Dublin airport. "How was your journey so far?" she asked with a lovely, lilting accent.

I smiled as our eyes met. "Not great."

She laughed and, after a bit of paperwork, handed me the key to my sensible subcompact. I was overjoyed – giddy, even. Skipped along, counting the parking spots before the car came into sight. But the darn thing was parked only three inches from the next one. There was no way of getting into the driver's side, even if I hadn't eaten at Taco Time. Maybe ten inches on the passenger side, so I squeezed myself into the tight space and then shimmied over the gearshift and middle panel before plunking myself heavily into the driver's seat. My second road trip had officially begun.

As I maneuvered around the parking garage – reminding myself to keep to the left – it dawned on me how much easier it is to travel with my wife. She knows whose advice to follow and what questions to ask. She can find a sick bag faster than I can, and has an amazing sense of direction. But this wasn't about taking the easy way. This was about experiencing Ireland in the raw. Though I would likely stumble and become lost (on numerous occasions), I had to journey alone – without any crux that might aid in my wandering ways. To best explore the internal as much as the external, I needed a significant push outside my comfort zone.

It may have been an awkward start to my solo adventure, but maybe that was okay. Maybe the best and most memorable journeys begin a little clumsily.

CHAPTER 6

A HINT OF SWEETNESS IN THE AIR

When my wife and I left the car park of Brú na Bóinne three years earlier, bellies full of scone and tea, we still had the afternoon in which to explore nearby sites. We narrowed the list, and with a couple guidebooks dog-eared and balanced on the dash of the car, drove twenty minutes north to Monasterboice (*Mainistir Bhuithe*).

"Please remember to drive on the left today," said Paula.

"Do not worry, my darling," I teased. "I shall do just that."

Though the rest of the day would be marked by a series of tourist destinations, my hope was that we could avoid the crowds. It's far easier to connect to something on a deeper level without the hubbub of day-trippers.

An early Christian settlement founded in the late fifth century by Saint Buíte, Monasterboice is famous for its tenth-century high crosses – one of which is Muiredach's High Cross. Featuring biblical carvings of both the Old and New Testaments, it has been described as the most beautiful specimen of Celtic stonework in existence.

Though time and the elements have smoothed down the details so that the figures seem melted and nearly indistinguishable, it wasn't difficult to find the five-and-a-half meter tall cross near the entrance. I could recognize Jesus with a bird on his head, Michael and the Devil, Moses, David and Goliath, and several others.

"It says here that many are concerned for the wellbeing of the cross and some are arguing that it should be moved inside."

"Uh-huh," muttered my wife as she focused in on the centre panel with her camera.

Leaving Paula to do her own thing, I wandered through the site, past the round tower that housed the library and other treasures; the West Cross that stands seven meters (making it the tallest in Ireland); and a sundial that would have marked the passing of time for the monks and indicated the times for prayers.

Ten minutes south is Mellifont Abbey, the first Cistercian abbey in Ireland. Built by monks originally from Clairvaux (in northeastern France) in 1142, little of the original abbey remains today save for a thirteenth-century lavabo (where the monks washed their hands before eating), some Romanesque arches, and a fourteenth-century chapter house. The original gatehouse was a great defensive structure, a necessity in the centuries when it stood on the border between the Pale (the part of Ireland under Anglo-Norman rule) and the territory under control of the native Irish chieftains.

Our last stop for the day was the famed Hill of Tara (*Teamhair* or *Cnoc na Teamhrach*). The complex was littered with sunbathers: bikini-clad women laying on beach towels and reading paperbacks, and shirtless men kicking around soccer balls. There were no bottles of sunscreen in sight, and I feared the pasty locals might soon ignite.

With our first full day slipping into an unseasonably warm late afternoon, we continued past the statue of Patrick and the nearby churchyard. The alabaster saint glowed against the stunning azure sky.

The area was revered as a dwelling place of the gods and an entrance to the Otherworld. According to tradition, it was also the seat of the High King of Ireland. Over the centuries, a hundred and forty-two kings are said to have reigned in the name of Tara. In the legends of St. Patrick's mission to Ireland, he is said to have first come to its ancient monuments to confront Celtic paganism in its most powerful place.

At the summit of the hill is the oval Iron Age enclosure known as *Ráith na Ríogh* (the Fort of the Kings). The remains of the two linked enclosures are easy to recognize from an aerial view, but difficult to recognize from the ground – especially when one is buried in a book. "It's pretty lumpy around here," I said. "And I don't see the fort."

"Get your head out of the book and watch where you're going," said Paula. "This *is* the fort, or what remains of it."

And this is why my wife always takes on the role of navigator, whether by foot or by vehicle, and I take on the role of driver or man-with-his head-in-a-book.

We found the standing stone, called *Lia Fáil* (the Stone of Destiny), where the High Kings were crowned. According to legend, the stone is said to 'scream if touched by a prospective king'. Looked around to see if anyone was watching and then, after a silent prayer to the ancient gods, carefully placed my hand on the stone and heard... absolutely nothing.

I later read that the stone will 'roar in joy' if the rightful

High King puts his feet on it, while another account mentions that it will utter 'a shout whenever a king of the true Scotic or Irish race stands or sits on it'. Maybe it warrants a second attempt. Or a third.

To the north of the ring-forts is a small Neolithic passage tomb known as *Dumha na nGiall* (the Mound of the Hostages). Constructed around 3400 BCE, its modern name comes from the medieval period as it was the place where the symbolic exchange of hostages took place. It is the oldest visible monument on the Hill of Tara, and it covers a passage tomb where human remains were buried for more than fifteen hundred years.

We made our way down the hill to the café for tea. On the way, Paula found some shamrock and carefully picked a few to press in her journal. I continued to fill the silence with historical bits from one of the guidebooks. "Earliest written records show that the High Kings were inaugurated here, and the legal text of the time specified that the king must first drink ale and symbolically marry the goddess *Medb* (Maeve) in order to qualify for high kingship."

Put my finger in to hold my place. "That doesn't sound so bad: a bit of ale and symbolically marrying some Irish goddess. How hard can that be?"

"Might I suggest you spend less time with your head in a guidebook and more time experiencing the country?"

She had a point. Tara is one of the largest complexes of Celtic monuments in all of Europe and I had spent more time reading about it than experiencing it. There had to be a better balance. After years researching Irish history and culture in hopes of one day visiting, I was now on Hibernian soil. Time to put my books aside and immerse myself in the moment. Move slowly, mindfully, and rely on curiosity to propel me forward – rather than adhere to a self-imposed itinerary.

Remind myself about the strange forces that drew me out of bed on my first morning to sit with the orange tabby cat and witness magic as the world woke up. Allow myself the space to feel vulnerable. Allow the natural world to comfort and guide me.

Keep reminding myself about what had happened when I took a moment to lose myself at the Neolithic carvings at Newgrange. Allow myself the space to look within and listen to the soft whisperings – the questions that echo off the walls of the internal chamber.

And yet I was continuing to walk around with my head in a book. Continuing to rely on my wife for some sense of direction. It was time to slow down. Be present. Be here now. I didn't want our time in Ireland to seem like a blur of rushing from one place to another, and then feel regret on the flight home for not allowing myself the time and stillness of mind needed to connect with the land and its people and the faeries that look on from the liminal borderlands.

An hour later, we drove into the town of Tullamore (*Tulach Mhór*) in County Offaly. Famous for its namesake whiskey Tullamore Dew, the town seemed like a nice place to lay our weary heads.

We hadn't bothered to make any reservations beyond our first night. Instead, we relied on our pre-purchased B&B voucher plan and a listing of approved accommodation in the convenient booklet. After a short walk through the quiet streets – the shops all closed for the day – we found a small country home outside of town.

The older lady that answered the door seemed

surprised to find anyone looking for a room at 7:00pm. She was already in her nightdress.

"Oh... um... you're very welcome," she said, a little flustered. "I'll have to make the bedding, if you don't mind waiting a few minutes."

"That won't be a problem," said Paula. "Sorry to arrive so late. We didn't realize the time."

"Not to worry, love."

By the time the room was ready, our hostess was all smiles and recommended a nice restaurant down the road.

After a fine breakfast of hot tea, freshly baked bread and assorted fried meat, we packed up and drove forty minutes to Clonmacnoise (*Cluain Mhic Nóis*), a monastery on the River Shannon. St. Ciarán founded Clonmacnoise in 544, and the strategic location helped it become a major centre of religion, learning, craftsmanship and trade. Scholars from all over Europe came to visit, and many of the high kings of Tara and Connacht (*Connachta)* were buried on the grounds. However, since it was situated where the major east-west land route meets what is the longest river in the country, it also allowed easy access for thieving marauders and the arrival of the plague.

St. Ciarán helped create the first church – a small wooden structure (now the site of a ninth-century stone oratory), and the first of many churches to be clustered on the site – but unfortunately he died that same year of the plague (just before his thirty-third birthday). Towards the close of the seventh century, another plague killed off a large number of its students and professors. But Clonmacnoise persevered. Because of its auspicious location at the crossroads of two major medieval traffic routes, the monastery became bigger and more important than any other at the time.

The period of greatest growth came between the eighth and twelfth centuries. However Clonmacnoise was also attacked frequently during this time: mostly by the Irish (at least twenty-seven times), the Vikings (at least seven times) and the Normans (at least six times). The early wooden buildings were replaced by more durable stone structures in the ninth century, and the original population of ten men grew to almost two thousand by the eleventh century. Artisans associated with Clonmacnoise created some of the most beautiful and enduring artworks in metal and stone ever seen in the country – as well as The Book of the Dun Cow, a vellum manuscript dating to the twelfth century.

Having reviewed the history, I decided to leave my guidebooks in the car. Wanted to focus my attention on the sacred instead: the ruins of the monastic site, but also the winding river where the whooper swans spend their winter months. And I wanted to give myself the time and space needed to slip away from the present. Connect with the spirits of those that once inhabited the area over the centuries: the monks, the traders, the metalworkers and stone carvers.

Walking the perimeter on my own as the sun reflected off the broad majestic Shannon (*Abhainn na Sionainne*), I relaxed my shoulders, closed my eyes, listened to the wind, and allowed the unadulterated beauty of the country to soak into my cells. There was a hint of sweetness in the air, as if someone not too far away were cooling soda bread on the windowsill. There was also the hint of a fine whiskey – a flutter of fruit and toffee and malt. And there was faerie music, or that of a hundred ghosts softly singing an old song together.

After warming my face in the sun's rays, I found ruins that featured a stoup but instead of holy water there were a few coins in the dry stone basin. As I pressed my palm against the cold stone, I thought on the founders of this once bustling community. What sights and smells would have assaulted the senses centuries earlier? What was it like to begin construction of the first church along the banks of a river named after the granddaughter of the sea god Manannán Mac Lir?

St. Ciarán may have chosen this particular site for good reason, but not all early Irish monks seemed so keen on being central. Many monasteries were built in isolated places – some on islands in the middle of lakes or miles off the western shores. Perhaps the other founding monks were more interested in praying and working without distraction than developing their meagre settlement into a major centre of learning.

As I thought about all the robed ramblers of yesteryear, looking for a place to call home in the unforgiving Irish landscape, I also reflected on my life back at home. About my school and the comfort of my second-floor classroom. How it overlooks the playground and – after reheating my coffee at recess – how I often watch young children play tag, or kick around a soccer ball, or just roll around on the grass. Sometimes they get sidewalk chalk and draw out a series of numbered squares. Though there is already a defined space in which to play, they agree to the boundaries and limits of the game.

In some parts of Germany, hopscotch is called *tempelhupfen* (or temple hopping). When children draw out a pattern on the pavement or designate a pattern on the floor within which they must stay to keep in the game, they are creating a space within which the rules of engagement apply, and opposites are held together. Derived from the Greek word *temno* (I cut), a temple is a place of order set apart from the chaos of the natural world – a place of safety or refuge.

Arranging the space around us is a basic instinct. St. Ciarán and his followers created their monastery on the banks of the river in the same way that children grid out a simple game of hopscotch. I wondered about the existence of my sacred space or my temple – and whether finding a physical place in the world that felt like home could help me find a metaphysical space in which to stake out the boundaries of the self.

As a teenager, I read *The Teachings of Don Juan: A Yaqui Way of Knowledge* by Carlos Castaneda. In the book, and subsequent others, the author spins extraordinarily rich, hallucinogenic evocations of ancient paths to knowledge based on what he described as an extended apprenticeship with a Yaqui Indian shaman named Don Juan Matus. Over the years, scholars and critics have debated whether Don Juan existed and whether the books are anthropology or fantasy – fact or fiction.

I only remember bits and pieces, but the one idea that has stayed with me is that of a personal 'power spot'. Castaneda never completely defined what a power spot is, other than it is a place you can discover by turning your vision inward and moving about until you settle upon a physical location in which you feel a deep comfort. It is a place that rejuvenates one's energy and allows one to tap into divine power.

Did St. Ciarán (or any of the Twelve Apostles of Ireland) feel that he had found his personal power spot after days or weeks of wandering without rest? Was he able to tap into divine power as he watched the birds land on the river or looked up at the sun on warmer days? Did he know, when he stopped to admire the way that light reflects off the water, or the wind whistles through the long grasses, or a mere hint of sweetness fills the nose, that this would be the place where his name would be forever tied to? Or was he merely hoping to find relief from a world that must have seemed chaotic, with the political landscape changing and the country still predominantly pagan?

Clonmacnoise was (and continues to be) a sacred site for so many, and I wondered if perhaps the entire country could be considered a temple for those like myself in search of Truth and Beauty among the forty shades of green. Would I find my power spot in a country far from my own? I couldn't deny that something magical had happened when witnessing the border between two worlds slowly close for another day in the company of a cat, or when I was lost in thought as I traced the ancient designs at Newgrange and envisioned my internal chamber, or when I strolled among the ruins on the shores of the Shannon and thought about my need for a sacred space.

It was cold in the shade and, wanting to warm my shoulders, walked up the hill, found Paula, and together we strolled around the stone churches, high crosses, grave slabs, a medieval residence, and the round tower before poking around inside the interpretive centre where the original high crosses have been moved. Like other important archeological sites in Ireland, Clonmacnoise warrants repeat visits but we barely had an hour before heading further west.

. . .

"Two hours to Connemara," I announced as we sped out of the parking lot.

"Why does two hours of driving seem like no time at all in Canada, but it seems like forever in Ireland?" asked Paula half-an-hour later.

"I believe it has something to do with the faeries," I answered.

Driving around the southern half of the country was already bittersweet. There was so much we wanted to see and do, and yet we also craved some time to sit and reflect. We were speeding around the country – ripping from one tourist hotspot to the next – and we tried to justify it by telling ourselves that this was merely to get the lay of the land before our next visit, but we had no idea when that might be.

We skirted around Galway *(Gaillimh)*, connected to the N59, and found the rolling hills of Connemara. The desolate beauty was a radical shift from the pastoral patchwork we had previously explored. The moody greens and browns that paint the area blend with delicious oranges and reds that punctuate the bogs scattered throughout the lowlands. The still waters contrast with the clear glacial lakes. Moor grasses, myrtle, sedges, and wildflowers surround the rivers.

Set between the foothills of the Twelve Bens mountain range and the Atlantic Ocean, Clifden (*An Clochán*) is not a big town but it serves as the administrative and economic capital. Agriculture and fishing continue to play an important role. Trading in cattle, sheep and Connemara ponies continues throughout the year. Traditional Irish music and song have long been associated with the area.

There was just enough time to buy a worry stone in a small store before the entire town closed for the day. The box mentioned something about myth and mystery, or serenity and good fortune, but I just thought it was pretty.

As I rolled the stone around in my pocket and pressed my thumb into its indentation, I thought back on the last few days. We had only scratched the surface as we sped across the country, and I feared we were no different than other tourists that flood in every summer in search of Riverdance and Claddagh rings and Bog Buddies – or gorgeous tavern-maids pouring pints of the black stuff and sheep farmers with shillelaghs greeting you with a top-o'-the-morning before breaking out into a stirring rendition of "Danny Boy".

But maybe being a tourist wasn't so bad this time around. Maybe we needed to embrace the gift shops, and order stew or fish 'n' chips for dinner, and take lots of photographs, and fork over fistfuls of euros to see antique treasures in glass cases. While we didn't want to be those who spend an entire holiday eating in chain restaurants and queuing for hours outside overpriced roadside attractions, we also didn't want to be those who spend their entire holiday sulking in hipster coffee shops and dodgy pubs to completely avoid a single famous attraction. There had to be a happy medium.

We soon spotted a sign with the approved accommodation logo and checked in. "If you're wanting to walk into town," the lady said after we dropped our bags in our room, "there's an alleyway that cuts through, and you can wind down the hill. You'll find it a little ways there. Not too far. The walk down is easier than the walk back up – especially if you've had a pint or two. But I'll leave the light on. Have a grand time."

A short walk at the end of the day was enough to remind us that we felt more at home in the wilds and small towns tucked in gentle coves than on stuffy busses with tinted windows and upholstered seating. Though the walk was longer than both of us expected, and were both hungry, we continued along the sidewalk framed in by low stone fences at a slower pace with our fingers linked.

We weaved through a newer residential area before spying the first of the town's two churches through the foliage. It was then that I knew Ireland was where I needed to be. No worrying about the past or dreaming about the future. Only aware of the present moment, holding hands with my wife on our way to dinner. It felt perfect.

After our meal we went looking for live music. Ambled past a formidable collection of small pubs and heard the muffled sounds of fiddles, accordions, guitars and bodhráns. We were a little ways down Market Street when a crazed fiddler suddenly burst out the red door of J. Conneely's Bar. He was playing a frantic reel and enticing anyone within shouting distance to come inside. "C'mon in, me lovelies. It's warmer inside and the beer and whiskey are flowin'. Y'don't want to be wandering the streets in the dark and cold. Y'want to be inside, so."

Paula and I looked at each other. We were both smiling. Here was the mad devil drawing innocent souls into the depths. It was exactly what we were looking for. We followed the fiddler inside and ordered a couple pints before leaning against the bar to watch him play in a dervish of flying fingers. He was lost in a beautiful trance, and his wide Cheshire grin lit his face as he jumped around the small musicians' corner. The place was dark and warm, and smelled of wet wool and alcohol. The music was loud, the bar was busy, and the dim lights reflected off the half-finished pints teetering on small round tables. Paula and I tapped our feet during the jigs and reels, and held hands during the slow airs. At set break, we discovered that the mad devil was none other than world-renowned musician Fergal Scahill.

Tired from a full day of exploring, and with a couple pints warming our insides, we walked back up through the misty streets and towards our B&B. Strolling uphill through quiet neighbourhoods was exhausting, but the music had soaked into our souls. We fell into bed with nothing left to give, and couldn't wait for tomorrow to come.

CHAPTER 7

A GLORIOUS CRESCENDO

The relentlessly unpredictable weather paints the wild Connemara mountains and nearby bogland in muted colours, and as we toured the countryside there was always a briny edge that permeated the area. But while the landscape is uninviting, and we never ventured far from the road, it is wonderfully uplifting when the sun breaks through the clouds and lights up the earth-tones. The turquoise sea, tranquil coves and little villages perfectly balance the brooding lakes, rugged hillsides and windswept wetlands.

Connemara is also famous for its ponies and Paula made me stop the car so she could get a closer look. Known for their athleticism, versatility and disposition, the breed makes excellent show ponies. The ones we found in the farmer's field were not show ponies, however. They were beautiful majestic creatures, but were covered in mud. Paula went over to say hello to a few lingering by the fence-line and a man in gumboots, frayed wool sweater, and old hat hanging over his eyes came by with a feed bucket.

"Good morning," said Paula. "I was just admiring your horses."

"Ah, yeah. Fine creatures, there are. But stubborn, y'know. I've been trying to separate one from the others for the last little while, but none too successful."

"Is there anything I can do to help?" she asked.

"Going to rattle the feed bucket and try me best to get to her, but she's shy. Or maybe she don't like me. Who's to know? But if you can feed these two a wee bit a grass, maybe they'll be distracted enough not to notice and leave me to do me thing."

A helping hand seemed to do the trick and the farmer waved goodbye as we drove down the road. Lured by the lovely white sand and clear waters, we were tempted to go for a swim at nearby Dog's Bay (*Baile Átha Cliath*). But a fierce cold wind cut through our wool sweaters and we couldn't imagine even dipping our toes in the water as we quickened our pace to keep warm. All we could think about was a nice cup of tea.

The cold didn't stop some locals. A few teenagers, made of tougher stuff than us, walked slowly into the Atlantic in nothing but their trunks.

Seven minutes down the road is the village of Roundstone (*Cloch na Rón*), popular as a holiday resort and renowned among artists and naturalists for the remarkable beauty of the surrounding mountains and seascapes. It is also home to the world-famous Malachy Kearns bodhrán studio.

After following the signs and turning off the road to find ample parking, we walked into the studio and accompanying gift shop. We were hoping to find the man himself, but he had left for the day.

His wife, a woman who seemed to possess endless

patience with the tourists milling about, was explaining the history of the handheld drums as we looked around. Though we stood at the far end of the shop, we could hear every word. "The bodhrán is one of the oldest Irish musical instruments," she began. "It is a one-sided hand-held drum that is made through traditional methods using goat's skin stretched onto a birch frame. It began as a skin tray used for drawing turf – or peat – on the bogs. In the hands of a skilled player, the bodhrán can be a subtle and exciting instrument."

Various sized drums and drum accessories echoed the woman's voice as she continued. "For over thirty-five years, Malachy has been a respected bodhrán maker, and he is the only full-time bodhrán maker in the world. These days, colourful designs are hand-painted onto the drum, including family crests by special request." She was droning on a bit, and we decided to leave empty-handed – curious as to what little treasures we would discover in the nearby village.

A few minutes later, after parking on the side of the road and walking down towards the water, we found a small area that had been transformed into a market with a dozen stalls under umbrella covering. There were various jewelry vendors, and other crafts of the Celtic and not-so-Celtic variety, but what interested us most was the food.

The briny ocean air filled our noses and the sound of crashing waves was a fitting soundtrack as locals came and went with their bags and baskets. After milling about and trying a few samples, we were soon tearing apart crusty bread with our fingers and hacking away at local cheeses with a flimsy plastic knife. Though we had eaten in some cozy pubs across the country, this was one of the culinary highlights so far.

We arrived in Galway an hour-and-a-half later. Being a college town, the streets are often buzzing with youthful energy. With a population of seventy-five thousand, it is hardly a sprawling metropolis but it did feel substantial after all the small towns, villages, and lonely cemeteries.

On and on we walked without purpose (which would have been a terrible idea had I been on my own), and managed to stumble upon the Spanish Arch. One of the city's historical gems, the extension of the twelfth-century Norman-built wall was constructed in 1584. It housed soldiers who kept watch and manned cannons on the roof.

Behind us, we heard some sort of non-Irish music and discovered that Galway was hosting their annual Little Havana Festival. Young people sat in groups and tapped their feet to the music, but we didn't join in.

Instead we found St. Nicholas' Collegiate Church. Built around 1320, and dedicated to St. Nicholas of Myra (the patron saint of children and mariners, and the model for Santa Claus), it is the largest medieval parish church in Ireland that has been in continuous use.

As we approached the front door, we could hear haunting Gregorian chants. "There are only a few things more enticing while ambling along unknown streets," I said, "than centuries old monophonic, unaccompanied sacred song."

"I assume that means you want to go inside?" asked Paula.

"It does, indeed," I replied.

There was only a smattering of people sitting in the pews, and we stood against the back wall as the voices filled the space in glorious crescendo.

"The central tradition of Western plainchant surpasses time and place," I whispered, "and I feel myself flooded with fleeting impressions and memories not my own, all contained within the vast web of the collective consciousness."

Paula knew I was being cheeky about the concept of past lives so, rather than responding audibly, she just squeezed my hand and smiled. My reluctance to accept reincarnation as absolute truth was something we had discussed just before leaving home.

Soon after my wife heads to work on a Saturday morning, I go through all my writer's rituals: burning incense, the smoke twirling and twisting in the sunbeams; lighting a beeswax candle, the flame flickering in a dark corner; placing an old recording of Gregorian chants on the turntable; stringing small wooden beads around my neck and covering my head with a light hood; sitting down at my antique roll-top desk, with its stains and scratches and long drawers full of forgotten treasures; and uncapping my fountain pen. It doesn't take long before the world becomes unfocused and I have tapped into the creative flow. Though I find myself at my most creative when my office area resembles a scriptorium, ancient sights and sounds and smells all around me, I have given little thought as to why.

I've spent enough time out in the woods or walking alone at night along quiet streets to observe the cycles of nature: the cyclic motion of the celestial bodies, or the way a beautiful flower returns to the earth after releasing its seeds so that new life may begin. I understand that our lives follow a fundamental pattern. There is change, growth, transformation and evolution. I understand that there is a constant rebirth of energy that occurs all around us in different shapes and forms. But it is here that I cannot go any further. It's comforting to believe that each reincarnating soul chooses a home and a family that can best fulfill its next step of learning and maturation, but there is still something preventing me from taking the final leap – from believing that the soul evolves from immaturity to spiritual illumination over several lifetimes.

Though much of my family followed a spiritual path that originated in thirteenth-century India – neither my brother nor I have much interest in walking the same path as adults. Though reincarnation and meditation and vegetarianism and karma were a part of our upbringing, the only thing that seems to have made a lasting impact on me is an affinity for Indian food.

I have never been able to wholly accept the idea that the non-physical essence of a living being starts a new life in a different physical form or body after biological death. Though I find the similarities and differences in ethics, metaphysics, and the nature and forms of salvation fascinating – and keenly observe human beliefs and practices regarding the sacred, numinous, spiritual and divine – I continue to observe them from a sociological point of view and not that of a seeker.

Recurring dreams, odd memories and feelings of déjà vu do little to prove reincarnation. But that doesn't stop me from continually researching the matter long into the night. I read recently that being an empath is a sign that one's soul has undergone many previous reincarnations. The belief that one becomes extremely sensitive after experiencing so many emotions in previous lives.

Then I read about the concept of 'soul age', which marks the soul's continued evolution as it gathers new experiences, makes choices, and learns life lessons. 'The primary way the soul evolves,' wrote one author, 'is by learning the ramifications of personal choice.'

Could my unexplainable attraction to a different culture

be considered past life residue, or was all of this a right load of old codswallop?

Though I have yet to accept a spiritual practice as my own, I have remained open. Maybe accepting that there *might* be a reason I feel so strongly connected to the stories, myths and magic of Ireland – beyond that which can be easily explained – is okay for right now.

As I refocused into the present moment, I turned to find Paula smiling at me.

"Welcome back," she said. "Where were you?"

"Not sure," I answered. "Somewhere else."

"Are you ready to continue on our journey?"

"I am, indeed," I said. "After you."

We ambled through the Galway Farmers' Market before continuing down busy streets, not-so-busy streets, and narrow alleyways. Then we walked past our parked car. "How did that happen?" I asked. "I thought our car was clear across town."

"No," said Paula. "I figured we were getting close to where we started. Have you seen enough or do you want to keep exploring?"

"I think I've seen enough. Let's get out of here."

DOOLIN IS APPROXIMATELY seventy kilometres south of Galway. Seventy kilometres on Canadian highways takes about forty-five minutes. In Ireland, the same distance takes over an hour-and-a-half.

Doolin (*Dúlainn*) is a quaint little town of approximately five hundred residents. Though traditionally a fishing village, it is now world-renowned as the music capital of the country. It seemed like the perfect place to spend the night.

We approached the first B&B that was listed in our approved accommodation guide and the innkeeper slouched up to the counter.

"Do you have a room for the night?" asked Paula.

"Ah, well, it is Bank Holiday, of course."

"Is it?" I asked, afraid of the answer.

"'Tis. But luckily for you, I think I have a room with three single beds. You'll have to hold hands if you're feeling amorous."

"That'll be fine," Paula laughed.

"Is there a pub nearby you would recommend?" I asked the innkeeper.

"Oh, aye. Just head down that way a bit," he said, pointing to the right. "There's a great little place about a five-minute walk from here."

We dropped our bags in our room and headed out for the evening.

Gus O'Connor's was packed with people. Not only was there nowhere to sit, there was nowhere to even stand. We wedged ourselves into one door, slithered through the throng of people, and then popped out the other.

A couple young men were finishing their pints outside, and balancing the glasses on the window ledge.

"Busy place," I said.

"Oh, yeah," said one man. "Bank Holiday, y'know."

"Is there another pub close by?" asked Paula.

"Oh, yeah. Five minutes that way." He pointed the way we had come.

"Red and white, so it is," the man said. "You won't miss it. Great *craic*, so."

We passed our B&B, and then headed across the north side of the village. It took over twenty minutes before we found the place. White with red trim. Lettering above the door and windows: Fáilte Mac Diarmada Dubhlinn.

"This looks like the place."

"It better be," said Paula. "I'm tired of walking and I need a beer."

As much as I am fond of a quaint pub, I am not a heavy drinker. After a beer or a thimble of whiskey, I tend to get sleepy and head to bed. But we were in Ireland – the birthplace of Guinness and whiskey – and maybe the village of Doolin was the ideal place to go a bit crazy. "Perhaps I should expand my drinking horizons tonight."

"Just don't get sick."

"Wouldn't dream of it," I said.

McDermott's Bar was crowded, but not as crowded as Gus O'Connor's. As I searched for a bit of bar space with which to prop our elbows, Paula spied our opportunity across the room. By some miracle she found a table for two near the small stage.

Only as we sat down did I realize that the bar was on the other side of the room and I would have to (not-so-gently) push my way through the crowd to get our drinks.

The opening act soon took to the stage. Amongst the loud din of the busy pub, an older gentleman plugged his guitar in, checked the microphone, and then sang an assortment of folk songs from Ireland and around the world.

We finished our pints, and I went up to get us a round of whiskey (or *uisce beatha*, literally 'water of life'). I chose the standard fare while Paula tried a peated single malt from Connemara. It tasted like the air smells in western Ireland – a mix of sweet earthiness, leather, vanilla and barley, with a touch of apple.

The older gentleman packed up his guitar and made

way for a merry band of teenage musicians that took to the stage.

Led by a commanding young woman that communicated to the soundboard operator and her band mates with a serious of subtle head nods, they played rollicking instrumental pieces with perfect timing – one song after the other without much of a break – and soon the bar was overflowing with holiday revellers. We counted ourselves lucky that we had snagged our seats when we did, and I went up for more whiskey.

During the set break, random members of the audience came on stage to sing. Feeling warm and fuzzy, and overly confident, I thought about performing a Newfoundland sea shanty but quickly convinced myself that another beer was a better idea.

A heavier-set man heaved himself up and took to the stage. His voice was deep and moving but, too shy to face the audience, he sang with his back to us. The crowd joined him for a stirring rendition of "Black Velvet Band", and then his drunken friend began yelling at him. "Turn around Kenny! Turn around! This is Kenny from Limerick, but the big bastard won't turn around! Turn around Kenny!"

He didn't turn around, nor did he seem fazed that his drunken friend was jeering him on. Maybe this happened all the time to Kenny. It would have done my head in, but Kenny is a better man than I.

During the second set, I had another beer and another whiskey. Not a great idea, but there you go. After that, we called it a night. Barely got undressed before passing out in my single bed.

CHAPTER 8

A SUBLIME ENIGMA

The next morning, I staggered out of bed and hoped a long shower would somehow wash away the sins of the previous night. It didn't, and I was unsure if I was going to finish my full Irish when we sat down in the breakfast room. "May have had a bit too much to drink," I told the innkeeper.

"Ah, you best be careful," he said, placing a plate of fried meat in front of me. "That stuff'll kill you."

After tentatively taking my first forkful, the innkeeper returned with another couple. He took their order and then turned back to me. "And you," he said. "You best eat as much as you can. Good soakage, y'know, and you'll be feeling better in no time."

I did as I was told.

After gathering our things and checking out, I began to feel my usual self. "Maybe more like 63% of my usual self," I muttered to Paula.

With the windows down, and the cold swirling inside the car, the world seemed a little less painful on the short drive between Doolin and the parking lot for the Cliffs of

Moher (*Aillte an Mhothair)*. Almost in good spirits as we walked across the street and along the wide path to the cliff's edge.

The path ends abruptly at a large billboard that warns visitors of immanent death, but dozens ignored the threat and shimmied around without a second thought. As we cautiously inched our way along the narrow path that parallels the edge, we hoped that no sudden gusts of gravity would cause our untimely demise.

The cliffs rank among the top-visited tourist sites in Ireland and receive more than a million visitors a year. Used as a backdrop for films like *The Princess Bride* and *Harry Potter and the Half Blood Prince*, they rise a hundred and twenty meters above the Atlantic Ocean and reach their maximum height of two hundred fourteen meters just north of O'Brien's Tower (eight kilometres further on).

The striated stone reaches its long fingers to counties Cork and Kerry, and we watched as some visitors carefully leaned over while others lay flat on their chests before inching their way to the brink of nothingness. The sheer drop is a haven for sea birds that catch the slipstream before nipping into their respective nests and hidey-holes, and we could see the Aran Islands (*Oileáin Árann*) and Galway Bay as we planted our feet so as not to be hurled over. Though uncertain about the prospect of a long wind-whipped trek along the clifftop, the invigorating freshness was certainly appreciated – especially given my current state.

"Apparently the Cliffs of Moher have been voted 'Best Cliff View in the World' by *Conde Nast Traveler*," I said. "So there's that."

"They are amazing," said Paula.

"But..."

"Well, it reminds me..."

"Uh-huh?"

"That I'm not a huge fan of heights."

"Shall we head back to the car and continue on to the Burren, then?"

Rather than answer, Paula spun around and hoofed it back to the paved path.

Maybe because I was still feeling a little wobbly from the night's frivolities, or maybe because we were competing for space with a heaving throng of tourists, but a quick peek was enough for me.

There are surely few places in Ireland more dramatic than the cliffs, which are constantly being lashed by the Atlantic waves and where one can feel as if they are braving the ocean from the prow of a magnificent ship, but we had lasted little more than fifteen minutes before hightailing it back to the car.

The Burren (*Boirinn*) seems a wasteland at first glance – limestone pavements with crisscrossing cracks. When Oliver Cromwell decided to export thousands of rebellious Irishmen from the eastern part of the country, he asked one of his officers to seek out a suitable location. After several campaigns across the countryside, in which he hunted small bands and destroyed foodstuff and crops, Edmund Ludlow reported back when he came upon the Burren. "It is a country where there is not enough water to drown a man, wood enough to hang one, nor earth enough to bury him. This is just the place you are looking for." Cromwell agreed and gave all the imprisoned Irishmen the choice: "To hell or Connacht."

On closer inspection, the Burren is not as bleak as it seems. The region supports an amazing variety of flora and fauna including Arctic, Mediterranean and Alpine plants as well as rare Irish species (some of which are only found in the area). In fact, three-quarters of the country's species of flowers are found here, and it's one of the main breeding areas in Ireland of the European pine marten. The sublime enigma of the Burren is that, in a desert of stone, rare living things and captivating landforms abound. The stark beauty apparently inspired Tolkien as he was writing *The Lord of the Rings*.

Though the Cliffs of Moher are certainly more popular, we both felt more at peace in the quiet of the Burren. More akin to the magic that creeps up gently between the cracks. The silence of the Burren is as layered as the undulating landscape – the pale grey stone ribboned with crags and crevices, and the miniature cliffs spread like mosaics as far as the horizon.

We had also come in search of a portal tomb called the Poulnabrone dolmen, one of approximately a hundred seventy-four dolmens in Ireland dating back to the Neolithic period.

Poulnabrone (which translates to Hole of the Sorrows) consists of a twelve-foot, slab-like, tabular capstone supported by two sets of slender upright parallel portal stones. Excavations revealed the remains of twenty-one people in the main tomb chamber; radiocarbon dating of their bones indicate that the tomb was in continual use between five thousand two hundred and five thousand eight hundred years ago. Some archaeologists speculate that the low angle of the capstone had to do with the ancient people's vision of the Underworld. Local deities were closely tied to the land and this was especially so of the Morrígan, the phantom queen associated with war and death (as well as regeneration and rebirth). The Morrígan and other deities, spirits, faeries and sprites were greatly feared, and defences were built against them at sacred sites throughout Ireland. Perhaps Poulnabrone (*Poll na Brón*) was constructed not to ease the passage of the soul to the next life but to discourage spirits of the other realm from entering the world of the living.

We crossed the eerie moonscape and made our way directly to the dolman. The barren land makes the powerful symbolic portal tomb even more impressive as it stands against a backdrop made almost entirely of rock.

I was curious what it might feel like to stand under the capstone, and position myself at the doorway between two worlds, but the iconic archaeological monument was cordoned off. Even though there was no one around, I respected the weathered rope. The Underworld would have to wait.

We walked around for a while, mostly with our heads down so as not to fall into any cracks and twist our ankles, and I wondered what the displaced Irish thought about stumbling across sites such as this one.

Paula must have been thinking the same thing, and looked out towards the horizon as she chose her words carefully. "Do you think they would have seen Poulnabrone as a place of safety and a promise of eternal rest, or do you think they would have feared this Neolithic dolmen?"

"I think it's a mistake," I answered, "to make a correlation between the Underworld and the Christian concept of hell."

"Go on."

"Well, the Underworld is not a place where souls are punished, but merely another realm of the Otherworld – and therefore not a place of death, but a celebration of life. For those that arrived with nothing but what they could carry, I think that ancient sites like Poulnabrone must have given them hope and allowed them to reflect on another – perhaps even better – world beyond this one."

Back at the car, we checked the map and calculated there were over three hours of driving ahead of us: south to Limerick, west to Tralee, and on to Dingle. We were less than halfway through our driving tour of the southern half of the republic, and already feeling the need for a break. We both needed a day away from the rental car and some time to kick up our feet. A day to soak in the beauty of the country without the rush of getting to the next place. But that was not something we had planned for.

After a quick snack of flavoured crisps, we headed towards the most westerly piece of land in Europe (unless you include Iceland).

Somewhere west of Tralee (*Trá Lí*), we fell silent as the most stunning coastline sped by. It was difficult to keep my eyes on the road when surrounded by such rugged splendour – where blues and greens and greys weave together in their eternal tapestry – and Paula had to remind me to stop looking out towards the ocean. This is probably why the main route from Tralee to Dingle has been called the most dangerous stretch of road in the county. Local *gardaí* hope that changes in driving behaviour and improvements to the road will stem the deadly tide, but I think the only solution is to block the view with hideous billboards advertising tech companies. (Note: Please don't do that. I'm only joking.)

As we neared Dingle, I felt my brain going numb. And then let out a long sigh.

"What's the matter?" asked Paula.

"We're surrounded by such intense beauty, and I feel such an inexplicable pull, but we have no time to appreciate it. We're just crossing things off a list, like any other tourist."

"Don't think of 'tourist' as some cringe-worthy word. It's okay to get an overview of the country and its people and the culture. And then we can come back and spend an extended amount of time in one place. You can even come by yourself next time, if you need to. Do your research, and then head off into the great unknown. I have no doubt that you'll get lost, but you should do what you need to do, and then come home and write all about it as you mumble at your desk. I'm okay with that."

"I do enjoy mumbling at my desk."

"I know, sweetie."

CHAPTER 9

AN INEXPLICABLE PULL

I was reflecting on that inexplicable pull three years later as I attempted to book myself into the same B&B as before and relive my first early morning in Ireland with the cat and the fog and the view of Newgrange. I wanted my second trip to the country to begin with the same sense of magic and mystery. To feel the same sense of peace, and witness again the softening of the border between two worlds.

But the owners had retired. The only other option within walking distance to the archeological site was listed as a hostel-like lodge. It didn't seem to have the same quaintness that the farmhouse had, but it did offer breakfast with the room. Maybe romantic beginnings weren't as important the second time around.

After finally arriving in Dublin and wedging myself into the rental car with sour-smelling jeans, I managed to get where I needed to go and didn't get lost once.

Thank God for small mercies.

Inside, a young man was more involved with the television than maintaining the front desk, but I arrived during the commercials and was checked in quickly.

"Your room is all the way down the hall," he said. "Have a good night."

"Thanks," I said. "I'm sure I will."

Shortly after, the quiet hallway was filled with someone singing. It wasn't a haunting Celtic ballad – which would have been a fitting soundtrack – but instead a Christian hymn in what seemed to be an Indo-Irish accent. Unsure if my sleep-deprived brain was playing tricks on me, I peeked inside the small conference room to confirm.

It must have been a family reunion, or a staff party, or something to that effect. An older woman wearing a *salwar kameez* made eye contact, nodded her head to say hello, and I nodded back before continuing on my way. The music echoed down the hallway, followed by applause and cheers. The question remained: Was I going to fall sleep at a reasonable hour? Possibly not. Still, could have been worse. Could have been country music.

Neither the stiff bedding and rough sheets nor the whooping and hollering from down the hall made it a restful night, but I managed a few hours of slumber. In the morning, I shuffled down the hall towards the dining room. The lodge advertises a breakfast buffet, so visions of locally baked bread, farm sausages, and half a dozen varieties of cheese danced in my head. While the Irish are not necessarily known for their fine cuisine, the full Irish breakfast is a thing of beauty and my heart quickened at the thought.

On display were grocery store sliced meats, process cheese still in plastic wrappings, and day-old bread that only softened when I dipped chunks into lukewarm tea. With enough calories to get me through the morning, I left the empty dining room and checked out.

My morning couldn't have been less interesting, and I was starting to doubt my solo adventure, but tried to remain optimistic while motoring down the road to the visitors' centre.

Later, after touring Newgrange and poring over my coiled map book, I figured the best way to get from Brú na Bóinne to the town of Dingle – estimated at about four and half hours – was to head back towards Dublin and connect to the M50 (the C-shaped orbital motorway that circumnavigates the city, and therefore is the busiest stretch of road in Ireland) before exiting onto the N7. While crossing the country, the N7 turns into the M7, which turns into the M20, which turns into the N21, and then finally turns into the N86 (because that's not confusing at all). If I didn't do anything silly, like stop for gas or anything to eat, I should be in West Kerry for a nice cup of late-afternoon tea – despite my terrible sense of direction.

With quick peeks at the map book laid flat on the passenger seat, I tracked my progress every fifteen or twenty minutes. Traffic was busy, but that didn't bother me. Nor did driving on the opposite side of the road to what I was used to.

A debate was raging on about water bills on RTÉ. Callers were complaining about having to pay or having to pay more than they should. After an hour of this, I turned the dial to some traditional music – mostly fiddle and accordion tunes – and tapped on the steering wheel as the road wound on and on.

Passed exits for Rathcoole, Kilcullen, Kildare and Rathdowney (*Ráth Cúil*, *Cill Chuilinn*, *Cill Dara* and *Ráth Domhnaigh*) – all places that would remain a mystery – and felt guilty for cruising across the country at a constant velocity without stopping to explore little villages along the way.

But I had limited time in the country and little villages along the M7 would have to wait until another time.

The first couple hours went by without a hitch and I was confident I would reach Dingle by mid-afternoon. It was almost too easy. Crossing Ireland should involve some sort of adventure. And that's when I noticed a posted detour.

A series of small signs directed me away from the highway, down along a series of country lanes. Soon there were only tall hedges and gnarly trees. The traffic had somehow thinned to nearly nothing.

"Perhaps I'll just continue on my way, find a local village, and there will be useful signs leading me back to where I need to go," I said to myself. Turned up the radio and drummed on the steering wheel to a rollicking fiddle tune.

Driving more like a country Irishman than a cautious Canadian is never a good idea, but nevertheless I flew over hills and around sharp corners. This reckless style can be excused if one is familiar with the lay of the land, but I wasn't. Didn't know, for instance, that a small village was just around the bend.

Sped right through it – far too fast to notice if there were useful signage. "I'll stop twice at the next village," I told myself.

After ten minutes of tall hedges and gnarly trees, there was another small village. This time I did slow down, hoping there was a welcome sign with the name in clear lettering so I could reference it on my map. There wasn't.

The road splits on the other side of the unnamed village. One road leads uphill and the other downhill. I chose the one that leads downhill. This was probably a mistake.

On the rare occasion the road allowed me a quick peek at the map book, I tried to figure out where I was. But I could have been anywhere. Had Ireland not been an island, I may have been in another country.

Earlier, I had made a conscientious choice to turn down any sort of GPS or sat-nav features with my rental car. Considered it cheating. Wanted to welcome adventure as I explored the lesser-known Ireland.

However, having spent close to an hour driving all over hell's half-acre, I was beginning to see the appeal of modern-day technology.

The road suddenly came to an end, and I found myself on the edge of a town of some significant size. Went looking for someone who could give me directions back to the highway and the first person I found was the local mechanic. He was wearing greasy overalls and was half-hidden under the hood of an old car.

"Excuse me," I began. "Um... I'm wondering if you could tell me where I am."

The mechanic snorted and grumbled, and then straightened up and turned around. Expected him to be gruff and unpleasant but there was a big smile across his face. He still hadn't said anything.

"I was following this road," I continued, "but now I don't know where I am."

Showed him the map book. He scanned the page.

"Ah, right... well... this is a good map," he said. "But you're not on it."

"I'm not?" I asked, looking down at the open page.

"Not to worry," he laughed. "Here's what you got to do: head all the way through town and you'll see signs connecting you back to the motorway at the other end. It's very simple. Sure, you won't even need your map book."

He was right, and in ten minutes I was back on the highway. Soon enough, skirting around Limerick and passing exits for Patrickswell, Rathkeale and Newcastle West (*Tobar Phádraig*, *Ráth Caola*, and *An Caisleán Nua Thiar*) – more places that would remain a mystery.

As I approached Tralee, an hour from the town of Dingle, I decided to stretch my legs and find a gas station.

Turned off the highway and found the small arrow indicating what side the tank was on but, when I turned off the engine, I couldn't find the lever to release the fuel door. It wasn't under the seat or under the dash. Popped the hood and the trunk twice, and found the fuse box, but there was no lever.

"Excuse me," I said to a woman in her early-forties who was filling her sensible four-door sedan. "Have you any idea where the fuel door might be? I can't find it anywhere."

"Sorry," she said. "I don't. But you could try the lads inside. They might know."

They didn't know.

Decided to pry it open with my car key, hoping not to cause too much damage, but it swivelled open after applying a little pressure with the palm of my hand. "That was a close call," I muttered while looking around to see if anyone had noticed.

Left Tralee without getting turned around (which was a huge success) and was on my way for the last fifty kilometres of the day's drive. Fought to stay on the narrow road as I admired the spectacular scenery.

A small sign pointed me towards Inch Beach, and I turned off somewhere between Camp and Annascaul (*An Com* and *Abhainn an Scáil*). Thought it might be fun to go for a quick cup of tea and a bit of a walk before arriving at my final destination. Judging by the map book, there couldn't be more than ten kilometres separating the N86 from the southern edge of the peninsula. Inch Beach should be easy to find.

Got lost anyway. Time and space bent into some alternate universe as I drove around in circles. Every road was narrower than the last. Eventually there was a ridge on what seemed closer to an animal trail. It was barely wide enough for my rental car, and got out at a little pullout to see if I could spy the beach. Instead, there was a muddy sheep.

Surprised to have a visitor, the sheep ran towards me. Wasn't sure if I should jump in the car and drive away before I was trampled or attempt some form of communication. Chose the latter.

The sheep stopped and looked at me quizzically when it realized I was a stranger. But rather than turn around and make its way back from whence it came, the sheep stared at me and I stared back. With no one around to talk to, and my brain soft from driving across the country, I engaged the sheep in conversation. "Nice view."

The sheep answered back, "Baa."

"You wouldn't happen to know the way to Dingle, would you?"

The sheep snorted in response.

Got back into the car and continued up the hill. Luckily, half hidden behind an overgrown bush, there was a faded wooden sign directing me to town.

It was then that I realized that I had no idea where my B&B was located. Had a name but no address. In my rush to cross the country, I had forgotten to look up the details.

There is a gas station on the edge of town and I hoped the friendly attendants could help.

A young man inside was leaning his head on his hand,

casually sliding lottery scratch cards between the counter and the Plexiglass. "How are ya?" he asked as I approached.

"Um... fine," I answered. "Actually, I'm looking for Dúinín House. It's a B&B somewhere in town. Do you know of it?"

"Isn't that Pat Nelligan's place?" he asked his colleague who was stocking chocolate bars.

"I think that's right, yeah," the colleague answered back, lifting his head above the top of the shelving unit.

The young man behind the counter looked out the window before giving me directions. "Just beyond us is a little roundabout. Head to your right, and that road is called The Mall. At the end, on your left, you'll see a bright yellow pub with green trim – that's An Driochead Beag."

"Okay," I said.

"Actually, it's not so much at the end of the road, but more like a bit of an 'S' curve, y'know. Anyway, cross the little bridge – the pub is named after it – and head up the hill. That road is Spa Road. Your B&B is just up there, so head up the hill and keep your eyes to the right. It's about a kilometre, maybe a kilometre and a half, I'd say."

His directions were perfect. An Driochead Beag was easy to find and so was Dúinín House. Parked the car, walked up the driveway, and knocked on the front door.

CHAPTER 10

A THOUSAND SUNRISES AND A THOUSAND SUNSETS

Normally, I would allow my body the rest it needed after flying halfway around the world, spending a restless night near Brú na Bóinne, and then driving across the country, but I wanted to wake up before dawn to join the fife and drum band as it made its way through Dingle on the morning of St. Patrick's Day.

In 1899, an ex-coastguard officer returned from the Boer War and introduced the fife (similar to the piccolo) to West Kerry. The Dingle Fife and Drum Band was soon born, and for over a century there has scarcely been any notable occasion that has not been honoured by their appearance.

Set my alarm, crawled under the covers, curled up, and slept undisturbed.

Morning sunlight filtered through the curtains. When I rolled over to check the time, the clock read 8:32am. The alarm had long given up. So much for that idea.

Pat walked in with a pot of tea soon after I sat down. "Big day, today," he said. "You'll be wanting to get into town for the parade, of course. Tonight, there'll be lots of music and... well... I imagine many of us will be having a few too many, if you know what I mean."

"I think I do."

"We won't wait up for you, then," he joked as he headed back into the kitchen.

Halfway through my meal, Pat sat down and I asked him about the events of the day.

"Well, the children'll all be there at the parade – lined up along the street – dressed in orange and green and waving little flags. There'll be a few bands. It's all a little... I don't know... silly, maybe, but it's a nice way to celebrate the morning. Wouldn't miss it. Anne and I'll be there. You can join us if you'd like."

The days of strolling around with one child on my shoulders and another by the hand, patiently waiting for costumed men and women to toss hard candy into the streets, were long gone. Made way for other things. Teenager things.

Maybe a small-town parade would be a lovely way to begin the festivities. Maybe watching the eyes of young Irish children light up with all the sights and sounds would be the perfect way to spend an hour.

Turned to Pat as he cleared another table. "I'll see you there."

Anne stopped me as I made my way down the hall. "It's tradition to pin on a bit of clover," she told me. "It is said that Patrick used the three leaves of the shamrock to explain the Christian holy trinity. Don't know if that's really true or not, but today you'll wear it as others have done."

While the fife and drum band had come and gone, I was excited to witness other traditions of the area. Layered up, pinned the clover on my wool sweater, and headed down the hill as the sun attempted to break through the morning fog. But as I neared the edge of town, there were no crowds of people or small bands marching through the alleyways. Just myself, wandering the streets. It was almost *too* quiet, as if everyone else knew something I didn't. Perhaps the tourists were savouring their second cup of tea, and the residents of Dingle were having a leisurely breakfast, tending to their lambs, or just watching the fog slowly dissipate.

Continued on my way, along the harbour, and then slipped into Murphy's Ice Cream for one of their Mayan hot chocolates. "Thought it would be a little busier in town this morning," I said to the young man behind the counter.

"There was the fife and drum band earlier."

"Right," I confirmed. "Slept through that."

"And, of course, the parade later this morning. And there's mass at St. Mary's if you're so inclined."

Finished my drink, nodded goodbye to the young man, and wove through the narrower alleyways that cross the town at odd angles where little shops and apartments are tucked into the brickwork. Then I turned down Green Street as a dozen men and women in their finest rushed to the front door of St. Mary's Church before disappearing into the darkness.

Having not been raised a Christian, much less a Catholic, I wasn't sure of protocol. But, after lingering on the sidewalk, debating whether they would recognize me as an outsider, curiosity won out in the end.

My eyes adjusted to the lack of light in the church as those ahead of me were dipping their fingers in the holy water and making the sign of the cross. Shuffled towards the back where casual viewers were leaning on one leg and then the other.

An altar server walked down the aisle, dressed in traditional garb and waving the incense pot, while the crowd repeated the liturgy. Mass was being conducted in the Irish language and, as the smells filled my nose, the soothing voice of the priest echoed off the walls of the neo-Gothic church.

I suppose it was a sense of community and history (even if neither were mine) that I found so moving.

Though the church is beautiful, and the service was fascinating, fifteen minutes was enough. Looked around one last time and slipped out.

The streets were slowly coming to life as I made my way down the road and into Strand House. Generally advertised as a ladies' fashion boutique and café, the first floor also includes men's fashion and a large selection of tourist tat.

My youngest had asked if I could find a snow globe. Unsure if there were snow globes in Ireland but, after a few minutes among the rows of baseball hats, bottle openers, cell phone charms, fridge magnets, and Celtic blessing wall hangings, I found a little Chinese-made snow globe with a mildly offensive preposterous-looking leprechaun inside. Happy to cross that off the list, I headed into the men's department in search of a smart-looking piece of Irish wear, so as to look more like a local than a tourist.

The tweed vest on the centre rack was more expensive than I had anticipated, but it fit well and made me appear slimmer (which is also advantageous).

After poking about another corner of the shop with the vest still on, and examining myself in a different mirror, an older couple approached me.

"Would you mind, if you're not too busy..."

Assuming they were talking to someone standing behind me, I slowly turned around. But there was no one there.

"My husband is looking for a size large, but there doesn't seem to be any on the shelf. We were wondering if there were any in the back?"

"I would check," I said, "but I don't actually work here."

"Do you not?"

"Um, no."

I liked being mistaken for a local. It made me feel – for just a brief moment – that I belonged somewhere. Though the older couple were only looking for some assistance in finding the right size, and I happened to be the nearest warm body in the vicinity, it made me feel that I was a part of the collective – not merely an observer of life, watching the world unfold from the perimeter. Maybe there were others like me. Those who also wandered aimlessly in layers of tweed and wool, balancing quiet moments of contemplation among the cold stone with trad sessions and pints in a warm pub.

I never felt that I belonged while growing up in the middle-class suburbs of Victoria. As some form of rebellion, I grew my hair long, strung wooden beads on hemp twine, read Kerouac and Ginsberg, and fled to Lotus Land to hang out in parks with bongo-playing, dreadlock-sporting hippies. But that world felt just as strange as the one I tried desperately to escape.

My first teaching job was deep in cowboy country. Ten months of chewing tobacco, bar fights, and honky-tonk country music. My second job was in a fly-in fishing village. Ten months of isolation, seasickness, and a tragic lack of sunshine.

Now, living in a rural farming town in southeastern British Columbia, where everyone fixes anything and everything with duct tape and binder twine, I constantly compare my soft hands to the calloused hands of those that sit nursing cups of diner coffee on days too miserable for haying. I listen in on conversations about tractor parts, grain prices and well pumps, and rarely have anything to add.

It would seem that I'm not alone. After checking my day-timer and making some coffee, I strolled through the school recently and asked my colleagues if they felt the same – whether they felt a part of the whole.

While they enjoy their jobs and feel a part of the school community, it's a different story when the final bell rings. They are various reasons for this: some told me that they don't have many friends nearby; that they don't feel any connection to a group or a club; that there is nowhere to go for dinner or a drink that feels familiar.

All these are issues that I also deal with. Most days, it doesn't affect me. I go about my business, either in the classroom or at home, and give little thought as to why I feel that I don't belong.

Sometimes I make a brave attempt: keeping an open mind when a new restaurant opens or there's some sort of social gathering. Still, that familiar feeling of being an outsider prevails.

But I don't feel out of place in Ireland. Don't feel the need to escape. The need to force myself to do something out of character. I can wrap myself in a lovely Aran sweater and walk along the wild western shores on my own, or tuck myself into a dark corner and read poetry. Listen to tunes that most here at home would describe as 'old-timey' without feeling that I'm the odd one out.

After leaving Strand House, with vest and snow globe in hand, more and more people filled the streets. Continued my walk around town and soon passed O'Flaherty's, one of Dingle's more recognizable pubs. With early Irish lettering above the door, beautiful stonework accented by red and white window frames, and the muffled sounds of competing conversations, it seemed like a decent place for a pint or two.

Inside, musicians were taking turns warming up their instruments, while others were chatting or finding quieter corners with cups of tea. It was crowded, and I went in search of somewhere to stand along the back wall – awkwardly knocking past a few people and bumping strangers with my backpack.

The bar is panelled in dark wood with framed photographs, antiques, and an old piano. There is a fine selection of whiskeys on display. It seemed to be the ideal whereabouts to keep warm until the parade. But, after looking around, I noticed that everyone was in some sort of matching jacket. Not only was every member of the news crew wearing insignia of some kind, so too was every patron. The only one *not* belonging to some group or organization was me.

Though no one said anything or even made a stinky face in my direction, I thought it best to slip out unnoticed.

Naturally I bumped into several musicians on the way out – causing them to spill their tea. Also knocked into an announcer from RTÉ. Not my finest hour. Luckily, I didn't trip over the cords snaking across the floor and cause expensive camera equipment to come crashing to the floor. Not surprisingly, all the good feelings I had from being mistaken as an employee of Strand House suddenly disappeared.

Families were setting up folding chairs along the parade route as a growing queue for Murphy's Ice Cream grew and grew. It was a chilly morning, and I assumed most were in line for hot drinks, but almost everyone leaving the shop was devouring frozen treats. Ice cream on a chilly mid-March morning seemed like a great idea to me as well, so I stood behind a louder couple in matching windbreakers.

"If I'm going to have ice cream," said the man in a Texan accent, "then it better be *darn* good ice cream."

"I'm sure it will be, my darling," said his wife.

A little while later, after scanning the flavours and choosing caramelized brown bread, I could confirm that Murphy's Ice Cream does indeed make *darn* good ice cream. The texture of this particular frozen treat is a little unusual because of the crumb, but the taste is heavenly.

A young man sporting an expensive camera around his neck approached me as I was standing on the sidewalk. "Excuse me," he said as he looked down at his guidebook. "I've got a question about this here. Are you a local?"

"I'm not, no," I said. "Are you?"

"No. I'm from Boston," he answered.

"Are you having a good time in Ireland?" I asked.

"Yeah, fine," he said. And then walked away.

Good feelings came back.

The parade was like any other small-town parade: floats advertising local businesses, children waving from slow-moving vehicles, and occasionally someone throwing hard candy at the crowd.

The Dingle Fife and Drum Band – sporting matching black and red jackets – led the parade. Various groups of children holding banners in Irish followed behind. Some of the children looked delighted to be the centre of attention; others did not.

A series of floats featuring ragged farmers playing a variety of instruments, or pretty girls in tight pants and dolphin costumes were next. Ever so often, a man dressed as the patron saint walked by. There were loads of tricoloured wigs, plastic hats, headbands, angel wings and flags and, just as the crowd was getting restless, it was over. It lasted about half-an-hour.

Families packed up their lawn chairs and bags of holiday sale items from Stand House and other little shops, and went home. I walked back up the hill, flung my pack into the car, and drove off to find the ruins of a twelfth-century church.

Ten minutes later, after parking close to some thorny bush, and digging in my bag for a few books full of torn up receipts that bookmarked any reference to the site, I managed to untangle my sweater and head through the modern area where shiny granite headstones stand next to Celtic crosses. Then another gate to the medieval section near the ruins of the church. Behind the statue of Mary is a tranquil spot on a low stone fence.

My interest in Irish history had led me to obscure literature – some found in used bookstores with creaky floorboards and disinterested black cats, and others ordered in slightly less romantic methods via the Internet – and now I was finally able to stand before that which I had spent hours researching.

My wife and I had walked the grounds of Kilmalkedar during our trip together when we had toured the peninsula. Though I didn't mention it at the time, there was something familiar about the site – the hints of burnt orange and mystic purple and early morning blue in the stones, the worn paths that weave through the grass, and the skeletal trees that stand stoic against the Atlantic wind. It felt like a long time ago I had witnessed a thousand sunrises and a thousand sunsets from this very place, and yet all I could recall was the movement of time. It felt like I had once known all the stories and all the songs, but now they were only hints of memories that moved like mist in the back of my mind.

Flipping through the pages of one book and then another, I hoped the history of Kilmalkedar would help unravel the mystery of why I felt an unusual connection to these particular stones or the ghosts that haunt quiet corners on the edge of the world.

Little is known of St. Maolcethair, said to be the son of an Irish king of Ulster and founder of Kilmalkedar (*Cill Maoilchéadair*), and little is known about the origins of the site itself. Maolcethair's death is recorded in the martyrology of Donegal in 636, but his life and deeds seem to have been lost to time. What would have been the original wooden church has also been lost to time, and now the ruins of a later twelfth-century church stands on the earlier foundation. Known for being a renowned school of learning in the medieval period, the site is also strongly associated with St. Brendan the Navigator who, according to legend, maintained a residence there. Archeologically speaking, there is no evidence to prove that St. Brendan lived or visited the Dingle Peninsula. But in order to draw pilgrims, historical evidence was ignored in favour of legend.

Built in the Hiberno-Romanesque style, the church at Kilmalkedar is said to resemble the more famous Cormac's Chapel at Cashel, County Tipperary. It features a round-headed doorway and high-pitched gables. The barrel vaulting, a lower section of the corbelled stone roof, and some carved windows have survived. The chancel still exists, as does the west doorway. The latter is decorated with chevron patterns and a carved human head (which may represent the founder, a local ruler, or even Christ Himself).

The original roof of the church has long given way but the east window, known locally as *Cno nan Snaithaide* (or eye of the needle), still remains. It has long been the tradition for pilgrims to pass through the window nine times, especially at Easter, when it was believed that doing so would grant the promise of eternal life.

Tracing the features of the church, smoothed over by time, I marvelled at how the stonemasons of an earlier age created something so seemingly simple and yet so stunningly beautiful – and that it would still stand almost a thousand years later. The east window appeared before me, but I decided not to attempt it after imagining myself getting stuck and having to holler for help.

In the chancel is the famous Alphabet Stone, dating probably from the sixth century. It was originally about four feet high but is now broken at the top. On its west face is the Latin alphabet and an earlier inscription DNI, which probably means *domini*. The north face has a thin, damaged cross while the south face has an equally thin Latin cross with scrolled ends.

A tall Ogham stone with the inscription ANM MAILE-INBIR MACI BROCANN (the name of Mael Inbir, son of Brocan) stands outside the church. The six-foot high slender stone is thought to date from the fifth or sixth century, and is unique to most Ogham stones as it features a hole near the top. Though the reason for the hole is not entirely known, it is thought that marriages and other important deals were finalized by touching fingers within it.

In the churchyard is a four-foot-high rectangular shaped stone with sundial markings. The half-circle was divided into four roughly equal parts, as is commonly the case with the Anglo-Saxon sundials, and the northwest face was decorated with a cross of arcs. It is now thought to be a symbol of pilgrimage as it appears on many stones associated with the early routes. St. Brendan's *Navigatio*, which specifically describes itself as a pilgrimage, pays great attention to the division of the days and the hours at which certain prayers should be said.

A large (possibly unfinished) ring-less cross is situated on the south side of the pathway. It's unusual in that the arms extend from the shaft about midway from the base. During excavations of a nearby gravestone, it was discovered that much of it is actually below ground. A number of early medieval grave markers in the form of crosses can be found on site as well. These probably mark the graves of the monks who lived at the monastery between the eighth and twelfth centuries.

I explored the rest of the site along the waist-high walls as the shadows weaved through the ruins. Nestled within the trees is a stone slab grave with no indication as to its importance or why it was tucked away on the edge. Someone had made a cross of white pebbles. A St. Brigid's cross, made of reeds and bleached by the elements, was balanced on top.

There is no doubt that Kilmalkedar is a place of exquisite beauty and serenity. Because it lies along the well-travelled trail from Ventry Harbour to the top of Mt. Brandon where thousands of Celts and early pilgrims walked as they prayed to their appropriate deities, it offers more than just the history of medieval Christians in Ireland; it offers a history that spans several thousands of years.

But the history did little to help unravel the mystery in any kind of significant way. I didn't feel any closer to understanding why this place felt familiar. Still wasn't sure why I felt a sense of peace, or that a weight had been lifted from my shoulders when I looked out towards the sea. Only knew that being alone at this sacred site – saturated in the voices of the past like an old concert hall still buzzing with music long after its doors are closed – felt like coming home after a long journey.

There was no clear answer, but maybe not knowing was okay for now. Maybe I didn't need to know why this place affected me on such a visceral level, and just trust that my heart (and my soul) needed to be there. Maybe remaining open was enough. As I stood up, and rubbed the cold from my legs, I gave myself permission to wander through the site again – this time slower and with more intention – and focus on all that cannot easily be put into words.

Near the car was a signpost for the Saints' Path. The bright yellow logo, featuring a figure with a staff, was half-covered in moss. The arrow pointed north to Mount Brandon. There was no other option but to walk.

The path soon disappeared. What I found instead were disinterested sheep. And mud. A lot of mud. Followed by more of the same. Opened a small gate and maneuvered over a series of low stone fences meant to keep in the animals. There was still no obvious route. And there was no mystery as to where the other walkers might be. As I slogged along – more and more muck sticking to my boots – I realized why the pilgrimage occurs in the summer and not in mid-March. Suffering for your gods is one thing in the warmer months, but it takes on a different tone as the soft spring soil sucks and slurps underfoot. My boots became heavier and heavier and finally, fearing I was lost, turned around and made my way back to the car. Took a few more photographs, tried to scrape my boots clean, and then drove away.

CHAPTER 11
A PINT OR TWO

Wasn't sure where to go next, so I drove west without a destination in mind. Twenty minutes later, I pulled into the empty parking lot of The Blasket Centre. Mine was the only car (as it was closed until tourist season), and I walked down the gravel road towards the shoreline. There, I was met with two options: the path to the right seemed the more obvious, while the path on the left seemed less so. I chose the one less travelled. There were no signs indicating how far it went or where it ended up.

It was narrow and full of puddles, and I had to leap over a small stream. Black, broken rocks jutted out of the earth, heavy and ominous – and soon the soft ground swallowed up my footprints. The path then seemed to disappear, only to reappear a little later, before it led me away from the water's edge.

As I rounded a hill, I came across a couple of small stone houses. It was difficult to determine if they were still in use or recently abandoned. Both had power lines and thin curtains drawn over the windows, but the whitewash and green paint of the windowsills was peeling. Either someone was living a simple life, or had recently vacated and left behind what they couldn't carry.

I imagined a young family leaving their home for the big city or a country far from their own, and was overcome with melancholy. No longer would they walk along the ocean's edge and listen to the waves upon the shore, or sing the old songs as the piercing wind cut through wool sweaters. No longer would they share stories at the local before staggering home to a faithful dog or disinterested cat. No longer would their ancestors guide them through difficult times on familiar soil – a place so entwined with one's own being.

My life is a series of chapters that take place in various settings, with various characters that weave in and out. Some chapters may be longer than others, but there is always a sense of impermanence. My name has no connection. I am not tied to one place. There is no land of my ancestors. My story is not part of a longer narrative.

Most days this doesn't bother me, and I chalk it up to one of the unfortunate aspects of living in the modern Western world. But when I do take a moment to think about it – looking out towards the setting sun, where the elements do battle in sea and sky – I wonder what it might feel like to know one's true place. To understand the significance of every lake and river and rocky outcrop, and know – at my very core – that history and mythology are not separate, unrelated entities. To know that the spirits of my ancestors will whisper guidance on days of hardship.

The Irish speak of all history – whether it happened a decade ago or a thousand years earlier – as if it only happened last week, and I came closer to understanding why. Like so many other tranquil places across the country, these simple yet beautiful stone houses on the edge of the Atlantic evoke an unmistakable sense of time and place. Not only did I feel a strong connection to the past, but there was also something wonderfully inviting about them – even in their current state. It would be a perfect place to write, with only the sounds of the ocean and the wind, and the setting sun lighting up the Blasket Islands every evening.

If history can be described as an endless long river, then Irish history seems to gently flow to the sea with little back eddies that loop around in mystical swirls. That which has come before determines every tiny movement in the water.

By the time I made it to my car, having stepped gingerly onto the drier patches of earth, it was time to eat. Parked at the pier in Dingle, headed to the second floor of Strand House, and ordered a small pot of tea and homemade pie. Halfway through my delectable dessert, I realized I was the only man in the café. All the other tables were occupied by groups of elderly women. The owner of Strand House must have noticed this as well because he soon walked by my table, placed his hand on my shoulder, smiled when I looked up at him, and then walked away.

My belly was full and I needed a place to lay my head – even for half-an-hour – so I drove back up the hill to my B&B, kicked off my boots, and picked up one of the books that Pat had lent me. A few pages in, and my eyes got heavy.

Woke up in a panic, thinking I had slept the remainder of the day away. But it was still light out. It had only been forty-five minutes. Relieved and once again hungry, I got up and rubbed the sleep from my eyes. It was time for a bowl of stew. And a pint or two.

. . .

HANGING out in bars is not my idea of a good time. In small town Canada, most serve beer the colour of weak amber, televisions are tuned to a hockey game, and patrons play pull-tab lottery tickets after a couple games of pool. They are sad places populated by either half a dozen older men drinking alone or by young men in oversized sports jerseys trying to impress the opposite sex that cluster together and look down at their cell phones all night.

But small town Ireland is different. While the number of pubs is falling because of the current economic times and changing lifestyles, the pub as an institution remains an important part of Irish culture. It is still the place where people across the country meet and stories are exchanged. Until recent years, Irish people rarely drank at home because the social aspect was a vital part of enjoying alcohol. The closest thing we have in Canada, besides the wannabe Irish pubs with their silly leprechaun salt and pepper shakers, are the coffee shops. For whatever reason, Canadians prefer to socialize over caffeine before dinner than socialize over alcohol after dinner. Maybe we just want to be home before it gets too cold and dark.

Calendars of Irish pubs usually feature one or two from Dingle. Over time, about half a dozen have obtained celebrity status because of their long history or unique character. While some do have televisions bolted to the wall, and maybe a pool table tucked away in a dark corner, most prefer to lure locals and visitors alike with a fireplace, a resident dog, a fine selection of beers and whiskeys, and traditional music every night of the week. I was looking forward to spending the next few hours in as many as I could.

Dick Mack's was my first stop. Some argue it is Dingle's most well-known pub, and for good reason. The pub has seen many reincarnations since the local stationmaster opened the bar in 1899 to provide light refreshments to its passengers. It was named after Richard MacDonnell (who established a successful boot store), and the family-owned pub carries on the tradition of also being a cobbler's with a small leather shop still on premises. As I approached, the sign outside read: "Where is Dick Mack's? Opposite the church. Where is the church? Opposite Dick Mack's!" Inside, the worn golden woodwork gives the pub a wonderful glow. The walls are lined with family memorabilia, old pictures, and rows of antique books.

I perched on a stool and ordered a Guinness. What a wonderful drink, Guinness is. A well-poured pint of the thick creamy stout is truly a thing of beauty. A pub is measured by how well they pour the ebony nectar, and shame to those that can't master it. Brewed in Dublin since 1759, Guinness had over a ninety-percent market share in Ireland up to the mid-1970s. Ten million glasses are consumed worldwide every day. Some claim it is an acquired taste, but those people are called wrong. Though many will complain of feeling full after a couple pints, the key to overcoming this hurdle is ignoring the stomach and paying closer attention to the taste buds that holler out for more.

The barman filled shot glasses and timed the two-part pouring so that every pint was perfect, and the patrons played out their familiar roles. The resident drunk with his beat-up guitar serenaded a couple girls in their early-twenties. They smiled politely for a couple songs before pulling on their jackets and heading out into the night.

"American girls..." I heard the drunk loudly whisper after the door had closed. "Fine creatures, they are... fine creatures."

Nodded my head and turned back to face the wall of whiskeys.

Three friends at the end of the bar were discussing how much they would spend on a single shot, and what significant events in life would warrant going above ten or fifteen euros.

"Gettin' married and all that. That'd be worth it," slurred one young man as he flipped his hair from his forehead.

"If anyone says yes to you, I'd be buying the first round," joked his friend.

"Yeah, bu' havin' kids and all that... that's obvious," said the third man as he scratched his nose and sniffed. "Wha' about all the other things? Littler things..."

"Oh right, yeah," said the first. "Well... I think... um..." He scratched his stubble, cracked his knuckles and then stared ahead, lost in thought. His friends did the same. I didn't feel the need to engage, and continued on my way.

My second pint of lovely, lovely Guinness was at An Droichead Beag. Anyone who has visited Dingle will know that there are several pubs between Dick Mack's and An Droichead Beag but my theory was that if I crossed town between pints, allowing for five minutes of fresh air, I could sober up a little and celebrate St. Patrick's Day until the pubs closed. It seemed like a sound theory after only one pint; wasn't so sure if it would hold by the fourth.

The streets, washed in spring mist, were quieter than expected. With nearly forty pubs to choose from in Dingle, no one needed to be wandering around.

An Droichead Beag is painted bright yellow with green trim. It's easy to find and is often full, especially during tourist season. The back half of the pub – with the large screen televisions, dance floor, and darker corners – was empty save for a young couple snogging and an older man on his phone. I leaned on the end of the bar and listened to the loud hum of a hundred voices competing with each other before finishing my drink and heading off in search of somewhere cozier.

Known for its rustic atmosphere and rousing sessions, O'Flaherty's boasts itself as the 'trad mecca' of Dingle. It features original Valentia Island (*Dairbhre*) flagstones from the 1860s and two mainstays in the bar rendered from a ship lost at sea. Opening in 1957, it was established when a local fisherman broke his leg and gave up his trade. It also featured a music shop at one point. Like Dick Mack's, it is layered with old bottles and clocks, framed photos and street signs, and is as much a museum as a pub. It was certainly livelier than when I walked in almost twelve hours earlier, and it was certainly cozier than An Droichead Beag, but I only stayed long enough to listen in on one conversation.

"What I'm sayin' is, y'know... I'm sayin' that Ireland is no more Celtic than any other nation in Europe. Is it? We just call ourselves Celts so that we can, y'know, sell tea towels to the Americans... or the English that don't know any better."

The man was excited, and his voice filled one corner of the pub. "To call Ireland Celtic is only falling for some silly advertising scheme, y'know. So we have our Irish breakfasts and our Irish teas... and it's somehow massively different than the English breakfasts and the English teas. We just didn't want to be English. That's all... and so we're Celts. We're Celtic and they're not... and that's the big draw."

It was difficult to determine if the man sitting next him was his friend or just trapped.

"The Celts – if you want to use that word, but let me tell you that they themselves wouldn't have used it, y'know – spread themselves across Europe... Turkey, even... but do the Turks call themselves Celts? They do not. But we do. Celtic this and Celtic that. Sure, they shared a similar language and artistic style. I get that. But they were nothing but barbarian tribes that arrived here, looking for... I don't know what. God knows, not the weather. Do you need another pint? I might need another – maybe two. I'll get this round; you get the next. Sure, it's going to be a great night... great *craic*, so."

He waved down the bartender and ordered two more pints. The other man had yet to say a word.

"Whoever they were... they certainly didn't *invade* Ireland, y'know. They settled here – no invasion – and they brought their families. Language travels with the women, y'know," he continued. "That's how you know. And don't tell me that they fought naked with just a gold torc around their necks. People still say that, but it's bollocks. I mean Turkey might be warmer... maybe they were naked there... but Ireland is cold, even with the endorphins pumping. I don't care who you are."

The other man nodded his head. His eyes wandered the bar, looking for rescue.

"And what the hell are people going on about the Celtic druids for? All the time I have to hear about something or other. Have you seen these New Age somethin' or others running around in white robes calling on the power of the moon or whatnot? Bollocks, so it is. Put some pants on and go to bed." The man paused to finish up one pint before starting on another. Reaching into his pocket, he paid the bartender with a fistful of coins.

Suddenly, he made eye contact with me. I froze. Wasn't

interested in being roped into a one-sided conversation so, before he could leave his perch, I nodded my head, finished my pint, walked out into the fresh air, and cut through town.

Despite the temperature dropping, my layers of wool and the beer in my belly kept me warm. Took a deep breath, smiled, and walked into the next place. It seemed that a dedicated effort had been made recently to modernize the inside of Paudie's Bar while retaining a traditional atmosphere. With large stylish leather seats, elm and walnut, and interior stonework, it seemed a little too polished for my liking but as the beer set in I decided that I didn't really care.

A couple young fellows were on stage singing Irish songs and other folk classics. Most of the music so far had been instrumental, so it was nice to hear something I could sing along to.

The band took a break after a few songs to introduce themselves.

"This is Dave," said one. "My name is Tom. And we are the Blow-Ins. The term 'blow-in' refers to a person arriving casually and unannounced – perhaps a stranger or foreigner – basically anybody whose ancestors have not lived within sight of the parish church for at least ten generations."

This received a round of applause and a couple whistles. Some lady behind me screeched with laughter. Didn't think the joke deserved such a reaction, but perhaps I hadn't been in Ireland long enough.

Lingered a while, thinking I might order another pint. But instead I headed out into the night.

Fifty-two meters further down the street is John Benny's. While the fresh air was nice earlier in the evening,

I was no longer interested in crossing town. My legs wobbled when I walked. The best cure for that was another pint.

Many of the tourists were already calling it a night. This was fine by me; it meant there was more seating available. The inside of the pub was dimly lit by dozens of candles in small glass jars and the gentle light made the old woodwork glow. Nabbed a spot near the small stage set off from the stone fireplace.

Settled into a chair as Ríona Ó Madagáin, a local singer-songwriter with a pleasing voice, a shy smile and gentle laugh, played an original tune called "Tom" about a homeless man she met on Grafton Street in Dublin. She followed this by another original tune about leaving boarding school called "Long Time Coming". Her sensitive lyrics merged seamlessly with her lovely voice and I was hooked. During her set-break, I bought her five song self-titled EP.

On the way out of town, I spied the blue exterior of O'Sullivan's Courthouse Pub. The chalkboard sign outside advertised the night's entertainment: Méabh Ní Bheaglaoich on accordion and vocals, and Matt Griffin on guitar. "Why have only five pints when I could have six?" I asked myself.

Inside, there are no televisions, jukebox or pool table. It doesn't have the feel of a museum that defines the pubs like Dick Mack's or O'Flaherty's, nor does it have the polished look of Paudie's Bar. It doesn't feature the open spaces of An Droichead Beag that seemed so uninviting earlier in the evening. With low ceilings, and an intimate front area where customers either lean on the L-shaped bar or sit around small tables with their pints, it feels snug but not too tight.

There was a significant amount of heat generated by

the little fireplace and the end-of-night revellers, so I stripped off some of my wool and found a seat near the front. It was easy to spot the owner, Tommy O'Sullivan. The tall singer-songwriter with a mop of curly hair wove through the bar and shook hands with the regulars before checking in with the night's talent.

Both musicians had obviously honed their craft over many years. Meabh's voice was enchanting and, though I couldn't understand the Irish lyrics, the emotion behind the words was undeniable. They played several tunes in the regional swing style of West Kerry, and a rousing collection of jigs, polkas and slides full of verve and vitality. The audience tapped their feet, whooping and hollering in applause. Meabh whooped and hollered right back as the tempo increased. This was not music for the head, or even the heart. It was music for the soul. I could have stayed until the sun rose over the mountains.

But, alas, the pubs close at midnight. I ordered one more at last call, and then left in a state of bliss as the band packed up.

On the edge of town, I turned around to give a drunken farewell. "Until tomorrow, fair Dingle..."

Spun back a little faster than I should have, and made myself dizzy.

The only light came from the occasional farmhouse set back from the road and, staggering along, realized that dodging speeding cars was one thing in the light of day but it was a different game altogether with no flashlight and seven pints inside me.

About halfway up the hill, I turned around to look up at the stars. Ancient magic danced in the eternal darkness. "May the road rise up to meet you..." I slurred. "May the wind be always at your back..."

Closed my eyes and breathed in the night air as I thought about all the colours that blurred in the encroaching fog and the lonely stones that stand stoic against the rolling hills of green.

"May the sun shine warm upon your face; the rains fall soft upon your fields; and, until we meet again, may God hold you in the palm of His hand."

In my stupor, I reflected again on the contrast that permeates everything in Ireland. As there was no one around, I offered my opinion to the hedgerow. "Everything has an opposite force working against it here, y'know... nothing can be taken as singular. Nothing is ever as easy as is seems. But... that's okay. I'm okay with that."

The road seemed to continue for far longer than I remembered.

"Savour the solitude of long walks along the ocean's edge," I continued, "but also feel welcome in a crowded pub... where every sad song has an element of hope, and every toe-tapping jig or reel comes from a time of hardship. Even the weather can never be trusted around here. Which is why I shall always invest in wool."

Finally made it to Dúinín House. Fumbled with my key, kicked off my boots, and tiptoed down the hall. My focus failed, I collapsed into bed, and fell instantly asleep.

CHAPTER 12

A GOOD DAY FOR THE MOUNTAIN

It seemed like a good day for the mountain. The morning fog that normally lays low in the town of Dingle was absent, and the stark blue sky promised an entire day of sunshine. I expected to feel last night's pints, but the light through my bedroom window promised adventure and I was soon awake and ready to conquer whatever lay before me. What lay before me was Mount Brandon (*Cnoc Bréanainn*).

Walking into the solarium for my breakfast, I was eager for my plate of fried meat and fresh bread.

"How do you feel?" asked Pat as he came out of the kitchen with a pot of tea.

"Surprisingly well... considering."

"Well, they do say that Guinness is good for you."

"They do," I said. "Just never believed them."

Pat laughed. "It's not always easy to know what to believe around here. I'll give you that."

"Do you think it'll be a good day to climb the mountain?" I asked.

"Oh, I think it might be, for sure," he answered. "A fine

day, indeed. Do remember, though, that the weather can change at any time – especially on the summit – even on a clear morning such as this one."

"How long does it take to get to the top and back down again?"

"Maybe four to six hours. Less, of course, if you're young and fit."

Wasn't sure if I qualified for either.

"Y'know, I was thinking of a good walk, meself," said Pat. "Best to make use of a lovely day."

As the solarium warmed up, I stripped off my sweater and finished my breakfast *sans* wool.

"Mount Brandon is an important part of the myth and identity of the Dingle Peninsula," continued Pat as he cleared the table. "In pagan times, it was one of two sites – the other being Croagh Patrick in County Mayo – where Lughnasadh was celebrated. That was the harvest festival to honour the Celtic god Lugh. Later, Catholic pilgrims used the same route to honour their god. Being so high and so far west, it is the last place where the sun can be seen before it sets. The older generations will still tell stories of those who walked up but never came back down; they may have got lost in the fog, or they froze, or the Little People took them away."

About halfway to the kitchen, he turned to me and with a mischievous smirk added, "But you'll have a grand time, I'm sure."

Had to at least make an attempt, even if it meant hours of wandering alone and possibly getting lost. I'm intimately familiar with all the emotions associated with being misplaced, for sure, and knew not to panic if I stepped off the trail and failed to find it again, but I was still hoping nothing too noteworthy would happen.

Pat caught up to me as I made my way back to my room. "I remembered something as I was washing up, and wanted to tell you – before you head out – about the last great pilgrimage to Mount Brandon. It was held in the 1860s when Bishop Moriarty of Kerry was carried on a sugán chair to the top of the mountain where he celebrated mass for twenty thousand pilgrims. However, such was the level of debauchery for several days afterwards that he banned the pilgrimage altogether."

"I'll hold off on the debauchery," I said.

"Good man."

A sunny day in March in Ireland doesn't always equate to a *warm* sunny day in March, so I opted for pants and a couple layers of wool (with a wool scarf and wool gloves) and then drove into town to stock up on supplies.

A small loaf of locally made soda bread, a chunk of cheese, and a bottle of water. That was all. Had I taken a moment to think it through, I would have realized that bread, cheese and water is not a lot for four to six hours of mountain hiking. Should have packed granola bars, trail mix, pepperoni sticks, various flavours of crisps and maybe some chocolate or a box of cookies, but I didn't.

With too much wool and not enough food, I drove to the base of the mountain and parked next to a stream. On the other side of the stream is a beautiful white statue of the Virgin Mary tucked into a shrine of brutal sharp rocks. Her eyes closed and her right hand outstretched.

Looked to see if there was anyone else around, and then hopped over the stream to get a closer look. Small mountain flowers surrounded Mary. Someone had adorned her with a string of simple wooden beads. Tipped my hat, nodded my head to say hello, and found the trail.

The slope began as soon as I stepped onto the yellow-green grass kept short by roaming flocks of sheep. At first it was difficult to determine where the path was, but then I noticed a series of short white posts at regular intervals and figured they were there to direct me. If I could keep those in sight, I would have less chance of getting lost. "And if I do get lost," I said to myself, "hopefully I can just walk downhill and end up at a village pub somewhere."

After ten minutes of hiking, it was time to unwrap my scarf, take off my gloves, pull the outer layer of wool over my head, and pack it all on top of the bread, cheese and water.

A few sheep were lazily grazing. Decided not say hello as they didn't seem interested in me. A little while later, I looked over the edge of a deep gulley carved by cold mountain waters. Not an exciting start, but I was content to be on the trail that so many had walked before.

It started getting warmer, so I stripped off my inner layer of wool and cursed my choice to wear pants. Shorts would have been the better option, but it had never been the right condition for them in western Ireland. Thought about continuing on in my underwear, but didn't want to run into another hiker and have to make small talk in my Calvin Kleins.

Further along, I stopped briefly to take a few photographs before checking the time. Maybe I'd been hiking for half-an-hour – perhaps longer – but no. It had only been fifteen minutes. Four to six hours in the oxymoronic Irish heat seemed even more daunting than before. Decided to put my phone at the bottom of my bag so as not to be tempted.

"Hiking," I told the mountain, "isn't about keeping time. It's about the organic flow of the universe. It's about stepping away from the confines of human existence. So

I'm putting my technology away. From now on it shall be just you and I."

The mountain didn't say anything in return.

A large wooden cross, its base covered by the same jagged mountain rocks that frame the statue of Mary, towers against the azure sky. Weathered by time, and with tips painted in flaking white, this is the first Station of the Cross. The Stations of the Cross, I discovered while flipping through my small guidebook, are a fourteen-step Catholic devotion that commemorates Jesus' final moments on Earth. At each station, the individual is meant to reflect on a specific event from Christ's last day. Prayers are recited, and then the individual moves to the next station until all fourteen are complete. As a non-Christian, I wasn't interested in the devotion. My first and only thought was one of horror. "There are fourteen of these," I said to the mountain. "Fourteen. And this is the first. This is going to be a long day."

After grumbling to the mountain and cursing the heat, I was surprised to discover that my body fell into a natural cadence. Slipping into a meditative state and, without too much effort, I passed the next two crosses – briefly acknowledging the Roman numerals nailed on the back when I turned around to see how far I had come.

The terrain, still largely made of short yellow-green grass, was dry and comfortable for the feet. The sun continued to beat down, but it was a little cooler with the increase of elevation. Felt I was making good time, even if making good time was no longer important. Began to almost enjoy myself.

Took an extended break at the sixth cross when I spied the ruins of a small stone hut a little off the trail. After a bit of bread and cheese, left my pack behind to dry my sweaty back and stepped away from the short white posts. For good reason, the hobbits in Tolkien's novel shouldn't have left the path and I shouldn't have either. Sank into soft bog. Water seeped up from the mud. Cursed under my breath, but luckily my new boots had a waterproof coating and my feet stayed dry as I circumnavigated the slope.

Didn't want to disturb the stones, or the moss and lichen, so I leaned on one leg and then the other while admiring the view – the ragged patchwork of greens and browns and yellows, stitched haphazardly and bordered by an array of blues that set poets ablaze.

A light breeze picked up as I looked down to the clusters of little houses below, and I thought of my life back home: the mountains and forests and golden fields of canola; morning walks with my students; the changing seasons and the fleeting nature of time.

Before leaving for Ireland, I mentioned to a colleague that I was interested in hiking Mount Brandon. An avid outdoorsman, he proceeded to outline all the benefits of leaving the comforts of modern living behind to spend time where few are willing to go. Was only half-listening by this point, since I had finished my cappuccino and needed to pee, but I do remember he mentioned something about patience, persistence and gratitude. "Mountains teach you to enjoy the small luxuries in life," he had said. "And they teach you about change. No mountain is the same as another, and no day on the mountain is the same as before."

Though less than halfway by this point, I knew that he was right. And perhaps I should have paid more attention when he discussed how mountaineering helps one overcome fears. That the road less travelled allows one to truly admire silence and to never give up. But I wasn't climbing

Mount Brandon in search of some life-affirming moment of clarity. Wasn't looking to overcome fear, or admire silence, or push myself physically or mentally. The truth is, beyond walking the same warm line that so many had done before me, I wasn't sure why I decided to abandon second-breakfast and elevenses to scale the second highest mountain in Ireland with a small parcel of food.

But maybe it wasn't up to me. Maybe there was some other force at work – a certain kind of magic that causes one to abandon reason. Had I unconsciously handed over the reins to the spirits that wait patiently for those wandering without direction? Was I finally learning to let go – to stop resisting? Though still finding it difficult to be completely open to connection – to feel a oneness with all things – some whisper from deep in the shadows of my internal chamber reminded me that I needed to be vulnerable and accept guidance if I was going to learn and grow. Took a deep breath, felt the wind on my back, shivered, and felt oddly at peace.

Turned my attention again to the ruins. There was no reference to them in my guidebook, so I let my imagination wander. Perhaps it housed a family escaping some tribal war, or perhaps it was a resting area for travelling monks guarding holy relics. It could have served as respite for those needing to stop and massage their feet, or perhaps some young entrepreneur sold cold mountain water and a bit of roasted mutton to those that hadn't packed enough sustenance.

Back at the cross, I slung my pack over my shoulders and continued on. The terrain soon changes. Instead of grass, the trail becomes rocky with small sharp stones. A little further, the trail more closely resembles a dry riverbed cut loosely into the mountain and the incline becomes steeper and steeper. Heaving myself up certain sections, and breaking my cadence with an occasional grunt, I passed another couple crosses. Stones crunched under foot. Once in a while, a soft breeze blew down from above. But the only other sounds were the drum of my heart and the rhythm of my breathing.

If was difficult to know how far I had left to go. Counted off the crosses, but wasn't sure if the last half dozen were spaced out further from each other as some terrible joke. The sky was a little hazy but most of the clouds were merely tufts that blew across the horizon. It was getting cooler, but I wasn't tempted to add any layers. Rationing my bread, cheese and water, I continued past jagged boulders and thought again of Tolkien's stories and the seemingly endless quest to the summit of Mount Doom.

As the terrain changed again, I stopped at every cross. The summit was still behind a series of ridges and, after passing the tenth and eleventh, had to give some credit to the early Christians; they weren't quite as cruel as I initially thought. The crosses seemed to be closer and closer together, and for that I was thankful.

I was tired and hungry. The muscles in my legs and my butt hurt, and I cursed the lack of food and drink in my pack. A trickling stream provided some cold mountain water and I splashed a bit in my face, combing it through my hair. A little further along, I watched a few sheep taking a drink and my thoughts again turned to food – specifically, lamb chops.

Continued on and on, watching the ground beneath me. Finally, the slope started to plateau. Looked up to find the smallest hint of the final cross, and then scurried up and even broke into a run.

A few minutes later, I stood on what is known locally as

Barr an Turas (the Top of the Journey). Slung off my pack and pulled my thinner sweater over my head before having a look around. Someone had placed a cheap string of plastic prayer beads at the cross. Sat next to it as I broke off chunks of bread and stuffed pieces of cheese into the soft crumb.

Had I the will or excess energy, I could have strolled for several kilometres along the ridge but instead I continued to munch away on my snack before peering over the edge to gaze out at the valleys, islands, and the enigmatic ocean below. The mountain drops dramatically and is punctuated by dark shadows and small crystalline lakes. Beyond the patchwork of farms and farmhouses are a few narrow roads cutting from one end of the peninsula to the other.

'Reaching the summit of Mount Brandon,' wrote one guidebook author, 'always allows for a healthy sense of achievement.' But what I felt could not merely be summed up so simply. While ruminating on what thoughts and emotions must have whirled in the minds of all those that came before me and all those that would follow, I looked out towards the edge of creation where the ancient gods and goddesses still engage in endless battle. Then sat down again where St. Brendan was said to have spent time in deep meditation before embarking on his great voyage to the find the Isles of the Blessed.

Thought about my hike, and all the stops along the way, and felt – for just a moment – part of a long line of human history. Whether those in ancient times journeyed solo or as part of a community, each would have stopped to reflect. Each would have taken a moment to connect with the divine. Some pilgrims may have stepped ashore in hopes of healing the body or the mind. Others may have offered prayers for a loved one. Some may have journeyed great distances and received great insight. Others may have only heard the faintest of whispers from within. Some, like me, may have cursed their choice to bring only a limited amount of food and water.

All would have felt a connection to the mountain, watching the ground beneath them as they continued their climb. All would have looked towards the summit and then up at the birds that soar above, and felt themselves free – grateful to be alive as they breathed in the briny air. All would have experienced overwhelming beauty at the edge of the world and wondered about what lay beyond.

Thought about the first few lines of what is considered Ireland's first poem. Said to have been spoken by Amergin Glúingel when he first set foot in the country, it begins

Am gaeth I mmuir (I am wind on sea)
Am tonn trethain (I am wave upon land)
Am fuaimm I mmuir (I am ocean roar)

Thought back to my first morning, years earlier, and wondered if this ancient bard had felt the same way I had while sitting with a cat as the fog slowly lifted. Had he stopped briefly to inhale the sweetness in the air and listen to the music of faeries? Had he witnessed the sun breaking through the clouds and lighting up the turquoise sea, tranquil coves, brooding lakes and the earthtones of rugged hillsides and windswept wetlands? Had he felt akin to the magic that creeps up gently between the cracks? Had he too felt guided to a place of openness and vulnerability? Had he too felt embraced and comforted, and no longer alone?

Tore off another chunk of bread, looked out towards the open ocean, and felt something I had never felt before. It was as if everything was a source of light: every droplet of water that churns in the river or falls from above; every stone that sits half-sunk in the sand; every blade of grass that dances in the wind; every mountain flower that brings hope; every tall tree that provides protection; every cloud that blows across the sky; every bird and beast that reminds one of beauty; every celestial body that causes one to dream. I felt as if the universe was a single connected consciousness – that there was no sense of one or the other, and no sense of time. I felt connected to eternity. It was a moment of secular holiness.

And then I felt a change in weather.

Pat had warned me, but was still surprised (and a little nervous) to find that the summit was suddenly enveloped in a freezing mist. Pulled on my heavier sweater, wrapped my scarf around my neck, and slipped on my wool gloves. It wasn't enough. Jumped up and down, and hugged myself to maintain body temperature. Wasn't enough. The sun was no longer visible; it had been completely covered by clouds of the darkest grey. Thought that the world was being swallowed by nothingness – that dark forces would soon be devouring me. Thought it best to get moving.

Adrenaline kicked in as the temperature continued to drop. Rushed down the rocky trail, scanning the ground to find the best footing. Slipped and felt one knee go funny. The ground was a blur while attempting to maintain control of my flailing body, running on the edge of control.

My lungs burned and I stopped to catch my breath. Bent at the waist and could feel my blood pumping, taking only a quick peek at the summit and the encroaching mist when passing another cross at a near-run.

Only when the darkness seemed to go no further did I slow to a walk and give myself permission to relax. Didn't want to overtax my wobbly body any more than I had to, take a spill, and end up rolling down the mountain (though it may have been a faster way to get back to the car).

As the rocky terrain turned to soggy bog, I thought again of the ancient men and women that had hiked up (and possibly ran down) the mountain before the early monks attempted to appropriate and Christianize the pagan ritual, replacing the worship of the sun-god with their own. During the Lughnasadh festival, the Celtic people would have walked the same route I had (and may have called the festival by another name – *Brón Trogain,* meaning the bringing forth of the fruits of the earth). While they celebrated the harvest, they also celebrated the temporary victory of Lugh the young, bright god over Crom Dubh the older, darker god. Other aspects of the festival may have included the sacrifice and eating of a bull, the cutting and presenting of the first corn, and a mythical dance. There was also general feasting, which is what I wanted to be doing.

As soggy bog became rolling grass, I emptied the last remaining drops into my parched throat. Though I was looking forward to a hearty bowl of stew and a fine pint or two, I also recognized the need to make the most of my time on Mount Brandon. May not have started my walk with a desire to learn anything about myself, but as I neared the final stretch I took a moment to reflect on my desire to travel alone and embrace quiet moments.

It took me years to understand the difference between being alone and being lonely. I had equated the two while growing up, and made several attempts to ward off loneliness by hanging out with various crowds of people. Hung out with other scrawny teenagers at video arcades on the weekends, plugging quarters until my allowance was used up, but often felt disconnected – like there was a dark veil between myself and the world.

In my twenties, I didn't feel comfortable in clubs, with flashing lights and throbbing music – and usually left long before last call. But kept going in order to avoid being alone. Continued to queue up, pay the cover charge, and then observe others saddling up to the crowded bar or making conversation with strangers. Kept paying for drinks that I didn't enjoy, and continued to wonder why I felt like an outsider.

Later, as a teacher, I finally learned to enjoy the peace and freedom found in solitude. Learned that there is a lot to be gained from knowing that you can comfortably spend time in your own company – especially out among the trees and turtles and dragonflies.

My time on Mount Brandon had reminded me that being alone is a state of *being*, and that loneliness is a state of *mind*. That walking solo among nature is far different than feeling lonely in the confines of video arcades and dance clubs.

Only with a certain amount of intentional time and space is one able to focus on what's important, and come to terms with one's true self. There are lessons that years to learn and those that take only an hour – like when to pack enough sustenance to sustain one's self during a strenuous hike.

It was then that I recalled a certain bottle of Vanilla Coca-Cola that I had stashed in the car. Hardly ever drink soda, but I bought a bottle in case a dose of sugar was needed. The vision of a syrupy carbonated drink made me salivate, but the car was still a significant distance away. "Perhaps if I power-walk," I told the mountain, "I can get there sooner."

My meditative state of mind vanished.

The distance from the first cross to the car park seemed painfully long and my vision blurred but, after three-and-a-half hours of hiking, I was back in the driver's seat. Guzzled the sickly sweet soda without restraint. It burned on the way down, but it was lovely.

Though the Little People hadn't accosted me (which was disappointing), I did feel a healthy sense of achievement for conquering Mount Brandon in all kinds of weather. Also felt an overwhelming sense of peace. Felt that I belonged to something bigger than myself. Felt present and connected.

I also felt in need of a break.

CHAPTER 13

A CUP OF TEA

Desperate for a cup of tea. And a scone. And maybe a slice of pie.

So perhaps it was kismet that I found a parking space in front of a small café named An Cupán Tae. With bold blue and red plastic chairs and clapboard doors in bright yellow, it looks closer to a ski lodge for school-aged children, but I didn't care. I was hungry and the food looked good.

Five minutes after ordering, the young woman behind the counter presented me with a pot of tea and a couple homemade baked goods. Perfectly content to just plunk my butt down, wrap my scarf around my cold nose, and flip through a book that outlined the mythical beginnings of Ireland as I wiped pastry flakes off my sweater. My feet were sore, but the sun was shining and the euphoria from summiting Mount Brandon had yet to fade.

Sociological and cultural critic Walter Benjamin once claimed, 'History is written by the victors.' I would argue that there are no clear victors in the long stretch of history –

especially Irish history. Irish history continues to weave and rewrite itself and the truth becomes more and more difficult to find – if it can be found at all. While archeological evidence may be more tangible, and can be documented and placed under glass cases, mythical evidence is just as valid. The two seem to go hand-in-hand in Ireland, and one cannot be studied without the other.

Lebor Gabála Érenn (or *The Book of the Taking of Ireland* or *The Book of Invasions*) was written in the eleventh century by a single anonymous scholar. Why he decided to draw from legends and bits of history to create a collection of fictitious, pseudo-historical poems and prose that tells of the mythical origins of the Irish people is anyone's guess, but he may have wanted to link pre-Christian history with Biblical accounts. Those interested in lengthy mythological narratives with medieval Christian overtones can look forward to five volumes of it.

I imagine this single anonymous scholar knew he was bending historical truth when he altered, changed or completely rewrote different sections to his liking, but many during the Middle Ages read it as truth and for six centuries Irish historians often regarded it as authoritative.

Lebor Gabála Érenn tells of Ireland being settled (or taken) six times by six different groups of people: the Cessairians, the Partholónians, the Nemedians, the Fir Bolg, the Tuatha Dé Danann, and the Milesians. The first four groups were wiped out or forced to abandon the island, the fifth group represented Ireland's pagan gods, and the final group represented the Irish people (or the Gaels).

Cessair (the daughter of Noah's son Bith and his wife Birren) and her people led the first 'invasion' and were the first inhabitants. Forty days before the Biblical Flood,

Cessair tells her people to follow the instructions of an idol when they are denied a place on Noah's ark. The idol tells her people to sail for Ireland, so the Cessairians load into three ships and navigate the stormy waters. Only one arrives safely; two are lost at sea. Forty-nine women and three men make camp, but soon Fintán mac Bóchra is the last surviving male.

Exhausted from having to deal with so many women, he decides to head off in search of peace and quiet. At some point he turns into a salmon, and survives the oncoming flood. The women aren't so lucky. Fintán eventually turns into an eagle and then a hawk before returning to human form. He lives for five-and-a-half thousand years (with or without women, we don't know) and is conveniently able to recount Ireland's history during that time. Many centuries later, he advises the Fir Bolg when they battle the Tuatha Dé Danann. He also survives into the time of Fionn mac Cumhail, and relays to him all that he has witnessed. But I'm getting ahead of myself.

After the Flood, Ireland is uninhabited for three hundred years (save for Fintán in fish or bird form). When the waters subside, the people of Partholón arrive (about nine thousand of them – five thousand men and four thousand women). They arrive from Sicily via Greece, Cappadocia, Gothia, and Spain. Why anyone would leave the warmth of the Mediterranean for the chilly drizzle of Ireland is anyone's guess. They finally land in South Kerry and construct early buildings, introduce farming and brewing, and somehow have the energy to defeat the demonic Fomorians, a hostile and monstrous supernatural race. After several years of building, farming, brewing and defeating a supernatural race, all but one dies from the plague in a single week.

Tuan mac Cairill is the only survivor. He is Partholón's nephew and also happens to possess the ability to shape-shift. Like Fintán, he lives for a really long time in order to conveniently dictate Irish history. As the lone human guarding the land, he grew hairy, clawed and grey (as one might expect). However, he later found himself reborn as a vigorous young stag, followed by a wild boar. It would seem he also turned into a magical hawk and, as such, hung out with Fintán in the skies above. Together, they spend their final days recounting stories and then decide to leave the mortal realm sometime in the fifth century, after Ireland was converted to Christianity. Again, I'm getting ahead of myself.

My tea was cold and my legs were twitchy, so I bookmarked the page, wiped some jam off the front cover, paid the bill, and walked across the street to the ocean's edge to watch the fishing boats bob in the harbour. The sun reflected off the still waters and painted the world in an amber glow. Closed my eyes, warmed my eyelids as I listened to the seabirds and lapping waves, and then found my place in the book.

Thirty years after the extinction (minus one) of the Partholónians, several ships set sail for Ireland once again. Only one is successful. The people of Nemed also battle the Fomorians, although they occasionally take breaks from fighting in order to intermarry. Unfortunately for the Nemedians, they are unsuccessful in defeating the Fomorians and must hand over two-thirds of their corn, milk and children each Samhain (marking the end of the harvest season and the beginning of winter). To top that, almost all of the Nemedians are then killed in a tidal wave. Only thirty men escape.

Some go north to Britain and become ancestors of the

Britons, and some go south to Greece. Those who washed up on Greek shores were enslaved by the locals and forced to settle on poor rocky land. Deciding to make the most of a bad situation, they sling bags of soil on their backs and proceed to make barren lands fertile. After two hundred thirty years, the Greek Nemedians sail back to the now uninhabited Ireland and become known as the Fir Bolg (Men of the Bags).

The Nemedians who sailed north became the supernaturally gifted Tuatha Dé Danann, and return to Ireland's shore – arriving with the mist in flying ships thirty-seven years after the Fir Bolg had settled in. While the Fir Bolg are described as short and stout, with darker skin and black hair, the Tuatha Dé Danann are described as tall and muscular, with pale skin, red or blonde hair, and blue or green eyes.

Led by their king, Nuada, the Tuatha Dé Danann fight the First Battle of Magh Tuireadh on the west coast, in which they defeat and displace the native Fir Bolg. Rather than completely wipe them out, the victors instead offer the Men of the Bags the province of Connacht. It is unsure how uncomfortable life in Connacht was for them but, as Cromwell's officer can attest, it probably wasn't great.

The Tuatha Dé Danann were said to be a civilized and cultured people, and their skills and traditions were held in high regard. They were skilled in art, science, poetry and magic. Not only are they fodder for storytellers and neo-romantic fantasy painters centuries later, they were also said to be in possession of four great treasures.

The first is *Lia Fáil* (the Stone of Destiny), later placed on the Hill of Tara. The second is the Sword of Light, capable of inflicting only mortal blows when used against the enemy. The third treasure is Lugh's Spear, which shot out bolts of fire, and the final is the Cauldron of Plenty. As the name suggests, it brought forth an endless supply of food.

With their golden locks, stunning eyes of emerald green and great treasures, the Tuatha Dé Danann enjoy a hundred fifty years of unbroken rule.

The Milesians were the last race to settle and they represent the Irish people. They are the Gaels who sailed from Iberia after spending hundreds of years travelling the earth. Again, for some reason, they choose the dreary weather of Ireland instead of warmer places. With magic swords and spears, the Tuatha Dé Danann should have easily beaten back the Milesians, but they failed. After several bloody battles, the two groups agree to divide the island. The Milesians take the world above, while the Tuatha Dé Danann take the world below. From then on, the Tuatha Dé Danann and their descendants become known as the *sidhe* or *aos sí*.

(*Sidhe* translates to 'a mound'. Since the Tuatha Dé Danann are associated with mounds, barrows and tumuli, they become known as People of the *Sidhe*.)

The *sidhe* (or fair-folk, or faeries) did not disappear altogether, however; there are many stories in which they interacted with humans – though not always favourably. As time passed, inevitably a distance grew between humankind and the supernatural beings.

I closed my book, wandered aimlessly around town, and somehow ended up in a little store filled with all sorts of tourist tat: lucky clover key chains, charm bracelets, and leprechaun stuffies. In a haze, I bought a street sign fridge magnet for less than three euros, and a few bags of crisps. Didn't see anything faerie-related, and wasn't about to ask.

Though the Catholic Church played a large part in the

shaping of modern Ireland, they failed to eradicate certain beliefs and traditions – including belief in faeries – and many archeological sites that would have otherwise been broken up and reused as roads or fences were left untouched for fear of disrupting a faerie fort.

W.B. Yeats and Samuel Beckett were both said to have had contact with them; Douglas Hyde (the first president of Ireland) admitted to seeing them, as did Éamon de Valera (the first *Taoiseach*, or prime minister of Ireland). In fact, de Valera's wife pressured her husband into establishing the Folklore Commission to research the wee folk.

Modern Ireland is still cautious about the *fae*. In 1997, work began on a new electricity substation in Kilkeel (*Cill Chaoil*) in an area known to be an old faerie fort. A chain of accidents soon occurred, and the fair folk were blamed for the failures of machinery and injuries to those on site. The substation was relocated and there were no further issues. In 1999, a ninety-million-euro highway in County Clare was diverted so it wouldn't uproot a lone Hawthorne tree said to be important to the *sidhe*. Folklorist Eddie Lenihan told the National Roads Authority that the tree was an important meeting place for supernatural forces in the region. He warned that the destruction of the tree would result in death and great misfortune for motorists.

In 2007, the *aos sí* were blamed for problems with electricity poles that were erected in Sooey (*Samhadh*) within twenty yards of a faerie fort. The two poles had apparently bent over by the wind. The contractors returned and straightened them, only to have them fall over. While non-believers blamed the wind, others blamed the you-know-who.

Whatever the case may be – whether it is a true belief in the faeries or merely romantic reimaginings – one is advised not to use the term 'faeries'. It's culturally insensitive. Apparently, they are not fond of the word and many of them consider it offensive. Instead, they prefer *na daoine maithe* (the Good People), *na daoine uaisle* (the Gentry) or *bunadh na gcnoc* (the People of the Hills).

CHAPTER 14

AN ARCHÆOLOGICAL TREASURE TROVE

It was days like this one that justified a diet of full Irish breakfasts. After hiking a mountain steeped in thousands of years of history and mythology, and feeling the warm glow of the universe as it held me in its tender embrace (only to be chased down by freezing mist), a large part of me was arguing for a mid-day nap. But my time in Ireland was limited, and I was desperate to find archeological sites beyond the half-dozen that were listed in glossy pamphlets or illustrated on grease-stained fish 'n' chip shop placemats. A myriad of colours reflected off the still waters of the harbour as I thumbed through the pages of a guidebook. The open road called my name once again and there was no other option but to answer.

The Dingle Peninsula promised to be an archeological treasure trove, with over two thousand sites found to date, but this meant discovering most of these with only basic directions. It also meant trekking through mud and muck and possibly fighting off the occasional sheep. And I'd probably get lost along the way.

Sure, this wasn't high adventure. My life was not at risk

in any sort of interesting way. Upon publication of this book, Hollywood will most likely not be knocking on my door – casting some up-and-comer with chiseled features and robust presence to portray yours truly.

My mother, who is nearing seventy, has recently been lowered into a gorilla's nest in Rwanda, tossed into a river while whitewater rafting in Costa Rica, and crashed in a hot air balloon in Turkey. Her next adventure will involve a trip down the Amazon with only her husband, a guide, and a dugout canoe.

My aimless wanderings offer nothing comparable. My occasional odysseys are more in keeping with someone twice my age. But perhaps an adventure in Ireland doesn't need to involve ground-dwelling, predominantly herbivorous apes or adrenaline-fuelled near-death experiences from the air. Perhaps an adventure in Ireland is more about walking in glorious silence, stumbling onto lesser-known archeological sites, and spending time in the realm of faeries.

With the car idling, I closed my eyes and let the fates decide. "I shall head off wherever my finger lands," I said to the empty seat next to me, thumbing through the book again.

Took a deep breath, opened my eyes, and skimmed the selected page. There was some passing mention of an early Christian settlement somewhere in Ventry. By the sounds of it, all I had to do was park by the quarry and head up the hill – though there weren't specific directions to the quarry or how far up the hill it was located. "Ah, well. Sounds like just the right adventure for me."

The village of Ventry, twelve minutes west, is advertised as having one of the most attractive and safest beaches on the west coast of Ireland, but I arrived to find nothing more than scattered holiday caravans wrapped in tarpaulins for the winter.

Could have asked for directions at the Ventry Post Office that doubles as the local corner store, but that would have eliminated whatever small fraction of an adventure this was. So instead, I puttered up the road until I found a big hole in the side of a hill. A dilapidated fence runs the length of the quarry, but there is no signage or anything else to indicate private property. Parked the car at an awkward angle, with the back half hanging out onto the road, and jumped the fence.

Dodging gorse bush and slogging through the mud and muck, I slowly ascended the steep embankment and kept an eye out for any kind of early Christian settlement. But after ten minutes, there was nothing matching the description in my guidebook. Concerned with my footing and looking down at my feet most of the time, it was difficult to determine where I was going.

After several more minutes, with boots weighed heavy by the soft soil, I got the strange feeling someone was watching me. Surely my awkward behaviour made for great entertainment – the *eejit* tourist trekking his way to nowhere. Imagined a local farmer's wife calling her husband from the sitting room to watch me from the kitchen window. They would follow with rapt attention as I struggled and swore under my breath. Then they would both double over with laughter as I suddenly stopped in my tracks when half a dozen large animals came galloping towards me.

Sheep were fine. Those that kept me company during my long walks along the shores of the wild Atlantic were usually docile, and we had an understanding: they kept to their business and I kept to mine. But these weren't sheep.

These were something else. Something bigger. Something far more menacing.

Tried to focus against the late afternoon sun, but all I could see were monstrous silhouettes and glowing red eyes. The thunderous noise grew louder and louder as the demon-animals roared down the mountainside towards me. The ground shook as if the world were splitting into a thousand fragments. The dark figures from the bowels of hell kicked up waves of dank earth. It was the end of days, and all I could do was wait for my demise.

"Please don't trample me," I whispered. "No one will find my body out here."

Only as they were closing in, did I realize that they were not demons but rather wild ponies. Maybe they weren't wild in the sense of undomesticated, but they were certainly wild in the sense of covered in mud and muck.

Identifying them didn't help as they came galloping towards me, and my muscles tightened as I held my breath. Closed my eyes. Braced for impact. But the thunderous noise suddenly was no more.

Peeked with one eye to find that the ponies had all slowed down when they discovered I wasn't their owner and hadn't come to feed them. Then they stood confused before snorting and walking away. Relieved to find myself un-trampled, I continued up the hill.

By now there should have been something – some wedge tomb or faerie fort or holy well – but all I discovered were thorns and cold earth. Hiked on and on, and still couldn't find a damned thing.

Tired and miserable, and a fine cup of tea was calling me. It was time to end my fruitless quest.

It was only as I turned around – defeated and wondering what would possess someone like me to hike up a random hill in rural Ireland – that the setting sun, in purest amber, lit up the rolling hills in an array of golden greens. The glorious splendour bounced off the wet rocks, igniting the world, and even the grubby ponies had a mythical glow. It felt as if I were invited, for only a moment, to witness the creation of existence – a reimagining of the world as the gods painted everything in broad strokes of colour.

I also spied a circular stone enclosure in the middle of a farmer's field.

It could have been an early Christian settlement, but it didn't really matter. Whatever it was, it was something more than gorse bush, and mud and muck, and wild ponies. And it warranted a quick peek – if making my way back to the car, driving further down the narrow country road, finding some sort of parking, jumping a fence, and running across a field where all sorts of wild animals may be waiting could be considered 'a quick peek'.

I was still thirsty for adventure. Some curious force pulled me onwards. It felt like I was just stumbling along, but that's okay. History is all about stumbling. Stumbling is about discovery, and it is discovery that makes history truly come alive.

Of course, one does not simply park on a narrow country road in rural Ireland. That would be too easy. After slowly inching along, finding nowhere to pull over, the only real option was to park at the quarry again and continue on by foot.

Had no trouble locating the site after peering through a sturdy steel gate. After looking around to see if anyone was watching, I hopped over and power-walked across the open field.

Not only was I trespassing, but there was no telling

what large four-legged animals were in the vicinity. Sheep and wild ponies were one thing, but I had read about encounters with bulls during mating season and had no desire to cross paths with such a thing. Adrenalin kicked in and I switched from power-walking to an all-out sprint, imagining all sorts of things behind me.

Thin wooden posts hold up a wire fence that surrounds the stone enclosure, and I stretched my tight hamstrings before flipping one leg over and then the other – careful not to snap the wire back while looking around. Ireland certainly has no shortage of fences.

Safe from any strange animals that might be lurking around, it occurred to me that I had no idea what lay before me. I was merely an exhausted, mud-caked wanderer in the final light of day and, at first glance, what lay before me seemed little more than a motley collection of stones.

My feet were sore and I was looking forward to something a little stronger than tea, but some whisper from within reminded me to relax and make the most of the moment. Still, I resisted. Still, I questioned.

'What am I meant to reflect on now,' I asked myself, 'as I stand here on the edge of a lesser-known archeological site, in the middle of a farmer's field, on the west coast of Ireland? Why can't I just be content to take a couple photos and call it a day? Why must I continue to search out meaning in the early morning fog, or along slow-moving rivers, or atop a mountain? Why must I continue to look for guidance from creatures great and small, or the spirits that inhabit quiet corners? Isn't there a hockey game on somewhere?'

And then it dawned on me, as I looked towards Ventry Harbour – the setting for mythical tales of mighty warriors and the start of the pilgrimage trail – that it was not a presence that led me here, but an absence. An acknowledgement of that which is no longer. An appreciation of all that has yet to happen. It was the space *between* that I was meant to focus on. Not the notes, but the beauty that lingers between them.

I HAD EXPERIENCED something similar when I was first introduced to Henryk Górecki's third symphony. It consists of three very slow movements, and each features the lamenting voice of a solo soprano over long-held string lines. The first movement is a great, complex canon of deep sorrow. It starts almost inaudibly with the basses and, with utmost slowness, progressively rises through the strings until the entire orchestra is involved. Even today, more than any other piece of music, I need to prepare myself both mentally and physically before placing the record on the turntable. Must be willing to do nothing but listen to the subtle complexities as the rest of the world melts away.

In 1992, a recording of Górecki's then fifteen-year-old symphony, also known as The Symphony of Sorrowful Songs, was released to commemorate victims of the Holocaust. Górecki had incorporated a fifteenth-century lament, a Silesian folk song, and words written by a teenage girl on the wall of her prison cell into the music. Despite the heavy tone, it has since sold more than a million copies.

But I didn't know any of that when I first heard the album in my early twenties – being of an age where everything needs to be loud and energetic. Had never experienced anything like it before. I was dating a woman eight years my senior. She lived on the twelfth floor of an apartment building that overlooked the park, and we spent afternoons watching the people down below as they strolled through the trees and over small stone bridges.

The inside of her apartment was stark. Except for one accent wall behind the couch, everything was white: the living room, the bedroom and the kitchen. There was no decoration on the walls or small appliances on the countertop. While it could have easily felt institutional, it instead felt peaceful. There was an absence of busyness and nothing competed for attention. One day, I mentioned the lack of colour and personal items in her apartment and how quiet the world seemed even though we could hear the hum of traffic outside.

Soon after, she lay me down on her couch and told me to close my eyes. "Don't open them until the symphony is over," she said. "Concentrate on the music, and nothing else. Feel it wash over you. Follow it in your mind and allow it to transport you. Understand the beauty of what isn't there – of the space between everything."

No piece of music had taken me to tears by this point in my life, but this one came close. Some may describe Górecki's symphony as meditative, but for me it was more than that. It took me to a place where time has no meaning – where the physical is of no importance. It was all encompassing. It revealed vulnerability. It celebrated that which splits the darkness. It reminded me that there is magic in the cracks that let the smallest amount of light in.

By the time the symphony was over, the world seemed a little different and I said next to nothing for the rest of the day – finding it difficult to focus as I walked home through the summer crowds.

About a week later, without any hint or preview, she packed up her entire apartment one night and drove off in search of a new life. Maybe Montreal or Toronto. Doesn't really matter. I never saw or heard from her again.

Looking around the stone enclosure, I thought about all the small moments that make up a life, and the connections we have to archeological sites or pieces of music or even each other. The beauty of what isn't there. And I remembered that sometimes the most powerful moments arrive when we least expect them. Often they are told in whispers rather than thunderous roars.

Made my way across the enclosure and found a carved boulder with two equal-sided crosses and a series of dashes cut along the spine. Recognized the dashes as the earliest form of Irish writing known as Ogham.

As I kneeled in front of the stone, I wondered how many had done the same over the centuries – all the men, women and children that had taken pause after walking up from the harbour. There is a naturally formed stone basin, called a *bullaun* stone, nearby and I wondered how many had dipped their fingers into the rainwater. Though the site had long ago been discovered, studied and catalogued, it felt as if I were unearthing some great archeological find – privy to a secret only known to a select few.

Back at the car, I searched through my books for reference to the site. Known either as Maumanorig or Kilcolman (*Mám an Óraigh* or *Cill na gColmán*), it likely contained the remains of several huts or a possible church. It lies on the pilgrimage route, called the Saints' Path (*Cosán na Naomh),* and was used by both pagans and Christian pilgrims who walked from Ventry to the summit of Mount Brandon. Travellers would have come ashore after days or weeks on the cold Atlantic and stopped at places like this one. They would then proceed northwards, stopping at Kilmalkedar and the Gallarus Oratory before reaching St. Brendan's Oratory on the summit of the mountain.

The Ogham stone reads ANM COLMAN AILITHIR ([written in] the name of Colmán the Pilgrim) and may commemorate Colmán Oilither, grandson of Díarmait mac Fergosa Cerrbéoil (who died sometime between 565 and 572). Most archeologists date the earliest Ogham stone inscriptions to the fourth century, although many argue that the alphabet was used centuries beforehand when it was first carved into wood. It is believed that Ogham letters were carved on wands of yew and used by the Druids for divination purposes.

Some have suggested that Ogham was created as a cryptic alphabet, designed by the Irish so as not to be understood by those with knowledge of the Latin alphabet, while others favour the theory that it was invented by the first Christian communities in early Ireland out of a desire to have a unique way of writing short messages and inscriptions in the Irish language.

According to mythology, Ogma of the Tuatha Dé Danann is said to have invented the ancient Ogham alphabet. Medieval folklore claims that it was conceived soon after the fall of the Tower of Babel, when a scholar created a language after comparing and selecting the best of all other languages.

Ogham is sometimes called the 'Celtic Tree Alphabet' based on a High Medieval *Bríatharogam* tradition ascribing names of trees to individual letters. Initially, eight letters were named after trees: birch, alder, willow, oak, hazel, pine, ash and yew. Their selection gives us clues as to the importance of these trees in early Irish society.

The original form of Ogham consisted of twenty

symbols arranged in four groups of five letters. Each letter was represented by one to five strokes to the left, to the right, across a central stem-line, or at an angle. The largest concentration of Ogham stones can be found in County Kerry (there have been almost seventy discovered to date on the Dingle Peninsula), but other clusters are found across Ireland, England, Scotland, the Isle of Man, and Wales. Used as grave markers or property markers, the Ogham stones now stand as direct links to Ireland's past and today many amateur archeologists are assisting in cataloging the stones with a phone app that creates 3-D imaging.

Still others argue that Ogham was a pagan alphabet, created before any real Christian presence in the country and only later did the early Christians stamp their mark upon the stones (rather than destroy them). This doesn't seem to be the case with the Colman stone since it fluidly incorporates two crosses into the overall carving – not to mention the term 'pilgrim'. What also makes the Colman stone unique is the shape of the stone itself. Most surviving Ogham stones are pillar-shaped, but the Colman stone is an irregularly shaped boulder with the inscription along the spine.

Dating the Colman stone has been difficult. It seems, perhaps because of the shape of the boulder itself, that whoever carved the inscription made spacing errors. Some words were broken by the angle of the rock, some letters were crammed, and other letters were warped in order to fix mistakes. Some scholars have attempted to date the stone by the crosses while others point to the use of the term ANM, which would place it sometime in the eighth or ninth centuries. The Colman stone is said to be of the scholastic period (from medieval Old Irish to modern day), rather than the earlier orthodox period (the Primitive Irish period) in which Ogham was used exclusively for recording the name of an individual either as a cenotaph, tombstone, or to document land ownership.

But the Colman stone is just one of hundreds of Ogham stones littered across Western Europe. It is neither the most important nor the most impressive. But it drew me in, and I wanted to learn more about the mysterious ancient alphabet, the pilgrimage route, and those that crossed great distances in hopes of connecting with the divine. Perhaps their search for Truth was similar to mine; while they were looking for guidance from a god (or *the* God), I was looking for guidance as to what drew me to a land and culture that was not my own. Discovering how this country could be as a catalyst for awakening self-awareness.

While sitting in the car, I wondered if my solo adventures could be considered a pilgrimage and whether any insights I had while walking through the morning fog were as valid as those experienced by the ancient Celts or early Christians. I wasn't taking part in any rituals involving the infliction of intentional pain (unless you include a sparse diet of bread and cheese), and yet I couldn't deny that this was – in the broadest definition of the word – a spiritual exercise.

Virtually all cultures recognize that there are certain transition points in our lives when we are meant to attend more carefully to matters of the spirit. Adolescents entering adulthood, seekers arriving at midlife, and those entering the last stage of their lives are all ripe for pilgrimage. So too are those who have had a transition thrust upon them unwillingly by death, divorce, or other personal trials. All of these experiences can open our hearts and souls to new insights.

My pilgrimage could not be considered a spiritual exercise or an act of devotion in the traditional Christian sense, but it could be considered a spiritual exercise in that I was open to a meaningful, transformative journey to a sacred centre. Mine was a journey of risk and renewal to a natural setting imbued with spiritual power. For thousands of years, many like myself – whose names have now faded from memory – journeyed to Ireland's shore as a rite of passage, an expression of faith and devotion, an answer to a sacred call, or merely to seek the spirit within.

While walking alone, I could feel the presence of all those that traced the same path before me and, like myself, entered a liminal state. Their identities becoming fluid amidst a myriad of possibilities. The distant hypnotizing rhythm of feet, the drum of countless hearts, but also the measure of a single breath and each ancient song that carried them forward all blended into a subtle symphony of sound.

Back in town, I strolled aimlessly in and out of shops. It was (probably) too early for a pint, and I was merely killing time before dinner. Slipped into one last store as most of the town was closing up, and found a collection of affordable jewelry made with silver and Connemara marble. Having lost myself in the Ogham alphabet, it was fitting to buy my wife a pendant that reads GRÁ (love). No one at home would know what it was, but Paula would and that's all that mattered.

My mind was numb, my feet were sore, and I had no desire to sit in an empty restaurant where I'd feel lonely and awkward and miss my wife. Didn't want to walk up the hill to my room and write in my journal before walking back down to have a pint or two. What I needed was some time and space to reflect on my day. Wasn't sure how else to do this except to follow the harbour.

Down Strand Street, past the pastel-coloured buildings, and I squinted against the low setting sun while strolling past Murphy's Pub. The Linen Chest and Paudie's Bar, and other stores selling a selection of scarves, caps and shawls in beautiful plaids and patterns. An employee of the Dingle Woollen Company was bringing in the rugby shirts set up outside on the sidewalk. The pub with John Benny Moriarty's name above the door, and the quintessential circular Guinness sign that hangs from the second floor. Then Harrington's Family Restaurant, and the smell of fried fish filled my nose.

Eventually the restaurants and pubs make way for three-story row houses, and I nodded hello to those walking their dogs before settling in for the evening or working up an appetite. The Dingle Oceanworld Aquarium and traditional houses with front lawns, well-trimmed hedges and wide driveways. Further on are smaller holiday homes and cream-coloured guesthouses.

My legs were on autopilot and it was only as the short stone bridge and the Dingle Distillery came into view that I felt a need to sit down and rest for a while. Had there been a nice wooden bench that looked out onto the water I may have watched the world go by. But there wasn't, so I simply turned around and went back the way I came.

It was nearing the end of the day, but I had no idea what time it was. Which was an unusual feeling. Despite being in Ireland on my own, with no set itinerary, I was always aware of the hour – whether it was lunchtime or teatime or dinnertime. Still felt the need to be somewhere by a certain hour. Still sought out a sense of order. Still needed to break up my days in bite-sized pieces so that I was back in town at regular intervals.

But what did it matter if it was a quarter-to-something, or a quarter-past-something else? What did it matter if I dined an hour before or an hour later? Or just ate a bag of snacks as I sat on cold stone and watched the sunset with disinterested sheep as the evening wind blew off the water?

Why couldn't I break away from this conditioning?

Maybe it comes from being a teacher for twenty-plus years. School starts at 8:45am. Math class soon after. Recess at 10:15am. Then Language Arts. The students eat their lunch at noon. I eat mine fifteen minutes afterwards.

It wasn't always like this. As a teenager, I often imagined my life as a wandering bard or a global vagabond. Never staying too long in one place. Nothing would tie me down. Teaching the local children about life, or telling stories to the villagers for the price of a meal, or saving some damsel in distress – and then I would pack up my meagre belongings and hit the open road. "My time here is done," I would say. "Best be moving on." The men would tip their hats, the women would dab their eyes with handkerchiefs, and the children would pass me some artwork they had done in crayon.

But I never got very far with that romantic ideal. Attended university, became a teacher, married, had children, and found comfort in the rhythm of my days and weeks instead.

While I don't mind the occasional free-form micro-adventure, I still find it difficult to go with the flow. Hardly ever join friends for drives out in the country – mostly because I get car-sick, but also because I want to know where I'm going and when I'll be back. Hardly ever join friends for hikes or camping trips – mostly because of the mosquitoes, but also because I want to know where I'm going and when I'll be back.

What would life without responsibilities even look like? A life without a significant other or kids or cats. Just me and the open road. My belongings on my back. But, honestly, that's no life for me. I'd get lonely. And despite myself, my days would start to follow a familiar pattern anyway.

I had always assumed that full-time artists and writers make the most of their freedom from a nine-to-five job by hanging out at home in comfy pyjamas or hanging out in dive bars with the seedy underbelly of society, but this is not usually the case. From what I've read lately, it's fair to say that most artists and writers treat their craft like any other job and follow a daily schedule.

Whether working at a place of employment that follows a strict schedule or not, we are all creatures of habit in some form or another and we all crave some sense of the familiar.

Among others, authors Stephen King and Haruki Murakami have discussed the importance of a daily routine when working on a new project.

"There's a certain time I sit down, from 8:00 to 8:30am, somewhere within that half hour every morning," explains King. "I have my vitamin pill and my music, sit in the same seat and the papers are all arranged in the same places."

When in writing mode, Murakami gets up at 4:00am and works for five to six hours. "In the afternoon," he told a reporter from *The Paris Review*, "I run for ten kilometres or swim for fifteen hundred meters (or do both), then I read a bit and listen to some music. I go to bed at 9:00pm. I keep to this routine every day without variation. The repetition itself becomes the important thing; it's a form of mesmerism. I mesmerize myself to reach a deeper state of mind."

While I had journeyed to Ireland in hopes of casting off this need to set certain parameters of my day, maybe that wasn't the lesson I needed to learn just yet. Despite the mountain teaching me that time has little meaning when on pilgrimage, maybe it was okay to hold on to a certain amount of control for now.

There were definitely moments in my life when I craved control – years adrift and desperate for some sense of normality. As a fledging teacher, waiting patiently for a position to open up, what I longed for was not only to obtain a position and have a meaningful impact on students, but to also know the parameters of my experience: to know how the year would unfold, and to have a space to call my own. I needed to know the order of my day and week – where the boundaries and limits are determined in advance, and where the emotional and psychological highs and lows are familiar.

It was difficult waiting for the phone to ring when on-call, only to receive a day or two of work. Difficult trying to connect with students when I was in someone else's classroom for a day (or even an hour). Difficult handing out some random worksheet on polynomial factoring, or playing some an out-of-date video on asexual reproduction, while I sat at someone else's desk with yesterday's unwashed coffee cup and papers piled high.

It was difficult waiting for positions to be posted and then waiting for an interview. Difficult hanging my head in disappointment when the position went to some out-of-town basketball coach who usually left at the end of the year in search of greener pastures. Difficult wondering if I had chosen the right profession.

I had almost no control over my career for so long, and would walk the empty streets at night for hours just to settle my mind. So I finally did something silly. Bought a pair of running shoes. And started small: a three-kilometre run. It wasn't easy. And my muscles were not pleased with me. But I set small goals, and soon pushed myself to run five kilometres, and then eight, and then ten. Discovered that no one but myself could control how far I went, how fast I ran, or whether I laced up once or twice or three times a week.

Ran the same route every time and learned to appreciate the subtle differences of the changing seasons. Found a sense of peace in the familiar. And I decided to set bigger goals, charting out my runs on a large poster board tacked to the back of the front door. Dared myself to run a thousand kilometres in ten months and, while doing that, adding more and more distance to each run. It seemed insane but I wondered if I could one day complete a marathon in less than four hours.

The more I ran, the less I worried about whether someone in a position of power valued me as a teacher. The further I ran, the less I worried about whether some boob in a suit thought I was good enough to join their team.

With only three days to spare, I completed my goal of a thousand kilometres. A little later, I crossed the finish line and collected my marathon medal after three hours and forty-four minutes (and forty-five seconds). It took me a week to learn how to walk again.

Both goals were insane. But I alone was in control. Didn't have to rely or worry about anyone else. And eventually I found a position in a school that appreciates my unique teaching style.

Even today, I still worry about losing control. Still wake up on rainy mornings, wondering if it'll all end – if the shadows will once again black out the sun.

So I run the same route, worry about my job every June, and feel uneasy when I'm away from home for more than a few hours.

For now, I am content to merely soften the parameters. Content to set out in the morning with my pack and camera and journal, and be open to what Ireland (or any other place) can teach me in safe little segments between breakfast and a pint or two.

At the thought of food and drink, I refocused into the present moment. It was with conflicted feelings that I walked up to the counter of Harrington's. Having dined in several award-winning fish 'n' chip restaurants all along the Pacific Coast, from northern British Columbia to southern California, I had never developed a taste for battered fish. Nevertheless, something quick and easy seemed perfect, and the restaurant does a high-caloric combo in a matter of minutes. It also offers Guinness on tap.

Fishing nets hang from the ceiling, a miniature rowboat hangs over the counter, the clocks are all nautical-based, and the chalkboards are cut out in dolphin shapes. The bright blue menus are under tabletop Plexiglass, and the meals are served in miniature slop buckets and fry cages. Not really my vibe, but I was open to new experiences.

Wish I could write that the fish 'n' chips at Harrington's finally made a convert of me. But I can't. Dipped half my thick-cut fries in malt vinegar and the other half in ketchup, and swallowed it all down with drink, but left about a third of my fish behind. It was enough to fill me up and still leave plenty of room for a few more drinks later in the evening.

There were still a couple hours before the music began so, rather than walk up the hill that seemed longer and steeper every time I hoofed it to Dúinín House in several layers of wool, I instead cracked open a couple books to review early Irish history. Wanted to anchor myself in the concrete, and attempt to untangle myth from reality. It's easy to get caught up in the fantastical while touring the country, and I wanted the opportunity to review the names and dates, and provide some sense of balance.

When the kids were younger and misbehaving in the back of the car, I would often threaten them with the audiobook of *A Short History of Ireland* by Jonathan Bardon. I thought it was great and couldn't get enough; the kids, however, did not care for it.

In the wake of its thirtieth birthday celebrations in 2006, BBC Radio Ulster embarked on the recounting of the history of the island nation. Two hundred forty short documentaries take listeners on a journey spanning the Ice Age, the arrival of Christianity, the Viking era, Brian Boru, the Normal invasion, the plantation and the famine through to the creation of the Irish Free State. Each program interweaves eyewitness accounts, letters and diary extracts with historical facts.

As a pack of teenaged boys saddled up to the counter and then hung around outside, and the sound of the fryer sputtering hot oil filled the otherwise quite restaurant, I made myself comfortable – wedged between the chair and the front window – and disappeared into the world of words once again.

CHAPTER 15
A PURE PART OF THE ABYSS

From about 2000 BCE, as mining techniques developed and the early people extracted copper, the Neolithic Age began to slowly make way for the Bronze Age. Bronze swords have survived from this era, as well as gold necklaces, pendants and armbands. Various dress fasteners, horns and trumpets, shields and axes all testify to a society growing in sophistication and technological development. Gold working was an important economic activity, and domestic pottery became even more varied.

The Bronze Age yielded to the Iron Age around 500 BCE, and with that change came the incursion into Ireland of the people (or peoples) with whom the island has been associated with ever since. The Iron Age brought not just a new metal and its associated technologies, but also the Celts (and with them a mythology forever linked with the country).

The drunken man's rant at O'Flaherty's has some basis in truth. The very word 'Celtic' is a tricky one. During his inauguration speech at the University of Oxford, J.R.R. Tolkien commented that "to many, perhaps to most people outside the small company of the great scholars, past and present, 'Celtic' of any sort is, nonetheless, a magic bag, into which anything may be put, and out of which almost anything may come. Anything is possible in the fabulous Celtic twilight, which is not so much a twilight of the gods as of the reason."

For many people, Celtic refers to a homogenized group located in the British Isles and Ireland. However, from an anthropological standpoint, it is far more complex. The term Celt derives from a label which one society placed on those outside its own community. The Greeks referred to certain peoples in western and central Europe as *Keltoi*. In modern times, the term has referred not to a nation or a group of related tribes but to a broad family of similar languages.

It is now believed that there was no sudden invasion of Ireland by conquering Celts. Instead there was a steady influx of related peoples over centuries. Because the early Celts didn't leave much in the way of written records, most of what we know of them was written by later societies – in particular, by those groups that conquered the Celtic lands. Nevertheless, we do know that these Iron Age people were highly skilled in metalwork, and their superior military prowess caused them to displace the indigenous population of Ireland.

Far out in the western ocean, cut off from European influence (not only by the sea but also by the wild highlands of western Britain), Ireland remained untouched and independent throughout the four centuries of Roman imperial rule over Britain, Spain, and Gaul. A distinctive aspect of Irish history is the absence of Roman rule – though the degree of influence on ancient Ireland is debated even today.

As the Empire grew weaker in the fourth century, and perhaps even before, the Irish began to attack Britain. Coastal forts built by the Romans to keep out the Irish (and the Picts from Scotland) were more and more ineffective as Roman power continued to decrease, and this left western Britain open to invading outsiders. There is abundant evidence of Irish settlements, and profits from the new settlements were used to fund dynastic wars while pirates continued to raid British shores.

Ireland at this time showed several characteristics of the older Celtic society on the continent. There was a tradition of bardic praise poetry, and there is some evidence of druids (or holy men) who provided the link between individuals and the pagan deities. Although fragmented, Ireland showed signs of cultural and political continuity. A primitive legal code, known as Brehon Law, developed though this could not be widely enforced because the country lacked any central authority.

It is not known exactly when the first Christian missionaries set to work in Hibernia, but a date in the late fourth or early fifth century seems most likely. Many sources discuss Palladius, who traveled to Ireland in 431 after being ordained by Pope Celestine. He landed in present-day Wicklow but was soon banished by the King of Leinster.

While Patrick may not have been the first to attempt to Christianize the island nation, he was certainly the most significant. Born into a respectable family in Wales (possibly in 405), he was captured by raiders at the age of sixteen and taken as a slave. Far from home, he clung to the religion he had ignored as a teenager. Even though his grandfather had been a priest, and his father a deacon and member of town council, Patrick admitted he "knew not the true God" until he suffered in virtual isolation.

Cold, hungry and having spent six years as a shepherd in the brutal landscape of the north, Patrick fought off loneliness by praying day and night. In his *Confessio*, he recounts a dream (or a vision) in which an angel of the Lord came in the night and told him of a pagan ship leaving Ireland. Patrick took a leap of faith and, after walking over three hundred kilometres to a port near Dublin and journeying across stormy waters, he arrived home and was reunited with his family and friends.

Not long after that, he then had another vision in which he heard Irish voices saying, "We beseech thee, O holy youth, to come and walk once more among us." This vision prompted his studies for the priesthood and, after four years, St. Germanus, Bishop of Auxerre, ordained Patrick before he left for Ireland as a missionary. Intimately familiar with the Irish clan system, Patrick's strategy was to convert the chiefs first. They, in turn, would convert their respective clans. There has been much written about how Patrick converted the pagan Irish, including the famous episode in which he explains the Trinity using a shamrock.

Patrick would go on to found Christian communities throughout Ireland, most notably his church in Armagh (*Ard Mhacha*) – which became the ecclesiastical capital. This is where Patrick would write, codify the Brehon laws, and finally retire. The church he founded, like that of Columba's in Scotland after him, differed in a number of ways from the church of Rome: most notably in its inclusion of women in church hierarchy, the dating of Easter, the liturgy, and the tonsure of monks (the practice of cutting or shaving some or all of the hair on the scalp as a sign of religious devotion or humility).

Though not well educated, Patrick encouraged learning in his adopted country. He favoured development of local Christianity around monastic foundations rather than bishops and their dioceses. He stressed asceticism (severe self-discipline and avoidance of all forms of indulgence), which may have been a result of his contacts with the monastic foundations in Gaul and their tough spiritual discipline.

In the sixth and seventh centuries, Irish Christianity entered a new and more expansive phase. The concept of *peregrinatio* – which meant that a monk would leave the monastery and his Christian country to proselytize among the heathens – became more and more popular. One of the greatest figures in this period was Columba (or Colmcille), born in County Donegal. He left Ireland in 563 and became the major instrument in the conversion of the Picts and his fellow Irish who had settled in Scotland. He did this by first combating the influence of the druid priesthood and then penetrating the royal court circles. Before he died in 597, Columba had begun the process of Christianizing all of Scotland and Northern England.

Christianity had to battle hard to survive in an era of magic, spells and ancient symbols. To be successful, Patrick's followers needed to find a middle ground between the church's teachings and the pagan belief system (though this would later bring early Irish Christianity into conflict with Rome). Rather than destroy pagan sites, the early missionaries combined their symbols with that of the early Irish. The Celtic cross, for instance, is said to combine the Christian cross with the pagan sun symbol. The druids believed that the number three was a magical number, and this proved advantageous for the early Christians when they described the holy Trinity.

Monastic establishments arose in the sixth and seventh centuries, such as Clonmacnoise (founded by St. Ciarán) and Glendalough (founded by St. Kevin). Monastic schools became centres of excellence. Many historians of the time reported that sizeable contingents of English students trained as missionaries in Ireland.

The great monasteries of the day, rather than the kings, were the main economic units in this society. A monastery could have many thousands of tenants and vast wealth. By now it was more common for a bishop to rule over these great kingdoms (or *túaths*), and the duties of bishops were clearly laid down.

Although Ireland did not see Roman rule, it did witness a wave of Viking incursions between the eighth and tenth centuries. The Vikings developed the finest fleet of seafaring craft in contemporary Europe, and the first recorded Viking raid occurred in 795 when they looted the island of Lambay (*Reachrainn*) – off the coast of north County Dublin.

The early raids were generally quick and small in scale, but the pattern of Viking attacks started to change after 836. In that year, they made their first big inland raid into the area ruled by the southern Uí Néills, carrying many people into slavery. Viking fleets soon appeared on both the Boyne and the Liffey, and the fierce warriors pillaged the surrounding areas, defeating the southern Uí Néills in the process. The Vikings wintered in Ireland for the first time in 840-41, and soon established a proto-settlement, known as a *longphort*, on the banks of the Liffey. A *longphort* was a defensible enclosure for shipping which offered adequate berthage and easy access to the open sea. By now the

Vikings had greatly increased the ferocity of their attacks throughout Ireland, and there was serious danger that they might conquer the entire island.

Irish kings began to fight back. While these attacks did not unite the warring Irish kingdoms against the Vikings, there were many instances of Norse-Irish alliances. More ships arrived (probably from Denmark) during the years 849-852, and many battles took place between these new arrivals and the more established Vikings. Despite this, many of the settlements developed and grew into towns. Their town of *Dubhlinn* (Dublin) had a thriving Norse community by the second half of the 800s, and had become the principal supplier of slaves in the British Isles. In time, it became a great merchant town – until it was defeated by an Irish attack in 902.

For a couple of decades afterwards Viking power was on the rise, but a struggle for domination between the Viking kingdom of Dublin and its rivals in Limerick and Waterford curtailed a Norse occupation of the country. The Vikings eventually settled down in the lands they had conquered. By 950 they had ceased raiding in Ireland, and developed instead as traders.

History books usually describe Brian Boru as the most famous Irishman before the modern era. They go on to detail his modest beginnings, how he rose to become king of Ireland, and his fabled death at the Battle of Clontarf. The stories and myths surrounding the man tend to dominate the history of Ireland in the two centuries between the end of the Viking excursions and Anglo-Norman intervention, possibly to the exclusion of other events. Yet much of his history is uncertain and disputed.

He was probably born around the year 940 in Munster. After his father passed away around 960, Brian's eldest brother (and successor) ousted the ruling Munster dynasty – making himself a powerful figure in southern Ireland. The Norsemen of Limerick murdered him in 976, and Brian's first act was to take revenge. Over the next three years, he conquered Limerick and the whole of Munster. This naturally brought him into conflict with the Uí Néills, who regarded themselves as the first family in Ireland.

In 1002, Boru established himself as High King of Ireland after successfully challenging the reigning king to the title and defeating him in battle at the Hill of Tara. As king, Boru was a generous benefactor. He sought to reorganize the church, rebuild the churches plundered by the Vikings, and uphold Armagh as Ireland's religious capital. He is said to have made a journey around the whole country in 1005, and the lesser kings soon recognized Brian as the supreme ruler. He managed to do what no other High King of Ireland had done: he established himself in more than just name by forcing all other challengers to swear allegiance to him during a ten-year campaign.

But Boru's rise to dominance was greeted with suspicion. (This was hardly surprising given the fractious nature of Ireland's dynastic politics.) In 1013, Brian was attacked by an alliance of Leinstermen and Norsemen from Dublin under Sitric Silkbeard, who brought in Norse warriors from the Hebrides and the Isle of Man. The decisive battle was fought on Good Friday at Clontarf (*Cluain Tarbh*), just north of Dublin. The Battle of Clontarf lasted all day, but in the end the Dublin-Leinster alliance was defeated.

It is estimated that between seven and ten thousand men were killed in the battle, including most of its leaders. Although Brian's forces were victorious, Brian himself was killed, as were his son Murchad and his grandson Toirdelbach.

There are many accounts of how Brian was slain, from dying in heroic man-to-man combat to being killed by fleeing Viking mercenaries while praying in his tent, but we do know that after his death his body was taken to Swords for the wake and then Armagh to be buried.

The battle of Clontarf has been the centrepiece for many Irish and Norse sagas but, despite the myths still propagated in popular histories, Clontarf did *not* mark the decisive victory of the Irish over the Vikings. Boru did not free Ireland from a Norse occupation, simply because it was never conquered by the Vikings. After establishing fortified camps that later grew into Ireland's first cities – Dublin, Limerick, Waterford, Wexford and Cork (*Baile Átha Cliath*, *Luimneach*, *Port Láirge*, *Loch Garman* and *Corcaigh*) – the Norse citizens had converted to Christianity, intermarried with the Irish, and often adopted the Irish language.

The battle *was* important because Boru's career effectively put an end to the Uí Néill claim to the high kingship of Ireland forever. After the battle, there was no longer any clear line of succession and the Irish were leaderless. Gaelic and Viking cultures were no longer contesting power against one another, and the title of high kingship remained unclaimed for a century and a half. Boru's reign had established a new pattern of fluctuating provincial domination.

The Norman invasion of Ireland, which began in May 1169, was helped and hindered by the country's disunity – helped because it made use of Irish dissensions and hindered because, unlike England, there was no central government for the Normans to take over. The real Norman opportunity was created by the feud between Dermot MacMurrough (*Diarmait Mac Murchada*), king of Leinster, and Rory O'Connor (*Ruaidri Ua Conchobair*), king of Connacht.

It was at this point in the story that I contemplated another pint, or maybe a deep-fried Mars bar, but instead my thoughts turned to the little town of Ferns (*Fearna Mór Maedhóg*). Paula and I had stopped there on our way from Kilkenny (*Cill Chainnigh*) to somewhere else. It seemed like a nice place to pull over and stretch our legs.

Compared to Blarney and Cashel, Ferns Castle didn't seem particularly impressive but we entered the visitors' centre, paid the fee, and were about to head towards the site on our own. Not allowed, we were told. We had to wait for the next available tour guide.

"Will that be long?" I asked.

"Four minutes."

Dressed in khaki shorts, wool socks, and black hiking boots, our guide was young and energetic. Her enthusiasm was contagious, even though it was late in the day and we were growing weary from the day's travels.

"Built in the early part of the thirteenth century, the castle was originally square-shaped with four large round towers at each corner," she began. "As you can see, the southeastern tower is still intact. The castle had three floors inside. On the first floor of the eastern tower is a vaulted circular chapel. If you look up, you can see eight heads staring down at you from the roof. Another feature of the castle is a fabulous gargoyle, extending out from the south side of the southwestern tower."

We looked around at the ruined castle and found the tower, the chapel and the eight heads. Then we walked around to view the gargoyle.

"The narrow winding staircase brings you to the very top of the tower where there are splendid views of the surrounding countryside – if you're interested."

I answered with a shrug.

"Great," exclaimed our guide. "Follow me."

We trailed behind, and from the third story we looked out at the surrounding lush landscape.

"This castle is considered to be one of the finest examples of Anglo-Norman fortresses in Ireland. Unfortunately, Ferns Castle was ultimately destroyed by Cromwellian forces."

We looked out again at the village as a late afternoon wind picked up.

"But what makes the area of Ferns particularly interesting, of course, is that it's the burial site of Dermot MacMurrough."

Paula and I looked at each other as if we should know who this particular character was.

"Do you know why he's important in Irish history?" asked our guide.

"His name sounds familiar," I lied.

"Dermot MacMurrough was the King of Leinster during the twelfth century, and is most remembered as the man who invited the English to Ireland."

"Ah... so he's not the most appreciated figure in Irish history?"

"No, he is not. But even before that he was known as a ruthless leader. After succeeding to the throne in 1126, he faced a number of rivals who disputed his claim to kingship. He decided to establish his authority by killing or blinding seven rebel chieftains in 1141. But the real story begins when he was involved in a dispute with Tiernan O'Ruark, King of Breffney.

"In 1153, MacMurrough abducted O'Ruark's wife. Whether the young lady consented to be abducted or not is unclear, but O'Ruark (understandably humiliated) appealed to Rory O'Connor, king of Connacht, for help. Thirteen years went by until finally the long-running and bitter feud resulted in MacMurrough being driven into exile by the Gaelic chieftains.

"He fled to France, but refused to accept his life away from Ireland and soon made his way to the court of Henry II of England. Henry had been too busy with other matters to give Ireland much concern, but now MacMurrough provided the necessary catalyst. While Henry was unwilling to intervene personally, he did provide MacMurrough with letters authorizing him to raise troops. In return, MacMurrough pledged to hold Leinster as Henry's vassal and to offer his daughter's hand to whatever military leader might be found."

I imagine our guide had told this story several times, yet there was no hint of waning enthusiasm. She barely took a breath before continuing, and we followed her as she led us away from the ruins and back towards the visitors' centre.

"MacMurrough raised troops in Wales, returned, and recovered some of his lands in 1167. He was reinforced by more Norman troops two years later. Their leader was Richard FitzGilbert de Clare, better known to history as Strongbow.

"The Anglo-Norman invaders soon won a string of fairly easy victories in the southeast. The original expedition had captured Wexford, so provoking a desperate measure by O'Connor who offered to restore MacMurrough as king of Leinster if he would send the Normans back home. Instead, more invaders followed and, to cement the alliance, MacMurrough married his daughter Aoife to Strongbow in Christchurch Cathedral.

"The local chieftains were not interested in allowing the invaders to settle without a fight, and they continually attacked and harassed the outsiders. At one stage, it seemed likely that they would be driven from the country were it not for the renewed support of Henry II. He had become concerned with the amount of power and influence that Strongbow was amassing across the Irish Sea and decided to intervene.

"By September 1171, the king decided to lead a military expedition. He wanted to establish control of both the Norman warlords and the native Irish. After landing at Waterford with a large army of at least five hundred mounted knights, four thousand men-at-arms and archers, and several siege towers, the Norman lords handed their conquered territory to Henry. The king let Strongbow hold Leinster in fief and declared the cities to be crown land. This was the first time a king of England had set foot on Irish soil, and it marked the beginning of English (and later British) rule in Ireland."

I CLOSED my book and looked out towards the harbour as a new wave of fried food attacked my senses and brought me back into the moment. The cold fish and puddle of ketchup was even less appealing than it had been earlier. After leaving Harrington's, I crossed the road to the tourist office, found the bronze statue of Fungie the dolphin, and sat down on a bench. There was no one else around.

As I re-wrapped my scarf and slipped on my gloves, I thought back on several millennia of blood soaking into the wet earth during times of turmoil; of ashes falling like dry leaves when the great fires marked the passing of the year; of melancholic reflection as the tide turned; of stolen moments among the stones; of tears for those that left too soon; and immense relief when light finally broke through the darkness.

Thought about all the cracked, calloused hands that helped built the dry-stone huts; the soft prayers made to various gods and goddesses; laughter in the rainstorms; all the stories and songs that spread throughout the land; the small pins and pendants lost and found again. Thought about those comforted in the arms of loved ones only to be struck with fear when news of outsiders spread in frantic whispers; about those with the courage to continue on with their daily lives, and those with the courage to change the course of history.

A pint at O'Sullivan's seemed like a better idea than sitting alone, so I crossed town feeling both infinitesimal and yet a pure part of the abyss – content to drift down the endless long river of history.

Like myself, there are many who want to be remembered for something they have created. It's a comforting thought that someone somewhere will read your book, or admire your painting, or use your hand-spun pottery long after you have shuffled off your mortal coil.

I often stroll through used bookstores, imagining where my tattered tomes might sit on the shelf. This book may one day find its way into the memoir section, or the travel section, or with the miscellaneous Irish paperbacks – waiting patiently for strange individuals like myself (and maybe you) who enjoy that kind of thing. It might snuggle next to H.V. Morton's 1930 publication *In Search of Ireland*. At the bottom of the first page is my favourite line. "I felt rather like the fool of the party," writes the author, "because I was bound on perhaps the most stupid and thankless task which a man can set for himself: I was going to add another book to that mountain of books about Ireland."

A tad disheartening, perhaps, as those words were penned almost a century earlier, but maybe I just need to have faith that my work will fall into the right hands. Despite those moments when all of this seems a waste of time, I will continue to plug away. And plug away some more.

However, my pursuit to be a published author shouldn't be the driving force in how I live my day-to-day. A life spent helping others and making the world a better place is ultimately far more important – reminding myself that, while my name may not be remembered a hundred years from now, hopefully the ripples of kindness and compassion will be felt in some small way.

CHAPTER 16

A GRAND DAY OUT

It seemed like a good day for Inch Beach (*An Inse*). Though I got lost when first arriving, I was now more familiar with the peninsula, and drove out of town with (somewhat misplaced) confidence.

Figured the five-kilometre stretch of pristine white beach should prove to be a good balance to yesterday's hike up the mountain. Famous for being the place where 'an inch is actually three miles long', it is advertised as a haven for surfers and other ocean-loving types. The nature reserve behind the banks of sand dunes is a popular attraction for birdwatchers, and the wetlands are important wintering grounds for many ducks and waders. It also featured heavily in the 1970 film *Ryan's Daughter*, directed by David Lean.

Lean had previously directed *The Bridge on the River Kwai*, *Lawrence of Arabia* and *Doctor Zhivago*, and international audiences were expecting another masterpiece with his Irish film.

I felt compelled to watch the movie before I left but, with a running time of almost two hundred minutes, I had to watch it in small doses over several sittings. The scenery is stunning, but the pacing is an issue. Film critic Roger Ebert was not impressed, either. He said that it was "a disappointing failure of tone, a lush and overblown self-indulgence in which David Lean has given us a great deal less than meets the eye."

Ryan's Daughter is set in 1915, against the backdrop of the burgeoning Republican movement and the First World War. The character of Rosy Ryan has an affair with an English officer to escape the drudgery of her marriage to a dull schoolteacher. After the village idiot innocently reveals their affair to the villagers, the husband ignores the scandal, assumes that the affair will pass, and that life will continue. However – without giving too much away – things don't work out too well.

Over breakfast that morning, I asked Pat about the filming of *Ryan's Daughter*.

"Ah sure, that was a great summer. Remember it well," he said. "I worked as a driver, as many did, and delivered cast and crew and supplies to different filming sites. Had a grand time and made a good bit of pocket money, too. Dingle was simpler then – not what it is today, y'know – and to have Hollywood types suddenly arrive at our door was something else, entirely."

"I heard that filming didn't go quite according to plan."

"Ah, so," laughed Pat. "Well, that certainly would be one way of putting it." He laughed again and sat down across from me after placing the breakfast tray on a nearby table. "Y'know, there were a number of stories floating around at the time, and many long afterwards. Most of them are probably true."

Pat looked out the window towards town. "It was the weather that was the real problem. The director insisted that many of the love scenes on the beach be shot in sunshine, a rarity on the west coast – as you may know – and so filming went on far longer than expected."

Lost in memory, Pat smiled to himself before asking, "You've seen the film, have you?"

"Yes, I did. But it took me about a week."

"Don't doubt it. It was not the director's best work – I know that – and I don't think the actors liked each other much. That couldn't have helped, either."

The film took two years to make and, in that time, the sleepy community enjoyed previously unimagined wealth. The drawback, however, were the wild antics of Hollywood actors.

The love scene played by Christopher Jones and Sarah Miles doesn't read well on film (probably because they didn't like each other) and the story goes that Robert Mitchum (who apparently played host to a number of girls in various rooms at a time and had a marijuana garden at a nearby residence) slipped an aphrodisiac into Jones' morning bowl of corn flakes to get him 'in the mood'. This was just the beginning of bad turns for Jones. He had a nervous breakdown after the film and never acted in a serious way again, even turning down a leading role in Quentin Tarantino's *Pulp Fiction*. It was later revealed that he had been having an affair with actress Sharon Tate, who was brutally murdered in her Hollywood home by the Charles Manson gang during the shooting of the film.

Critics lambasted *Ryan's Daughter* and Lean did not make another feature film for fourteen years. It also signalled a decline for Miles' career. After having multiple affairs with many of Hollywood's leading men (and one young writer who was mysteriously found dead in a bathtub), she is now an alternative healer and therapist. She married the writer of *Ryan's Daughter* twice. Their son, after recovering from heroin addiction, has became an antique watch expert.

The final cost of *Ryan's Daughter* was around $74 million in today's prices – largely because of Lean's perfectionism – with hundreds of retakes and delays for 'the right clouds to come'. He built elaborate sets and even felt the need to retake some shots in South Africa. In time, the film eventually covered costs and is now reviewed more favourably.

Pat merely nodded his head when I relayed what had become of the director and lead actors. "It's not a life I would choose for meself, y'know. Had fun driving around, but I don't remember ever wanting to change places with anyone – even as a young man."

He stood up, collected the tray, and looked out towards the ever-changing skies. "No regrets – none at all. I like where I am and how I got here."

"Not everyone can say that."

"Just so. Anyway, you enjoy your day. Inch Beach is beautiful and you'll have a grand day out."

I returned to my room and was contemplating which wool sweater would be best for the morning's excursion but, as I readied myself and put my belongings in order, the skies darkened and a freezing rain forced me to reconsider my plans. However, as I was considering an alternative that didn't involve the outside world, the rain stopped as quickly as it had begun. As a precaution, I packed two sweaters and two scarves to counter the cold.

It wasn't difficult finding parking. Besides a few other cars, there were only a couple orange vans with surf school logos. Made directly for the beach and watched kayakers and windsurfers battle the sea. The wet sand glistened in the sunshine and the trails of a dozen footprints hinted as to who or what had strolled along earlier in the morning. A few people were emerging out of the water in wetsuits.

The lapping waves and the long stretch of gently sloping sand, nestled underneath a swath of rolling mountainscape, lulled me into a contemplative state. Looked down at the shimmering reflections of the shoreline, like the sweet nectar of stolen fruit, and then out towards the strand. It was a wild sanctuary that drew me ever onwards, and the rhythms of nature became the soundtrack for a thousand nothings. Poetic imaginings sparked and caught ablaze as the biting wind blew off the ocean.

At one point, I stopped to wash a little shell in the palm of my hand and thought back on my childhood. Growing up on Vancouver Island, I was never far from the calm waters of the Pacific. The rocky beaches and tide pools were my playground. Filled my days making sandcastles, strolling along the breakwater, and watching the ferryboats go by. Never did I think that one day I would live ten hours inland. That I'd miss the briny smell, the sound of gentle applause, and the great mysteries that lie beneath the surface.

Whenever I visit, I make sure to include long walks along the shoreline. Sit on worn wooden benches and look out towards the open water as I sip my coffee. The consistent ebbing and flowing de-stimulates my brain. The smell of the ocean breeze soothes my troubled mind.

Since ancient times, we have assigned healing and transformational properties to water. It has also symbolized rebirth, spiritual cleansing, and salvation. We are naturally drawn to aquatic hues; staring at the ocean has been known to change brain wave frequency, and put many into a mild meditative state. We turn to water for a sense of calm and clarity. Whether we are merely walking its shores, or refreshing ourselves with long showers and soothing baths, we often build our homes and our lives around being near water.

Canada has almost thirty-two thousand lakes, so one is not usually far from a significant body of water. But, for me, it's not quite the same. While I appreciate a good lake or two, there's something about the infinite nature of the sea that I still long for.

Or maybe it's something as simple as salt. As author Karen Blixen (writing as Isak Dinesen) once penned, "The cure for anything is salt water: sweat, tears, or the sea."

At the America's Cup Dinner in 1962, President John F. Kennedy remarked, "I really don't know why it is that all of us are so committed to the sea, except I think it's because in addition to the fact that the sea changes, and the light changes, and ships change, it's because we all came from the sea. And it is an interesting biological fact that all of us have in our veins the exact same percentage of salt in our blood that exists in the ocean and, therefore, we have salt in our blood, in our sweat, in our tears. We are tied to the ocean. And when we go back to the sea – whether it is to sail or to watch it – we are going back from whence we came."

The importance of water to physical survival in Ireland was reflected in the spiritual importance attributed to the source of water. Votive offerings – the ritual sacrifice of valuable objects – have been found everywhere across the country. Wells, fed by underground springs, were especially venerated. (A nineteenth-century survey stated that Ireland has no fewer than three thousand.) The emerging water was said to have originated in the Otherworld; not only did it preserve life, but special healing powers were often associated with it. Even with the conversion of the populace to

Christianity, belief in the supernatural qualities of the wells remained strong.

Renamed in honour of local or national saints, the magical water from these holy wells was credited with curative properties for healing ailments from headaches to rheumatism. At some, certain patterns (devotions that take place within a parish on the feast day of the patron saint) are still held annually and retain vestiges of the pagan past – walking three times clockwise around the well while reciting particular prayers, or tying scraps of cloth to an adjacent tree.

Looking down at the shell in my hand, and then out towards the horizon, I thought back to all those times when water guided me. Helped me reflect and feel strong, and reminded me that I had the power to heal myself. Taught me to let go and have faith.

I thought back to my time in the Sultanate of Oman – swimming out beyond the waves and floating alone in the quiet coves along the southern coastline. The feeling of no longer being a part of the physical realm. Surrendering to the ocean, and giving it permission to lead me away from the darkness and into the light. Holding me and whispering everything I needed to hear.

I thought back to my experiences in sensory deprivation tanks, and how difficult it was to quiet the mind. But then, once finally relaxed, I could trust that the journey from here to there wouldn't be fraught with peril. Wouldn't be a journey I would have to take alone. Some mysterious power would always be there – especially when I needed it the most.

I thought back to the first time I sat in the cave at the local hot springs – where the Ktunaxa First Nations peoples found respite after long days of hunting, fishing, and gathering roots and berries. After battle, warriors would soak in the spirit waters (*nupika wu'u*) to ease their wounds. I am no warrior (or hunter, for that matter), but I always feel grounded and that the wounds of my heart are being cared for at Ainsworth.

After almost an hour of ambling along the golden sands, I turned around and headed back. I was hungry and was thinking of the little eatery next to the parking lot. Desperate for a scone and a pot of tea.

The only other patrons were an elderly couple staring out the window and a younger couple outside, weighing down their napkins so they wouldn't blow away. Under the glass counter, next to the register, were the typical Irish mid-day desserts – tarts, pies and crumbles – but I opted for the daily soup special instead. With a couple slices of soda bread, a pad of butter and a pot of tea, I warmed myself up and joined the two couples that gazed out at the battling blues.

While quaint villages are not as they once were, and there are no longer little pockets where time stands still, rural Ireland still offers a way of life different from that in the bustling cities. Simple pleasures like going for a walk, looking out at the open ocean, or having a cuppa still rule the day.

With my belly full, and my nose no longer frozen, I walked back to the car and drove off.

While heading back west to Dingle, I thought more about *Ryan's Daughter* and the dramatic shots of Rosy Ryan walking along the beach with her parasol. While the village set was torn down after a neighbourly feud, the schoolhouse built for the film still stands and finding it seemed like the right kind of adventure for me.

After stocking up on junk food at Garvey's SuperValu, I

asked the cashier if she knew where to find it. "I do, indeed," she said. "And it's an easy walk, so. You park at the Blasket Centre and just head down to the ocean. There's a path that leads to the right. Haven't been in a long time meself, so I can't say much on the condition of the place. But, as far as I know, it's still there."

Paid for my cookies, crisps and carbonated soda and headed out of town.

Mine was again the only car in the parking lot at the Blasket Centre (*Ionad an Bhlascaoid*), but this time I found a helpful map on a lamppost. It showed nearby walking routes. Some were short; others were longer. None made a left at the ocean.

The path to the schoolhouse follows the cliff's edge and then continues over the main road before eventually dropping towards the Centre again. It seemed simple enough. There was no chance of getting lost.

Walking along where the churning waters tear away at the earth was a little worrying. A sudden gust of gravity might send me into the inky darkness below. But neither the heights, nor the wind, nor the possibility of my untimely demise seemed to bother the resident sheep.

"You're brave," I said to one as she pulled up grass.

The sheep looked up at me and blinked. "Baa."

Didn't appreciate her tone.

And then decided it would be best to stop talking to the sheep.

The path is easy to follow, but still has an air of mystery. As with many in Ireland, this one crosses a number of farmers' fields. There are no fences but instead small stepladders or stone slabs built into low rock walls, similar to those at Kilmalkedar.

The rhythm of my walk and the muffled arguments of

sea gods caused me to become lost in thought. When I refocused, the sun was behind a curtain of grey. The farmhouses that dot the landscape were now out of focus. The nearby mountains were no longer visible.

The fog became a heavy blanket that muffled every sound and muted every colour. Solid shapes blurred in the fuzziness. The grey devoured everything. There was nothing but whispers. Lost all sense of where I was, and where I was going. At some point, I needed to stop for a while, calm myself down, and look down at my hands to confirm that I was still a part of this world.

In Irish mythology, there is mention of a magical mist or veil called *féth fíada*. Anyone shrouded by it would be rendered invisible to the human eye. It was gifted from the sea god Manannán mac Lir, ruler and guardian of the Otherworld and the one who ferries souls to the afterlife. Blurring the borders between the world of the mortal and that of the *sidhe*, Manannán's cloak acts as a conjuncture of the two.

Though uneasy, I also felt that I had been invited to not just walk the border between the earthly realm and *Tír na NÓg* (Land of the Youth), but somehow slip unseen between the two. The softest hint of flowery meadows and a forested wilderness beyond the sea. The faintest flutter of birds singing, and the trickling waters of a fountain. A sweetness in the air – of endless orchards, of golden apples upon silver branches.

But as soon as all the sights, sounds and smells of this supernatural realm seemed to solidify, they disappeared altogether. As if waking from a dream. It was then that I finally understood why so many myths, traditions and superstitions continue in rural Ireland – why so many stories of lone travellers disappearing and never being heard from again are still told around turf fires.

Not long after, I spied the ruins of the schoolhouse. Only the bare bones are left. The roof beams are stacked and left to rot; the tiled floor of the living quarters is now hidden under a film of green. No efforts have been made to preserve the building. Though the movie had been a catalyst for tourism, the only remaining set piece didn't look like it had many years left before it was unrecognizable.

Over the years, there has been talk of renovating the schoolhouse but nothing ever came from it. As a movie set, maybe it doesn't really matter in the long run. Most residents, I suspect, have little to say regarding the matter. Though *Ryan's Daughter* helped modernize the town of Dingle (and the surrounding area), it is what it is today not because of a Hollywood epic but because of its rich history and friendly locals. While the movie may have brought awareness to West Kerry, it is the true essence of the peninsula that makes it so welcoming.

The path took me away from the ocean and up towards the main road. After scampering up the steeper bits, I continued to a nearby viewpoint, where harsh jagged rocks seem to tear out of the ground. Imagining it as a place where otherworldly creatures live, I went to explore. But no faeries invited me dance or sing, or feast on fruit tarts. There was only cold hard stone.

However, while wedging myself into the rock and finding shelter from the wind, I felt a part of Ireland's history once again.

Long before the earliest people settled along the western edge of the island, some inexplicable force caused this small formation to surface from the world below. Here it remained until time was no longer measured in millennia, but in centuries. As I leaned into the throne of a thousand blades, I wondered if this was where Fintán and Tuan mac Cairill perched in bird form to watch time pass. Wondered what frail animals in search of refuge had made their beds here, and what lone travellers like myself had found momentary comfort from the Atlantic storms. And I thought about a future far from now – and whether this lonely outcrop would exist far beyond humankind, when the earth finally reclaims herself.

(I read later that the rocky outcrop is called An Mionnáin Mor, but I couldn't find any further information. It would have to remain a place of mystery. Think I prefer that, anyway.)

While I appreciated the mystical fog-entrenched countryside, I began to question my sanity and whether what I had experienced was true or just a figment of my overactive imagination.

Back in Dingle, I went looking for a bit of the *craic*: the latest news, gossip, entertainment and enjoyable conversation (usually with a pint). It is often used with the definite article – *the* craic – as in the expression 'What's the *craic*?' (meaning 'How are you?' or 'What's happening?'). There are, of course, various levels of *craic*. Good *craic* refers to a decent night out, but nothing too memorable. Mighty *craic* is better, but not quite as good as savage *craic* or deadly *craic*. Nothing, however, tops 'The *craic* was ninety'.

Walked down Strand Street and noticed a little souvenir shop cheekily called the Craic House. It offers an odd array of tourist tat. There's a selection of t-shirts, penny whistles and fridge magnets, but also some more obscure and interesting items – including a framed photograph of the schoolhouse, taken during production. It shows the building soon after it was constructed, with laundry hanging on the line. Glued to the photo was a piece of 'authentic wood' taken from the set. I could have easily framed a piece of wood and a picture myself, but it was selling for a little more than the frame was worth.

"Are you a fan of the movie?" asked the man behind the counter.

"Sort of," I answered. "Watched it a couple weeks ago."

He scratched his unshaven face before continuing. "Haven't been to the schoolhouse in a while. Looking a little rough last time I was there."

I showed him the viewer screen of my camera. "It's not doing well."

"Ah. 'Tis a shame, really. But it does reflect the state of the country in many ways, y'know. Everything's going to ruin."

"I guess so, yeah," I agreed. Then poked around the shop some more. Flipped through a handful of CDs featuring local musicians and a rack of t-shirts. The man behind the counter continued to talk, but I had stopped listening. Just grunted in agreement ever so often and that seemed to satisfy him. Paid for the framed photograph, some music, a t-shirt that read 'I had the *craic* in Dingle', and was on my way.

CHAPTER 17

A CURIOUS SIGHT INDEED

While poking about the little shop, I had spied a photograph of the pier at Dunquin. Many have been taken (and continue to be taken) of the pier, but what makes this particular photograph unique is that it features a herd of sheep clogging up the narrow walkway that leads up to the village. A small figure of a shepherd in a dark coat, holding a *shillelagh*, brings up the rear with his trusty dog. He is of an older generation, and may have come from the nearby islands. It is a unique moment in history, and a postcard-sized copy now hangs over my bookcase at the top of the stairs.

The pier is where the traditional rowboats, known throughout Ireland as *currachs* (but locally as *naomhóga*), would have come ashore from the nearby islands. While the pier is only used during the summer months now, when boats take tourists to see the ruins of the village, it makes for a beautiful place to contemplate the sub-culture of the Blasket people.

After winding the car through the stone-lined streets of

Dunquin (*Dún Chaoin*), I parked next to a small shack strapped down by boulders so the wind doesn't carry it away during frequent storms.

Again, there was no one around and the only sounds were the sea below, the occasional shriek of seabirds, and wind blowing over long grasses. The walkway is steep but I found footing in the deep ridges. About halfway down, I stopped to capture with my camera the calm ocean in darkest blues and greens, and rocks like monstrous teeth. Further down, the islands revealed themselves like songs long forgotten. No boats were scheduled until after Easter, so the pier was as close as I could get.

Tucked against the cliff, lacquered in black and flipped over to dry, were a few rowboats. They looked like large beetle shells. It would be a curious sight indeed to see them 'scuttling' across the beaches when two or three fishermen carry them on their backs. I looked towards the horizon again before dipping my fingers into the water, wondering how many had lost their lives to the consistent inconsistency of the ocean. And then I reflected on the spirits that linger long in the blurred borders between their world and ours.

Growing up in a middle-class suburb of a mid-sized city in the Pacific Northwest, I had little (if any) interaction with the men and women who sail the salt sea. Knew none of the songs or stories passed down for generations. But the more time I spent on the water or walking the rugged shores of the wild Atlantic, the more I understood why the ocean is a cruel mistress. It gives and keeps on giving, and yet constantly asks for more in return. There is stillness in its depths, playfulness in its turbulent mischief, and a myriad of colours in its abundance of prismatic, vivacious marine life. There is a level of comfort that only the sea's soft sway can provide, as it cradles us and lulls us to sleep. And yet, as we dream, we can never fully relax. No matter how much we long to understand its mysteries, and unravel the enigma of its beauty, we return heartbroken and disconsolate.

Back in the car, sheltered from the cold wind, I read from a couple accounts of those that had lived on the islands.

In the 1910s, a number of anthropologists, linguists, musicologists and writers came to the Blasket Islands (*Na Blascaodaí*) to study and record a culture largely untouched by the modern world. They came to see the disappearing village life and to hear a form of Irish Gaelic (*Gaeilge*) not heard elsewhere for centuries.

These scholars encouraged the islanders to write down their stories and in the 1920s and '30s the Blasket Island people produced books now deemed classics in the world of literature. They wrote of living on the very edge of Europe, and brought to life the hard times on the far reaches of civilization. Sadly, the community declined as a result of the persistent emigration of its young people and eventually the islands were abandoned in 1953 when only twenty-two inhabitants remained.

Despite being so isolated, the archipelago of seven islands were inhabited throughout history. The first people to live on the Blaskets herded animals, grew crops and hunted. Early Christian monks lived there in the fifth and sixth centuries, and the Vikings later used them as jumping-off points for raiding the mainland in the ninth and tenth centuries. The Ferriter family controlled the islands as far back as the thirteenth century, and maintained their own castle. A recently discovered document records people living there in 1597.

The population grew with the influx of tenants evicted from their holdings by Lord Ventry during the first half of the nineteenth century, and many others followed because life on the islands was better than what they had to endure on the mainland. Nevertheless, island life was a constant hardship and struggle. Islanders had to cross an often-perilous five-kilometre crossing, followed by an eight-kilometre walk to the nearest priest or an almost twenty-kilometre walk to reach a doctor.

The number of people living on the islands ebbed and flowed over the centuries. There was a population of about a hundred and fifty in 1840, but after the Great Famine that decreased to only a hundred. (The population is said to have reached its peak in 1916, at a hundred and seventy-six). From then on it was in decline until 1953-4 when the Blaskets were completely abandoned.

Today, with easy access to electricity, central heating and flush toilets – not to mention health professionals, teachers, and nearby grocery stores – it's easy to forget how difficult (and dangerous) life was a century ago.

Whether they liked their neighbours or not, the Blasket people relied heavily on them and that reliance created a unique bond. This may be part of the reason the Blasket culture continues to fascinate so many of us (including myself).

Until the arrival of the seine boat at the beginning of the nineteenth century, the islanders fished only from the rocks with hard lines. Though heavy and requiring eight men to row it, the seine boat gave them the means to take to fishing as a way of life, and they gave up tillage almost completely apart from potatoes, a little oats, and some vegetables. The land was poor and sandy, and garden plots were scattered here and there. Some islanders had a cow or two, but a year's supply of manure would not go far on the smallest holdings. The dung had to be supplemented by material from the beach: mussel shells and seaweed, and even the soot from the chimney was spread as fertilizer.

Pigs and horses may have been on the islands at one time, but not in more recent years. Donkeys took the place of horses and carried turf from the mountain. There were rabbits for hunting. There were also plenty of sheep, as they were an important indicator of a man's wealth. It was said that one should possess 'a sheep to sell, a sheep to shear, and a sheep to eat.' The islanders had little trouble selling and trading their wooly wonders, as Blasket sheep had a great reputation for their flavour.

In the late nineteenth century, the Blasket Islanders discovered the *naomhóg* (or *currach*) and soon replaced their seine boats with the smaller, more agile rowboat. In *The Islandman*, Tomás Ó Criomhthain states that the first *naomhóg* was brought to the island by two men who purchased it while under the influence of drink in Dingle. Whether that story is true or not, the rowboat caught on quickly and a distinctive regional type soon developed. The *naomhóg* was an easier craft to handle and required only a three-man crew. It could take sail when the wind was right, and when needed it could be taken closer to the rocks. It also widened the range of work and variety of catches. The only major drawback was that it made transporting animals more difficult.

A big change came in the early 1930s. Not only had the Great Famine affected the islanders, but young people were also lured away when letters arrived from relatives who had found a new life either in Dublin or in the United

States. They also wanted a wider selection from which to choose a lifelong mate; only two couples married on the Blaskets between then and the time of its abandonment.

At its peak, there were thirty houses. All had a large kitchen, with enough room to host a dance or a wake. It also had to be large enough to accommodate animals at night or during bad weather. The narrow loft was used for storing nets, fishing lines, trawl lines and other goods. As there were no shops, islanders had to go to the mainland for household goods they didn't make themselves.

In the nineteenth century, the islanders ate only breakfast and dinner. Both meals consisted of potatoes and fish, with the occasional bowl of sour milk. Though terrible storms meant the islanders were cut off from the mainland, these same storms often presented gifts of food, drink and other goods from nearby shipwrecks. It was only after a tea chest washed ashore that tea became a drink of choice. The islanders had little experience of alcohol apart from what the Frenchmen would give them in exchange for their lobster and crayfish, or the infrequent barrel of wine and spirits that was gifted by the sea.

While the men went fishing, the women congregated during the day. Some fetched water, some washed clothes, and others talked and gossiped. Chores were often completed in a communal manner. Spinning, knitting and patching were the main nighttime occupations. Their lives would change dramatically when the last of the visitors left at the end of summer and the long dark nights set in. Life closed around them and from then on it must have been a dreary, depressing time.

The last of the islanders were taken to the mainland by the Irish government in 1953 when it was agreed that the population was too low to sustain themselves. They moved into government houses at Dunquin, or moved in with family that had settled elsewhere. From their new homes, many could still look across the hauntingly beautiful Blasket Sound towards their former residence that held so many memories.

The islanders' cultural output was immense, including works by Tomás Ó Criomhthain, Muiris Ó Súilleabháin (*Twenty Years a-Growing*), Peig Sayers (*Peig*), and many others. No other island of this size has yielded such a literary wealth. At the heart of each book is a love for the beauty of the writers' surroundings, a profound respect for their cultural inheritance, and a powerful depiction of community.

They were also master musicians, and wrote songs that are still performed today. *Port na bPúcaí* (*The Music of the Fairies*) is one of my favourites. It's a haunting tune and, like many things in Ireland, is steeped in local folklore. The story revolves around some men that were out fishing in their rowboats near Inishvickillane (*Inis Mhic Aoibhleáin*) – one of the smaller islands. A fierce storm broke out, and the men feared for their lives. However, as if by magic, the wind suddenly died down and they were enveloped by evocative, otherworldly music. The island fiddler was amongst the crew and, when they arrived safely back on land, he was able to recall the tune they had all heard. While some swear it was the work of faeries, others believe that what the fishermen actually heard was the song of humpback whales reverberating through the hulls of their boats. Whatever the truth may be, *Port na bPúcaí* has since passed into the traditional repertoire.

Looking out across the water to the islands, towards the ruined houses and winding pathways that speak to the rhythms of a life now gone, I thought about the hardships and long winters – but also about the sense of community. The fantastical stories and tales of survival. The more I delved into my research and the more early photographs and film reels I discovered, the more I thought about the strong sense of community on the Blaskets. Though life was incredibly difficult, the islanders were strongly connected to each other. They relied on one another to fend off hunger and loneliness and, in doing so, must have also felt that they belonged and mattered, and that their needs would be met through their commitment to each other.

Today, communities have been replaced with networks in which we keep in contact with only our closest friends and family. At a time when we can swipe a touchscreen to connect with people, products and information from anywhere in the world, we are in danger of disconnecting from our own neighbourhoods. With the entire universe at our fingertips, we are losing sight of what is outside the four walls of our homes.

It's an important part of human life to feel that we belong to a certain group of people – especially at a young age – but with the development of technology we tend to transfer our lives into virtual worlds and then justify that one is the same as the other. As much as I enjoy scrolling through social media, and marvel at how much information is available at the click of a button, I am also appalled at how much time most of us (including yours truly) spend on a screen: groups of teenagers that sit around at the skate park and stare down at their phones, or entire families in restaurants playing idiotic games before their meals arrive.

I don't mean to romanticize life on the Blasket Islands. Certainly have no desire to eke out a living from the anemic soil or row across the tumultuous sea in a traditional rowboat. I'm happy to have running water, central heating, and a coffee shop up the street. But I do appreciate what the islanders had: their music and stories and sense of belonging. Perhaps, someday soon, we will possess the willpower to step back from our screens, find a healthy balance, and establish strong community connections once again. Or perhaps we will sink further into the tar pit of technology and exist each as our own island, entire of itself.

CHAPTER 18

A STILLNESS HERE

As the haunting tune took me back in time, I flipped through some brochures I had picked up during my travels and discovered that there is now simple, self-catering accommodation available in three restored houses at the top of the Great Blasket village. Lodgings are equipped with basic amenities but 'no more than what is needed to enjoy a peaceful and relaxing getaway'.

I wondered what emotions I would experience if I ever had the chance to stay for a few days. Imagine that anyone who spends time there is overcome with a sense of impermanence as the wind whistles through the stonework during long walks or the embers glow in a blackened fireplace when the sun dips below the horizon.

It's difficult to say if loneliness would creep in, or if I could embrace the solitude.

As I looked out towards the islands one more time, my thoughts turned to the busloads of GORE-TEX-clad tourists buzzing with excitement as they queue up outside the Guinness Storehouse on the other side of the country.

Perhaps they will later gaze in awe at the Book of Kells or pound back pints in Temple Bar. Most will purchase one or several of the following: a Guinness pint glass, a 'Kiss me I'm Irish' t-shirt, a turf candle, a tin of tea, a pair of Celtic cross earrings, a bar of whiskey chocolate, a penny whistle, a copy of *Ulysses*, a Claddagh ring, a Waterford crystal decanter, a worry stone, a snow globe, or any other item that would remind them of their time in and around (but not much further than the borders of) Dublin.

And that's okay. It is the Ireland that many come looking for, and it is the Ireland that I had spent time in, but it wasn't what I ultimately fell in love with during my travels. Though all the tourist hotspots, visitors' centres and gift-shops that my wife and I frequented have their place and are usually worth the expense, my Ireland is ultimately about quieter moments devoid of the hustle and bustle.

My Ireland is more about sitting outside in the early morning fog before the farmhands slip on their muddy boots. It is more about celebrating the simplicity of bread and cheese at farmers' markets by the sea, and walking at the close of day along low stone fences. It is more about the stories of the stones, and the flowers that grow in the spaces between. The unraveling of mysteries, but never fully succeeding in discovering an ultimate truth. Narrow paths full of puddles and small streams, which lead us ever onward – all the mud and muck and wild ponies, and the beauty that can be found in the absence of all things. It is more about looking out across the Blasket Sound and listening to the voices of the dawn.

My mind wheeled with the stars and, having no idea where to go next, drove off without direction. Which is how I got lost. Again. This came as no great surprise. By this point, it was unnerving *not* to get lost. Though Ireland seems deceptively small compared to Canada, there is still amble opportunity to become misplaced in fog and mist and wet greenery – or even sunshine and blue skies, for that matter.

I wasn't *lost*-lost. Merely temporarily misplaced as I drove around the back roads of rural Ventry, hoping to stumble across something interesting. And this is when the jagged silhouette of Rahinnane Castle came into view.

Of course, ruins of castles aren't that difficult to find in Ireland. There are over thirty thousand in various states, dotted across the landscape. Some are important and have received government funding in order to be restored; others have not. Rahinnane Castle (*Caisleán Ráthanáin*) falls into the latter category.

The farmhouse seemed an appropriate place to ask for information, so I turned off the road. Was tempted to jump the fence and run across the field, as I had done earlier, but it occurred to me that I should a bit more ethical (and legal) about it all.

A small hand-painted sign reads 'Tourist Parking'.

That sounded promising.

Knocked on the front door, but there was no answer. Knocked again and waited until the silence became uncomfortable.

Halfway back, a voice behind me called out. "You're very welcome."

I turned around. "Uh... hello."

"You're to be looking for the ruins of the castle, are you?"

"Thinking of it, yeah."

"You're welcome to take as long as you like. That'll be two euros."

"Two euros? Oh, okay." Felt around in my pockets, but

there were no coins. "I've got some change in the car," I said. "Be right back."

After paying the lady of the house, she pointed me a little further up the driveway. "It's just the other side of the old shed."

By 'old shed' she meant the centuries old farm hutch and by 'the other side' she meant the near side and not the far side where another hand-painted sign reads 'No Tress-pass: Danger Bull'. Didn't feel the need to correct the spelling, and didn't feel the need to be told twice. Turned around, headed to the opposite side of the shed, and found my way to the castle.

Taken by Sir Charles Wilmot in 1602, and then destroyed during the Cromellian Wars, Rahinnane Castle now has the look of a rotting tooth with various shades of green growing in its dank corners. More than half of the walls of the two-story building still exist, however, as does the staircase.

The Knight of Kerry chose the site for Rahinnane Castle in the fifteenth century. Built within an earthen ring fort that dates to between 300 and 1000 CE, it was separated by a wide ditch (or *fosse)*. The two earthen banks, about thirty feet deep, enclosed a busy farmstead with houses, sheds, workshops and animal pens long before the castle was built. The ring fort was not for military purposes, but rather to keep out wild animals and as a protection against cattle raids that were common in Ireland at the time. Inside the fort is a *souterrain* – an underground stone-lined passage that was a refuge in times of attack as well as a place to store food. It has been suggested that *souterrains* might also have been cozy sleeping accommodations during inclement weather. The ground floor was probably used for storage, while the hall was situated on the upper floor. The old ring fort defences were strengthened when the castle was built.

There wasn't much else to do but take a few photos of where the second floor windows allow a little sunshine to highlight the stone. Walked around the castle one more time, bid adieu to the spirits, and then strolled back to the car.

As I drove along Slea Head Drive (*Slí Cheann Sléibhe*), there were signs for Dunbeg Fort. Seemed like a good place as any to explore. Parked the car, unbuckled, and tossed a few coins in my pocket.

The date at which the fort was built is uncertain, although its structure resembles other western stone forts built within the Iron Age. (A sample of wood found in a ditch lying partly under the wall was dated to around 580 BCE.) Recent excavation has shown that Dunbeg continued to be occupied at intervals at least until the late medieval period. It was rarely, if ever, a place of prolonged habitation. At some stage, the rampart was reinforced and may have served as refuge during times of danger.

The fort's wall cuts off access to the triangular promontory, which was later occupied by a single beehive hut. On either side of the entrance, there are small chambers inside the rampart, and the entrance itself features holes in which a wooden bar could have been inserted to support a door. The rampart, *fosses* and banks would have served as substantial defences. The *souterrain*, too, was probably defensive – a hiding place in time of attack, or possibly even a means of surprising attackers from behind.

The reasons for creating such elaborate defences like Dunbeg Fort (*An Dún Beag*) on a rocky outcrop remain far from clear. Archeologists argue as to whether this housed and protected the last of the people in retreat from Iron Age invaders, or if it was the first fortified footholds of the invaders from which they advanced to control the area. Dunbeg may have been used for ritual or even status purposes to show the wealth of the tribe.

During tourist season, the nearby visitors' centre features audiovisual displays, a craft room, a small café, and a seafood restaurant. Since it was not tourist season, mine was the only car and everything was closed. I did, however, find a bit of company. The resident cat – orange with a snow-white chest and feet – was lying on her back, basking in the late-afternoon sun, where picnic benches are set out during the warmer months. She seemed content, in the absence of noise, so I sat down quietly on the brickwork next to her.

Her eyes smouldered with a quiet intensity. The golden hues burned like hot coals that could reignite the bonfires of Beltane at any given moment. And yet there was a hint of playfulness – of mischief managed, of forbidden adventures, of secret pleasures. The suggestion that not everything is as it appears to be.

I warmed my fingers in her fur before she sat up, and together we looked out at the wild Atlantic and watched the dark grey clouds envelope the land and sea. The islands were no longer clear on the horizon, but a blur beyond the tumbling of the tide. What had been delicate muslin folds above us was now the weight of slow, dirty tears. There was no longer the roar of wind or of water. The world fell into an immortal silence.

We walked across the road and I paid the man sitting in his shack a couple euros, which seemed to be the going rate to trek across someone's field and have a look at ruins. With the cat beside me, down the slope we went and along a pathway fenced on either side. We followed a narrow stream that runs parallel to a low stone wall and, though the sun was no longer visible, the waters reflected a dreamy glimmer as it cut into the earth.

The ground seemed to heave and swell as the ancient structures came into view and I had to stop a moment to centre myself. As we arrived at the outer defensive banks, it felt as if we were momentarily leaving behind one world and entering another.

Though Paula and I had walked through the rampart passageway years earlier, as the early people would have done, it was now no longer possible. This section of the fort has since been wrapped in fencing and closed off to the public after much of the western wall fell into the sea due to storm damage. The Office of Public Works and National Monuments Service sent personnel to investigate damage to the site shortly after the storm, but there was nothing they could do to prevent more from eventually falling away. One day, the entire structure may fall into oblivion and future generations will have to rely on photographs.

Within the earthen banks, I could spy the sea through the linteled doorway. Thought back on those that took part in the building of this ancient site – placing and balancing stone upon stone to create a solid defensive structure without mortar of any kind. Wondered how difficult it was to maintain hope in this unforgiving landscape. It would have taken enormous courage and fortitude to make a home thirty meters above the unyielding and unrelenting waves that crash against the black rocks.

After following the fencing, I managed to find a way in and discovered the ruins of the *clochán* (dry-stone hut) at the centre of the site. The interior of the wall slopes, forming steps, presumably to give access to a parapet or for seating during communal events. Plunked myself down and the cat sat at my side as I tried to imagine what daily life was like at Dunbeg – what sounds competed with the constant roar of the sea and howl of the wind. Was the crackle of the fire and the sharpening of bronze and iron with circular stones a soundtrack for the women who wove or dyed cloth with cold, cracked hands? What stories did they as tell as darkness fell? What lullabies did they sing to their children? Did they look out towards the open ocean and wonder what lay beyond? Did they feel a presence guiding them during quieter moments of reflection?

Together, the cat and I mused on the passing of time – the ceaseless transition of season to season, but also the long history that turns all to dust. "Then shall the dust return to the earth as it was," I whispered, "and the spirit shall return unto God who gave it."

The cat looked up at me, and we made eye contact before both turning again to the churning waters. The Celts considered cats to be guardians of the Otherworld, and keepers of ancient secrets. I half-expected my furry friend to clear her throat before engaging in metaphysical debate. But she didn't say anything. Instead, by giving me permission to sit with her, I was gifted with the knowledge of continual present – with no sense of the temporal distinctions of past, present and future. "It feels as if nothing exists but right now," I said to the cat. "All memories and worries are nothing but illusions."

Tears of peaceful contentment rolled down my cheeks as we continued to look out towards the unrivalled beauty that can only be found at the stark edge of creation. "There is a stillness here," I continued. "And maybe, in that stillness, a little bit of magic that allows one to get in touch with the sacred experience of life."

The cat stood up in response, and then yawned,

stretched her back, and sauntered around the wall. She waited for me to follow and, as it is no use arguing with a cat, I stood up and rubbed the cold from my legs. Instead of walking with me, the cat took the lead and I followed behind.

We were about halfway up the hill, when she turned around, sat down, and gazed out towards the promontory. She looked up at me as I approached.

"I believe it was Polonius..." she began.

"Pardon me?"

"Polonius... who told Hamlet, 'To thine own self be true.'"

"Ah, right."

"It begs the question, then: How often do you feel you can truly be yourself?"

"Is this something that's been on your mind lately?" I asked.

"Not really. Just the last little while."

"Oh, I see."

"Philosophers throughout history have held the idea of authenticity in high esteem. There is our *outer* authenticity – how well what we say and do matches what is really going on inside us – and our *inner* authenticity. This refers to how well we actually know ourselves, and are aware of our inner states."

"Why are you telling me this?" I asked.

"I'm getting there," she said. "Have patience."

"Sorry. Go on."

"No one is fully authentic all of the time in their outer presentation. Sometimes we need to put on an act to get by. But some people spend more time living inauthentically than others."

"Do you think that is *my* problem? That I'm not living authentically?"

"I think that there is a part of you that feels you must now rush off to town because you need to somehow justify being out here. Despite all that you have learned, there is still a level of resistance. There is still a little voice inside you that stirs doubt in your heart. But you need to tell yourself that it's okay to spend your days walking up mountains alone or wandering through archeological sites with strange animals. You don't have to feel embarrassed or ashamed that you need more of that in your life than the alternative. I know that you want to push yourself outside your comfort zone, and make conversation in crowded pubs, but that is not the reason you came here – even if you think it is. The reason you came here – to the edge of the world – is to listen, observe, and reflect. You came here to understand that you are connected to everything and everyone by golden threads, even if sometimes you don't feel it. You came to find solace in all that you can see with your eyes, and all that you can feel with your soul. And then you will go home, pour yourself a thimble of decent whiskey, and write."

"I've been trying," I said.

"Yes... well... in the words of one legendary Jedi master, 'Do. Or do not. There is no try.'"

"Mmm," I said. "Very good."

"Anyway, as I was saying... If you ever feel trapped – in your job, or in a relationship, or in the culture in which you are living – and rarely get the chance to be yourself, then you damage the true essence of who you are. More damaging, however, is when you don't know yourself and it is your inner authenticity that is compromised."

"I appreciate your concern," I said, "and your words of

wisdom. But I'm not rushing. Though I may not always feel connected to the place I call home, I *do* feel a connection to *this* place – and maybe that's enough for now. Even if I'm not able to return for many years, I now understand the connection I have to the natural elements: the eternal battling of light and shadow across land and sea and sky. To all the stories of the stones, carved by those that lived and loved so long ago. To that which exists just beyond the borders of this world – where time moves in mysterious ways. And maybe, by spending a few more days here in Ireland, I will confirm who I am and how to best follow my inner authenticity."

"Hope so," said the cat. "Remember that conformity is a form of cowardice. Don't feel you have to be something that you're not. Remember what Alan Watts once wrote: 'Waking up to who you are requires letting go of who you imagine yourself to be.'"

"I will," I replied. "Promise."

There was suddenly a sharp noise behind us. I turned around, looked down the path and out towards the never-ending blanket of grey. Couldn't locate the source, but there was now a subtle hint of blue on the far horizon. The patchwork of farmland once again became a verdant applause.

When I turned back, my feline companion was gone. Figured she had either concluded our conversation and gone in search of adventure, or had merely continued up the hill.

A few minutes later, after crossing the road, there she was – lying on the brickwork, where we first met. Sat down next to her and, after warming my fingers in her fur, she looked up at me. But she didn't say anything further.

It was time to take my leave. I was getting hungry, and was looking forward to a couple pints, so I patted her head one last time and whispered a thank you. Stood up, rubbed my eyes, and took a couple deep breaths as I looked out at the setting sun. In a haze, I buckled myself into the rental car and drove off.

It was only when nearing town that I began to doubt what had happened. Could neither confirm nor deny that I had spent time with the *cait sidhe* (the fairy cat). What had earlier seemed so clear was now beginning to fade away, like the last remnants of morning fog. Had our strange conversation actually happened, or had I imagined the entire thing?

Perhaps, I concluded while crossing the stone bridge on the edge of town, it doesn't matter. Perhaps, like so many other aspects of Ireland, it doesn't need to be explained. Doesn't need to make sense. It just needs to be felt.

CHAPTER 19

A WONDERFUL PLACE TO BE AN INTROVERT

Rural Ireland is a wonderful place to be an introvert. There are multitudes of quiet corners tucked away in back alleys of small towns or among the stonework built thousands of years ago where the wind howls and the rain falls and there is an absence of artificial noise. There are countless holy places for those inclined to communicate on some level with the spirits or gods. It is no surprise that Ireland is known as the land of saints and scholars – there's not much socializing or small talk required to be either one.

Except for my morning conversations with Pat at Dúinín House, poking around a few stores and an ice cream shop, and sitting in empty restaurants for dinner or ordering a couple pints at the pub, most of my time in Ireland had been spent wandering through fog and discovering ancient sites on my own (with the occasional animal as company). Though I was certainly comfortable continuing in this manner, I didn't want to leave without some attempt at conversing with the locals.

The Irish people are said to be some of the friendliest people on the planet. They are engaging, polite, and genuinely interested in others. Ask someone for directions and they will probably take you themselves. They are proud of their history and want you to enjoy yourself while being a tourist or a traveller – or whatever it is you want to call yourself. More importantly, they want you to feel at home while on Irish soil.

A large part of travelling solo is having the opportunity to engage with complete strangers, and that's what I set out to do this fine morning (even if it meant doing something touristy). Besides, my feet were sore and I wasn't sure how many mountains or random hills I wanted to climb.

But there was no rush. The town would be quiet at this early hour. Locals don't feel the need to leave the comforts of home on dewy mornings (unless it's tending to their animals) and, since tourist accommodation comes with a hearty start to the day, there is no need for mediocre American-style breakfast joints with bad diner coffee and pancake syrup.

Sat at my regular table, and Pat came in with my daily plate of fried meat. As he had done throughout the week, he plunked himself down for a chat. Somehow the topic turned to the trials and tribulations of teaching, and Pat mentioned that he too had taught public school. "I was born here, y'know – well not here, exactly, in this house – but above The Mighty Session (one of the pubs in town). Me family still own it, and me brother runs the place. Anyway, as a young fellow I had to find work somewhere else, and so I took a position as a schoolteacher in Dublin. That was back when it was more a town than a city. The rare ould times, and all that."

"And how did you find life in Dublin?"

"Ah, well... Dublin was full of life and music and food I had never tried before. Ah, sure, it was all grand. But those were different times. Not sure I could live there now. Glad I went, but I'm more than happy to be home."

"Is life in a smaller town more your speed?"

"'Tis, so," he replied. "Couldn't imagine living in the hustle and bustle of Dublin at me age. Everyone is off running in some direction or another."

"I agree. Could never live in Vancouver or Toronto. Couldn't imagine spending so much of my day in traffic."

"Indeed, not," he said with a chuckle. "Not much traffic here. Summer's a bit different, y'know, but still..."

We both looked out the windows of the breakfast room before Pat turned to me and asked, "What is the population of the town you live in?"

"There's about five thousand people – maybe fifteen thousand altogether in the valley. Most times I like living in a smaller town. It's a nice place to raise kids, and there's a lovely used bookstore, but other times I am desperate to get away."

"Can understand that," said Pat. "Anne and I – we pack up the car a few times a year and head north. Explore the countryside, y'know, that kind of thing. As they say: it's nice to leave and nice to come home."

"What is the population of Dingle?" I asked.

"Oh, I'd say maybe two thousand people."

"Is that right? It seems bigger, for some reason."

"Does it? Maybe that's because it's a tourist town. Hasn't always been that way – but it is now, for better or worse. Lonely Planet called Dingle 'quaint, yet cosmopolitan'. Suppose that's accurate."

"It is a beautiful town."

"T'is that," replied Pat. "Indeed."

"Small towns in Canada stretch along the highway, growing over time to accommodate the increase in traffic – all those speeding from one place to another. While the valley itself is beautiful – with the farmland and surrounding woodland – you'd be hard pressed to call the town itself beautiful. There's no cohesive identity. I could explore Dingle all day, down the back alleys and into secret corners. Not so much at home."

"There's no back alleys and secret corners?" asked Pat.

"Not really, no. It's very much a car culture, or a truck culture. Back home, it's not uncommon for people to drive to their post office box, just down the street, and then hide in their houses with the telly on. I've seen far more people walking here than back at home – whether it's to pick up a few things at the store or just stroll in the sunshine."

"They say Ireland has always been a nation of walkers. Sure, you've done your fair share these last few days."

"I've done that," I agreed.

Pat stood up and picked up the tray. "Best let you get on with your day," he said. "Unless you'd be needing anything else."

"No," I said. "Thank you."

He disappeared into the kitchen where traditional music played softly on the radio, and I headed down the hallway to my room.

The weather continued to play out its daily battle as I tucked my camera into my daypack.

My first stop was Murphy's Ice Cream for their Mayan hot chocolate. There isn't much liquid in the cup, but it's thick and rich and velvety – with just the right balance of sweet and spicy. Though hardly authentically Irish, it seemed like a luxurious way to start a stroll through town.

I was the only customer poking around the shop.

"Tried your brown bread ice cream a couple days ago," I began, "and it was really good. One of the best I've ever had."

"Ah, yes – the *aran donn*. Thank you," said the young man. "It's one of the favourites."

"I'm almost tempted to have some right now."

"Ay, well, I'm not one to judge."

"Maybe in an hour or so, then."

"You'd be surprised how many people come into the shop saying the same thing," he said. "But there's no great secret. We use local ingredients and keep the recipes as simple as possible. There's no additives or fillers or what-not. We don't use colourings or flavourings, or even powdered milk."

"Usually the old ways are the best ways," I said. "Unless it's dentistry."

"Right, you are," he laughed.

"Anyway, you were saying..."

"Ah, right... well... our ice cream – it's made with farm milk, local cream, free-range eggs and organic sugar," he continued proudly. "Whatever we need to do, we do ourselves. We bring everything raw and extract real ingredients. We temper chocolate, infuse alcohol, and scrape vanilla beans by hand. And we even make our own salt from Dingle sea water and distill the rain to make our sorbets."

"Really?" I asked. "You're joking."

"Oh, I don't joke about our ice cream."

Waited for him to crack a smile. He didn't.

The young man's co-worker – a beautiful raven-haired woman with a shy smile – straightened out a few items before returning to the back of the shop. She didn't seem interested in adding anything to the discussion. Imagine she had heard it all before.

"That's impressive."

"Impressive, yeah, and a lot of work, if you don't mind me saying," the young man continued. "In the summer season, I'm breaking eggs all day. There's a little device in the back of the shop that separates the whites from the yokes as they go down a ramp. It's mesmerizing to watch for the first hour or so, but we go through a lot of eggs."

"Right... yeah," I said. Didn't know what else to say. While I appreciated the young man's passion and attention to detail, I didn't know for how long I could maintain a conversation about ice cream or eggs. The gift of the gab was alive and well in West Kerry, and I still had much to learn.

After finishing my drink and thanking the young man, I stood for a moment on the corner of Strand Street and Green Street, noticed a sign for Tim Hortons coffee (which reminded me of home), and then passed several buildings in bold colours with contrasting doorways – yellows, greens and blues – until I spied the familiar logo of Subway sandwiches. Tried to ignore it, for it broke the spell. Dingle, for the most part, seemed immune to multinational corporations.

Hurried past a pharmacy before stopping in front of Brian de Staic's jewelry shop to gaze at his fine works of silver and gold. There were pieces featuring Ogham, the carvings at Kilmalkedar and the Riasc Stone, as well as the

Neolithic art of Newgrange. Though stunning, they didn't fit into my meagre traveller's budget.

The buildings further up the street relied on the charm of old brickwork – including one that housed a Chinese restaurant. Passed the Lisbeth Mulcahy weaver shop and, as I approached St. Mary's Church, there were more buildings in bright colours that housed Dingle Crystal, Dingle Pottery and Dick Mack's.

The door to the Dingle Record Shop had been closed on my previous jaunts around town. Either the owner – local legend Mazz O'Flaherty – had closed her shop to run an errand or she was recording a live session inside (which she later posts for free on her website). Dubbed 'the smallest record shop in Ireland', the walls are covered by compact discs and vinyl records as well as framed photos and concert posters. Hand-written notes, re-taped and warped over time, direct wayward audiophiles to different areas of the store.

Mazz's shop, in its charming, organized chaos, is the central vortex for the local music scene. But it's not just a way station for upcoming acts. Musical royalty – the likes of Paul Simon, Bono, Donovan, Arlo Guthrie, Mary Black, Christy Moore, Dervish and Glen Hansard – often come to say hello and play a few tunes.

I was happy to find it open.

Mazz was standing behind the counter, warming her hands on a cup of tea. "You're very welcome," she said. "Just taking a cuppa. Have a look around. Take your time. I'm here if you're in need of anything. You let me know."

"I will," I replied while narrowing in on the stacks of records.

Mazz took a couple quick sips, but couldn't resist the urge to help.

"A record is it, you're after? Just got in a couple that you might like. If you're looking for a compilation of fine tunes, I have this one here. Hard to find, if you fancy yourself a bit of a collector... or not, it doesn't matter. Still a good record." She said this all with a playful grin that I'd come to expect from West Kerry residents.

Then she handed me *Another! Feast of Irish Folk*, released in 1980. The purple cover features bubble lettering, indicative of the time. There seemed to be a good cross-section of traditional tunes.

"Also have this one here, that just came in. Do you know John McCormack? He was an Irish tenor. Very famous, he was. Sure you've heard of him?"

"Of course, yeah," I lied.

She saw right through me.

"Right, so. That's a good record in your hand. Think you'd enjoy that one."

"Okay," I replied. "I'll take both of them." Looked around the shop again before making eye contact with Mazz. "I'm also looking for a compilation album of local musicians. Do you have something like that on CD?"

"I *did* have something like that, yes. Not sure if I still have a copy. Might be out, but give me a second here. You do have a second, don't you?"

"Take your time," I replied.

Mazz poked around her shop, moving various piles here and there and looking behind boxes. She scanned the stacks that crowded her desk. "And where are you visiting from?" she asked from behind the counter. "Where do you call home?"

"Canada," I answered. "British Columbia. Near the Rocky Mountains."

"Ah, right. That's a beautiful part of the world, so it is. Haven't been there meself. I hear it's lovely, though."

"It can be," I answered.

"Cold, though, I imagine."

"Yup," I agreed. "It gets cold."

After some more digging, she eventually found a copy of *The Music of Dingle*. It was behind a stack of CDs, near a little note taped on the shelf that reads: Local Musicians and Friends (and their friends) are our friends.

"And what are you up to this afternoon?" she asked.

"Not sure," I answered. "Think I might go horse riding tomorrow. Don't know why. But maybe the best reason is no reason at all."

"Right," she laughed. "Wouldn't know much about horse riding. Not much of a horse person, meself. But come in afterwards and let me know how it went – let me know that you survived and all."

"I will."

A hundred meters further up Green Street is the Dingle Bookshop.

The small store is stocked with books on Irish history, coffee-table books for tourists, guides to the peninsula, and a substantial number of works by local writers and photographers. It is well organized, and I easily found what I was looking for. Even so, the lady behind the counter asked if I needed any help.

"I'm just where I need to be," I answered. "I'm looking for books by the Blasket Islanders – specifically *Twenty Years a-Growing*."

"Should be right in front of you, so."

And it was.

Was about to pay for my book and head off for the

continuation of my walk, but couldn't help listening in on a conversation between father and son.

"When he chose to be a poet, he chose a very different path from his father's or his grandfather's. He's not digging potato drills or digging peat. Instead, he's digging into the past – his father's past and his grandfather's past, sure, but also Ireland's past – with his pen. Do y'see?"

"I think so, maybe," answered the son.

The scene reminded me of the long conversations about poetry I had with my father when I was of a similar age – a taciturn kid, merely grunting in response when my father introduced me to the works of Milton, Byron, Keats and Tennyson. A lesser man would have given up, but my father fought on. He was desperate to pass on his love for words. And, despite my desire to be anywhere else during our one-sided discussions, I too became an aesthete.

"There is a sense of deep loss and even moral guilt in Heaney's earlier work," said the father. "He continues to encounter a growing distance between the world of language, y'know, and physical world he sees around him. Heaney must also come to terms with who he is, and that his education and gifts of language have excluded him from the agrarian society in which he was raised."

The son put his hands in his pockets and shuffled his feet. He was trying to pay attention, but I could tell his thoughts were elsewhere.

"Never mind his use of the poetic devices I was telling y'about earlier. Doesn't 'squelch and slap' bring to life the noise of soggy peat? Look how carefully he uses both onomatopoeia and alliteration at the end of the line, there. Do you see it, son? Do you see why "Digging" is such a great poem? Have I convinced ya?"

The son shrugged his shoulders. He would lie, just as I

did, and say he understood so he could get back to playing video games. But I knew the seed was planted, and he would later hunt down the poet's work in his own time – just as I did.

After paying for my book, the owner told me to take a couple bookmarks as needed. I took ten when she wasn't looking.

On Main Street is a small craft store called Commodum with little hand-knit lambs in the window. Inside there is a wonderful selection of wool clothing and woollen goods. Poked around the shop and spied a pair of fingerless gloves the colour of seaweed with an Aran diamond design on the back. Paula had crocheted me a thin pair before I left, but the cold wind often made me wish for something a little more substantial.

Further up the road is another inviting store called An Gailearai Beag, selling goods from the West Kerry Craft Guild. Walked in to find a number of small wooden pieces, as well as felted hats, aprons, leather keychains, photographs and prints of watercolour paintings. Next to An Droichead Beag, and tucked behind a row of buildings, is Cúl Gáirdín Café Gallery. The back garden reminded me of little coffee shops back home. The inside features freshly cut flowers and tables for two, but I sat outside where the daffodils were in bloom among the totem poles and tikki heads. The menu advertises vegetarian, vegan, and gluten-free delights.

After tearing open a couple sugar packets that read 'spoonful of Irish', and stirring my cuppa as I settled into my chair, I thought back on my drive east from Dingle with Paula three years earlier. By this point in our travels, I was finally comfortable with the idea of a whirlwind tour – punctuated by top tourist attractions – and was content to spend time with my wife in one of the most beautiful places in the world. There was a noticeable lightness to the rest of our holiday together. It helped knowing that I would one day return to explore the lesser-known corners – allowing myself a moment or two to sit on cold stone and watch the world go by. Allowing myself to stumble and become lost, on numerous occasions and in all sorts of weather, between the stones and the sea. And I would love every minute of it.

CHAPTER 20

AN ADVENTURER'S BEST CHOICE

Once we had checked out all the cultural highlights in and around Dingle that we could manage within half a day, Paula and I stopped in Killarney for a later lunch.

Like many other towns and villages across Ireland, Killarney (*Cill Airne*) began as an important religious settlement when St. Finian the Leper founded his monastery on nearby Innisfallen Island (*Inis Faithlinn*) in 640. Today the town has a population of about fourteen thousand.

The sun shone off the wet cement and brick sidewalks, washed by the morning rain. The mid-day energy of the downtown core seemed contagious as we walked hand-in-hand, listening to the lovely lilt of those who strolled along. As we passed a pub, a small dog stepped out onto the sidewalk beside us. "How many pints do you think that fellow has had?" I asked.

Paula looked down at the dog, its tail wagging. "Enough to wash down a couple biscuits, I would think."

No matter where we went, or for how long we lingered, the dog remained by our side. He sat next to us when we stopped at street corners, and hurried along when the traffic lights were about to change. We continued down tighter alleyways and across busy streets, and still the dog kept us company.

"What are we supposed to do with him?" I asked as we got further and further along.

"Just leave him," Paula answered. "I'm sure he does this all the time."

"Do you think he'll find his way back?"

"Odds are he has a better sense of direction than you," she teased.

"I suppose you're right."

The dog followed us for another ten minutes, as if he knew exactly where he was meant to be. And then suddenly he was no longer with us. We turned around as the dog's back end disappeared around a corner.

"There he goes," said Paula. "Off on another adventure."

"Terrible tour guide," I replied. "Didn't learn a thing."

"But he was cheap, and it was nice to have a bit of company."

"That's true."

On the way back to the car, we found the Aran Sweater Market. Unable to pass on a treasure trove of lovely woollen goods, I dragged Paula inside. I was on the lookout for a sweater with suede elbow and shoulder patches.

A stylish young woman was organizing a collection of longer scarves.

"Ah, sure, are these what you're after, then?" she asked me after I enquired. She unfolded a dark grey sweater with black suede patches.

"That's exactly it."

"Grand. I'll leave you a moment to find the right fit."

She returned to the scarves and I read the informative hangtag.

'The timeless ribbed wool sweater was designed with the great outdoors in mind, taking inspiration from the life and needs of the fishermen on the Aran Islands. The rib pattern creates a tight-knit effect allowing for extra warmth, while still remaining breathable. The sweater is finished with suede patches on the elbows and shoulders to ensure durability and convenience. The design is an adventurer's best choice, as it is both hard-wearing and practical.'

There was no way anyone could resist.

While contemplating another scarf to add to my collection, two women who I assumed to be sisters on holiday came barrelling into the store.

"Perhaps the most sought after by tourists are the more authentic styles modelled on the very sweaters, hand-knit by the women of the Aran Islands in 1892," read one sister. She had a guidebook in hand and was holding her place with her finger.

"And did you know," she continued, "that on the Aran Islands the sweater patterns were closely guarded, and kept within the same clan throughout generations? They were often used to help identify bodies of fishermen washed up on the beach following an accident at sea."

"Is that true?"

"Sure, it is."

The two sisters looked at a few items near the entrance and then left without purchasing anything.

"It's actually not true," said the clerk.

"Is it not?" I asked.

"Not at all," she answered.

. . .

Nearby Ross Castle (*Caisleán an Rois*) was open to visitors, but only by guided tour. The next one was not for forty-five minutes. "That's okay," I said to the young woman at the front desk, glad to have some time to use the restroom and stretch my legs.

The castle sits on the banks of Lough Leane (*Loch Léin*), overlooking the lake and Inisfallen Island (home to a seventh-century monastery). Though it could be argued that the castle is more English than Irish, I had to admit that it was a pleasant scene with the little wooden bridges, rowboats and horse-drawn wagons. We pottered around the perimeter to check out the formidable stonework and thick wooden doors with decorative metal studs before meeting the guide at the appointed hour.

During the tour, we learned that the castle is a typical example of the strongholds of Irish chieftains during the Middle Ages. Winding stone stairs still lead from the basement to the battlements. To the south of the tower is a range of added chambers, and from here one can see traces of a high-pitched roof on the tower gable.

The front door, on the inside of the anteroom, was constructed of two layers of thick Irish oak. Windows at the lower levels are vertical slits preventing entrance into the structure but allowing those inside to aim and fire in case of attack. The windows on the top levels are larger to allow in light. The spiral staircase, located in the front left corner, was built in a clockwise direction. This allowed defenders a greater range of movement when they wielded their swords with their right hands. These types of stairwells also diminished the ability of attackers to properly swing their swords, since right-handed fighters would have to contend with the walls while making their striking motions. Even the stairs themselves served as a defence, as each step was designed to vary in size. While the castle's inhabitants would be familiar with the smaller and larger steps, invaders could easily lose their footing and slip during battle if they misjudged a step.

Ross Castle also features a murder hole. This is an opening in the ceiling of a gateway or passageway in a fortification through which the defenders could fire, throw or pour harmful substances or objects such as rocks, arrows, scalding water, hot sand, quicklime (calcium oxide), tar and boiling oil down on attackers.

The castle was built in the late fifteenth century and is thought of as the ancestral home of the O'Donoghue (*Ó Donnchadha*) clan – though ownership changed hands during the Second Desmond Rebellion of the 1580s). It also played a big part in the Cromwellian wars, and was the last fortress in Ireland to surrender to the Parliamentary forces. After their defeat in County Cork in 1652, Lord Muskerry withdrew what was left of his Royalist soldiers to this stronghold, and seemed to be in a good position to resist General Ludlow for an indefinite period. However, an old legend about Ross soon helped the Cromwellian general to a quick victory. Whether he knew of the legend, or benefitted from it by sheer luck, we shall never know.

The Irish had a prophecy that Ross could never be taken until a warship could swim the lake.

Ross may all assault disdain
'Till on Lough Leane strange ship shall sail.

This seemed an implausible prospect, and those that had faith in ancient prophecies felt themselves safe.

Ludlow marched to Ross with four thousand foot soldiers and two thousand horses, but it was by water that he attacked the stronghold. Several boats from Kinsale (*Cionn tSáile*) were sailed to Killorglin (*Cill Orglan*) via the River Laune (*An Leamhain*) and then dragged by oxen to Ross Castle. The sight of the ships unnerved the onlookers and those within the castle soon submitted.

Another story regarding Ross Castle is steeped not so much in history but in folklore. It tells of O'Donoghue's attempt to restore his youth through the use of black magic. Rich and powerful, he was said to be the wisest man of his time who could do wonders by the power of the black arts – but neither his wealth, power, nor wisdom could prevent him from growing old. One day, O'Donoghue shut himself away in his grand chamber at the top of the castle with his magical books and vowed to have no contact with anyone until he'd discovered how to make himself young again.

Several weeks passed, and finally O'Donoghue called for his wife. "You must cut me up into several little pieces," he said, "and put me into a barrel in this chamber. Then you must lock the door and stay away for seven weeks. When you return, you will find me alive and well – but no larger than a three-year-old child. If you become frightened and try to enter my chamber before the appointed time, all will be lost. However, before we begin, I need to test your nerve. To do this, I shall read to you from one of my books. You will see and hear strange things while I am reading, but you must not cry out or I shall be taken from you forever."

O'Donoghue began, and his horrified wife saw the most terrible things and heard the most dreadful noises. But she kept her nerve and not a sound escaped her lips – that is, until she saw a vision of her own child lying dead on the table. She cried out in anguish and, with that, the castle shook. O'Donoghue fell out of the window and disappeared into the lake along with his horse, his table and his library.

To this day, he remains in a great palace at the bottom of the lake where he keeps a close watch over the area. Every seven years, on the first morning of May, he reportedly rises out of the waters on his horse, circles the lake, and then disappears again. Any soul who spots him will reportedly have good fortune for the rest of their lives. As it was mid-March, we didn't stick around. And, besides, it was getting late and I was hungry.

AFTER FINDING a place to lay our weary heads, and after consuming an enormous amount of food the next morning, we made our way northeast.

Our next stop is impossible to miss, as it casts an imposing shadow across the land. You would have to be terribly distracted to drive past it.

"Look at that unusually distracting cow," I said as we raced past green pastures.

"Yes," said Paula. "That is an unusually distracting cow. Let us both take a minute to gaze at it and be totally unaware of where we are."

"What a great idea. Say... I wonder when we'll arrive at the Rock of Cashel."

"Must be any minute now," said Paula.

Neither of us can remember whether the above conversation unfolded in exactly this way but, for some reason, we both became interested in a random bovine and didn't notice the ancient royal site. Only when checking the rearview mirror did I notice the spectacular collection of medieval buildings getting further and further away.

According to local mythology, the Rock of Cashel (*Carraig Phádraig*) originated in the Devil's Bit, a mountain thirty kilometres north. Satan was enjoying his lunch when

St. Patrick appeared and ran him off. The fleeing demon took an angry bite from the summit of the mountain, but later dropped it during the chase.

Geologists like to mention that the Devil's Bit is made entirely of sandstone while the Rock of Cashel is a limestone crop. Those enchanted with Irish myths should probably ignore the geologists. Whether or not Satan was involved with the placement of the enormous rock, Cashel is also reputed to be the site of the conversion of the King of Munster by St. Patrick in the fifth century.

The Rock of Cashel was the traditional seat of the kings of Munster for several hundred years prior to the Norman invasion, including Brian Boru. It was in the early twelfth century, however, that the Rock began to develop into a major Christian centre and the majority of buildings on the current site date from around this time.

The oldest and tallest of the buildings at the Rock is the well-preserved round tower, dating from 1100. Experts once believed that the round towers were designed for protection against the Vikings, as the doors are usually located twelve feet off the ground and a ladder could be pulled inside in case of attack. However, as all of the surviving towers postdate Viking times, and would have been virtual death traps in times of strife, this theory has been discredited. They were certainly symbols of prestige, power and wealth – not only of the ecclesiastical community that built them, but also of their patrons. Some acted as treasure houses. The high doorway would have allowed relics to be displayed above the heads of those that gathered.

There is ample parking and we walked up the hill with the tourists who had *not* driven past because they were looking at distracting cows. As we walked near a tour group, we overheard a guide explain that there are three weather systems on top of the Rock: either it's *very* cold and windy, *unbelievably* cold and windy, or so *brutally* cold and windy that even the ghosts require woollen pants. Though the arrival of the Black Plague in 1348 certainly played a role, rumour has it that the real reason the Irish lords began building their own houses at lower elevation was because they were tired of the constant cold and wind. The castle-like structure was undesirable to the archbishop of the time as well. He also abandoned his residence and built himself a palace closer to the village.

Despite the cold and wind, we explored the entire walled plateau and extensive graveyard that includes a number of high crosses. Scully's Cross, one of the largest and most famous high crosses at the site, was originally constructed in 1867 but was destroyed in 1976 when lightening struck the metal rod inside.

While Paula was taking photos of the stonework, I decided to get within earshot of another tour group – partly for a history lesson and partly so they could block the wind.

"Work began on Cormac's Chapel – the chapel dedicated to King Cormac McCarthy – in 1127 and it was consecrated in 1134," began the guide. "The Hiberno-Romanesque chapel contains one of the best-preserved Irish frescoes from this time period. Unfortunately, the chapel was constructed primarily of sandstone that has become waterlogged over the centuries, significantly damaging the interior. Restoration and preservation requires the chapel to be completely enclosed in a rainproof structure with dehumidifiers to dry out the stone."

(While the frescoes inside Cormac's Chapel were not available to the public when Paula and I toured the lower half of the country, they were three years later. Following an extensive conservation project, experts tenderly wrestled the eight-hundred-year-old frescoes back from the hands of time. They cover the walls and ribs of the chancel, and have been restored to reveal two layers of painting: including geometric and floral motifs, as well as figurative scenes including the baptism of Christ and possibly Solomon and the Queen of Sheba with the temple of Jerusalem. These brush-to-wall images are the earliest of their kind on the entire island.)

The tour group shuffled from one frozen perch to another before huddling into each other like emperor penguins that stand with their backs to the wind as they incubate their eggs. Every few minutes, they reordered themselves so that everyone had a change to cycle through the warmth before the guide continued.

"The Cathedral was built between 1235 and 1270. The Hall of the Vicars Choral was built in the fifteenth century."

"I think my lips are blue," uttered one woman.

The guide ignored the comment and continued. "After the English civil war, when Parliament emerged victorious and King Charles I was beheaded, Oliver Cromwell brought over his army to crush the Irish rebellion. Cromwell's troops enthusiastically slaughtered the Irish people and destroyed everything in their path. Cashel was one of several villages that were sacked and, when Catholic soldiers and the town's people sought refuge in the cathedral, Cromwell recognized no sanctuary, ordered his troops to pile turf around the building, and set it afire – killing all within."

"At least they were warm," said the blue-lipped lady.

The guide didn't laugh, and instead continued where she left off. "Arthur Price, the Anglican Archbishop of Cashel, arrived to find the immense medieval gothic cathedral in ruins. Since Cashel was a small town and could not possibly afford to repair the building, Price sought money from both the Irish parliament and the British parliament. But they refused. In 1749, Price then sought and received permission to remove the expensive lead from the roof (so it could be used for ammunition). He planned to use the proceeds to build a new, smaller cathedral. Unfortunately, he died before the building was completed and it remains unfinished today. Price's decision to remove the roof on what had been the jewel among Irish church buildings was heavily criticized during his time and ever since."

Then it started to rain, and I soon lost feeling in my fingers and nose. Broke away from the tour group and took refuge in a lonely corner of a rock wall. The birds found their nests in the cracks, and I kept myself warm by jumping up and down like a crazy person. Quickly lost patience with my wife as she continued to take more photos from different angles. The romantic notion of living at an ancient royal site on top of a rock dropped by the Devil suddenly lost its appeal entirely.

There are countless historical sites in various states of ruin or reconstruction across Ireland – all of them fascinating in their own way – but there is something particularly enticing about the Rock of Cashel. When dressed appropriately for the brutal weather, one can appreciate the unique character of the complex and the remarkable collection of art and medieval architecture. As I was *not* dressed appropriately (even though I was sporting my new sweater), my only thought was the comfort of the car. Sprinting down the hill, I tried to warm my hands with my breath as some feeling returned to my lower body.

"Slow down," yelled Paula. "My legs aren't as long as yours."

"Freezing. Need tea," I yelled behind me. "Or soup. Preferably both."

That evening, we plunked our bags in our room and headed out for dinner. After a short walk to aid digestion, I jotted down a few notes about my day and then researched the origin of the myths surrounding Aran sweaters. It seemed appropriate, seeing as I spent most of the day huddled for warmth.

There is some debate about when island residents first started making the sweaters and whether some stitch patterns were believed to have a traditional interpretation (often of religious significance). It was later discovered that these interpretations were fabricated by Heinz Edgar Kiewe, a Prussian-born self-styled 'textile journalist' and yarn shop owner who noticed a chance resemblance between Aran stitches and Celtic knotwork. He assumed Aran knitting was at least as old (if not older) than the knotwork it resembles, but his thesis has been thoroughly debunked by modern historians.

The misconception regarding Aran sweaters was also fuelled by J.M. Synge's 1904 play *Riders to the Sea,* in which the body of a dead fisherman is identified by the hand-knitted stitches on one of his garments. On closer reading of the play, the garment is actually a plain stocking and the number of stitches identifies it rather than a decorative pattern.

"So Aran sweaters didn't identify families of fishermen, just like Vikings didn't wear horned helmets," I said to Paula. "How much of this Irish identity is steeped in history and tradition, and how much is just a construct?"

"Mmm," answered Paula in a disinterested tone as I continued to flip through various websites.

Some online sweater markets entice shoppers with

various symbolic patterns, or 'stitches inspired by life on the islands'. There's the Irish moss stitch, which represents a type of carrageen moss found on the cliffs (and often gathered as a source of food). The diamond stitch represents the enclosed stone walls that were built to divide the lands of different ruling clans. Stitches such as the cable and the trellis symbolize the ropes of the fishermen who risked their lives on the Atlantic seas.

Whether this too is a modern construct meant to boost sales of 'authentic' Irish textiles and crafts is debatable, but it probably doesn't matter.

The first Aran knitting patterns were published in the 1940s and *Vogue* magazine carried articles on them in the 1950s. Exports of ornate knitted sweaters from the west of Ireland to the United States began around the same time. Grace Kelly had one. So too did Steve McQueen. The Clancy Brothers wore them while performing (though they must have roasted under stage lighting). So popular were they that some companies had difficulty filling orders.

While in the past the majority of sweaters and other Aran goods were knitted by hand, today the majority of items for sale in Ireland and abroad are either machine-knit or produced on a hand loom. Gone are the days of wearing something lovingly toiled over by somebody's dear grandmother for weeks on end – rocking chair, turf fire and all. However, the patterns, designs and embossed decoration in every garment still reflect the loves, lives, losses, and defiance of community at the very edge of the Atlantic.

CHAPTER 21

A MANGY BOULDER

The next day, we journeyed east to the town of Blarney (*an Bhlarna*). For over two hundred years, world statesmen, literary giants, and legends of the silver screen have joined millions of random nobodies to kiss the Blarney Stone and supposedly gain the gift of eloquence. Naturally, the stone has been named the world's germ-iest tourist attraction (with some four hundred thousand tourists snogging it every year).

Originally known as *Lia Fáil* or the Stone of Destiny (*another* Stone of Destiny, apparently), the Blarney Stone probably dates back to the twelfth century. Many believe it to be the original Stone of Scone upon which the first King of the Scots was seated during his coronation. It is said that in 1314, Robert the Bruce presented part of the Stone of Scone to Cormac McCarthy (*Mac Cárthaigh*), the Lord of Blarney Castle, after the king of Munster sent five thousand men to support Robert the Bruce in his defeat of the English at Bannockburn. Some claim it is the stone that gushed water when struck by Moses; some say it is Jacob's Pillow, brought to Ireland by the prophet Jeremiah; others claim it is the Stone of Ezel, brought back from the Crusades; and still others believe it to be the deathbed pillow of St. Columba on the island of Iona.

The origin of the stone is of no major concern for those that join the never-ending queue to plant their lips upon the side of the castle. Up until recently, one had to be held by the ankles and lowered head first over the battlements in order to make contact, but the fine folks at Blarney Castle are more cautious of visitors' safety these days. The stone is still set in the wall below the battlements and one only has to lean backwards (holding onto an iron railing) from the parapet walk.

We arrived at the front gate, paid the entrance fee, and then made our way across manicured lawns and gravel walkways to the imposing castle. After staring at the tall wall of stone for a few minutes in quiet solitude, I finally broke the silence. "That's a tall wall," I said.

"That is indeed a tall wall," replied Paula.

Slippery, steep and narrow, some sections of the castle stairs have a safety rope but we took it slow and steady. Although the original wooden floors are gone, there is a second spiral staircase to accommodate tourists returning from their smooch. Like many castles built within the similar time period, Blarney sits atop a rock – in this case, an eight-meter tall rock – and the walls gradually angle inwards to form the original four-story rectangular keep.

I soon joined the three-person queue. "One has to do these kinds of things when one has the chance."

My wife disagreed. She wasn't interested in making out with a mangy boulder.

When it was my turn, I handed Paula my glasses and laid down on my back. Shimmied into position and the friendly Blarney Castle employee told me to give a stretch.

Casting from my mind the countless others that had slobbered all over this particular chunk of stone, I quickly made contact and then came back up a little dizzy. Refocused, slipped on my glasses, and we made our way back through the castle.

"Do you feel any different?" asked Paula. "Do you feel more eloquent?"

"Definitely," I answered.

"Really?"

"Ah, no. Not really."

As we crossed the manicured lawns, I read from one of the dog-eared guidebooks. "Those that quickly visit the castle, kiss the stone, and drive away miss out on exploring amazing gardens, incredible trees and local folklore. The castle should serve only as a starting point."

"We have nowhere to go and all day to get there," said Paula.

"Well, then... let me relay some local history."

"Please do."

"The first castle, built in the tenth century, was a wooden structure," I began. "It was replaced by a stone fortification in 1210. In 1446, King Dermot McCarthy demolished the stone structure and enlarged Blarney Castle, reinstalling the fabled Blarney Stone. So..."

"Go on."

"It would appear Blarney Castle has seen its fair share of ups and downs."

"You're hilarious."

"I did kiss the stone, y'know."

"I remember."

"Anyway... in 1586, Queen Elizabeth I commissioned the Earl of Leicester to take the land from the McCarthy Clan, but the clan found ways to delay negotiations. These constant delays frustrated the Queen, and the family held onto Blarney Castle until the Confederate War (1641-52). When Cromwell's general, Lord Broghill, besieged the castle, he fired down from Card Hill above the lake and broke the tower walls. However, when he entered the castle, he found only two trusty retainers. The main garrison had fled through Badgers Cave."

"That's embarrassing."

"Indeed. But the story continues. When Oliver Cromwell died in 1658, the McCarthys reclaimed Blarney Castle. This victory did not last long, however. When Donough McCarthy joined forces with the Jacobites of Scotland, the Duke of Malborough took him prisoner in 1690. Imprisoned in the Tower of London, McCarthy escaped in 1694 to James II's court. He returned to England in 1698 to finally begin married life, only to be turned in to the authorities by his brother-in-law, Lord Spencer."

"Sometimes castle ownership is just not worth the hassle."

"True. Speaking of which, Blarney Castle changed ownership numerous times over the next two centuries. The Hollow Sword Blade Company of London purchased the land soon after the McCarthy Clan left and in 1703 Sire Richard Payne, the Lord Chief Justice of Ireland, bought the land from the company. Afraid that the McCarthys would one day return, Payne sold the land to Sir James Jefferyes, governor of Cork City. They subsequently turned the property into an estate village with ninety houses, a small church, and three mud cabins. In the 1800s, the Jefferyes family married into the Colthurst family and their descendants maintain ownership of the castle today."

"That was a thorough history," said Paula. "And now it's time to put the book away and go exploring."

She was right. Threw back a handful of trail mix, zipped up my bag, and we trotted off together with book in bag.

After exploring the caves under the castle, we found the Poison Garden hidden behind the castle battlements. It contains an interesting and informative collection of deadly plants from around the world, and we both felt like students at Hogwarts as we peered into small cages that hold wolfsbane, mandrake, opium and other plants labelled with information about their toxicity as well as their traditional and modern uses.

One plant had been recently removed by the authorities and was no longer part of the collection. Wondering what could be so dangerous that it had to be taken away in the dead of night by a special operations force, we leaned over to read the small official notice. It was the *cannabis* plant – probably the least dangerous in the entire collection.

We then found the Fern Garden, with over eighty varieties of ferns, and the Rock Close where majestic yew and oak trees grow around an ancient druidic settlement. The bog area features two waterfalls, and a raised wooden boardwalk led us through large groups of giant rhubarb. While many of the rare and unusual trees on the property were planted in the late 1970s and 80s, other trees such as the yews, limes, Spanish chestnuts and various conifers are over six hundred years old.

An archway of limestone rocks directed us to the Wishing Steps where, legend has it, our deepest desires would come true within a year if we walked up backwards with our eyes closed. It is said that the resident witch grants these wishes as her way of paying for firewood. It is the same witch who discovered the powers of the Blarney Stone and revealed it to the McCarthys after she was saved from drowning. If one arrives early enough in the morning, and is open to the existence of such things, one may spy the dying embers of her fire.

Though Paula and I knew that any reference to the resident witch had very little, if any, real basis in Irish history or mythology, we still walked up the stairs backwards with our eyes closed. One must do these things when one has the chance.

While the grounds are peppered with what seems like Ireland's greatest hits – a Druid's circle, witch's cave, faerie glade, dolmen, and wishing steps – we enjoyed spending the afternoon wandering the grounds and finishing our walk by circling the mighty trees. The yews and Holm oaks are particularly impressive.

Both Druids (with their belief in reincarnation) and Christians (with their teaching of the resurrection) regarded the yew as a natural emblem of everlasting life. In the Brehon Laws it is named as one of the Seven Chieftain Trees, with heavy penalties for felling one; and in Irish mythology the yew is one of the five sacred trees brought from the Otherworld. It is considered to be the most potent tree for protection against evil, a means of connecting to your ancestors, a bringer of dreams, and a symbol of the old magic.

Of all the trees in Ireland, the oak was considered king. Famed for its endurance and longevity, even today it is synonymous with strength and steadfastness in the popular mind. In the Classical world, it was regarded as the Tree of Life as its roots penetrate as deep as its branches soar to the sky. Ancient writings mention that Druids performed all of their religious rites in oak groves, where they gathered mistletoe from the trees with a golden sickle.

Whether the casual tourist takes a moment to ponder the authenticity of the witch's cave or the historical uses of the mighty trees is of no matter. The castle and grounds are worth the admission fee, and we were glad to have stopped before finding a quiet place to spend the night.

THE NEXT MORNING, we needed to make up some miles. In Canada, 'making up some miles' translates to five or six hours of driving. In Ireland, this is closer to one or two.

Tucked in County Wicklow, and situated on the river that carries its name, the village of Avoca (*Abhóca*) was immortalized by Thomas Moore in his famous song "The Meeting of the Waters". (The title of the song derives from the meeting of the Avonmore and Avonbeg rivers.)

Television viewers will recognize the village as Ballykissangel. The BBC television dramedy of that same name ran from 1996-2001, and had ten million viewers at its peak. The original story revolved around a young English Roman Catholic priest as he became part of a rural community. Viewers will also recognize the pub Fitzgerald's (originally called The Fountain, but given a new name for the filming of the show). Assumpta Fitzgerald was half of the dynamic love story that spanned the first three seasons. When tourists began to flock to Avoca, their first port of call was the pub and so the owners have simply left the Fitzgerald's sign up all these years.

We decided it would be our first port of call as well.

"Are you fans of the show?" asked the waitress as she came around to get our drink order.

"Yes, we are," I answered.

This isn't totally true. While I had watched all six seasons, Paula had only seen one or two episodes. She didn't see the appeal in quite the same way.

After a pint and a bag of crisps, we walked halfway

across the stone bridge, looked down at the river for a while, walked back again, and then headed up the street – past the corner shop Hendley's, the *gardaí* station, and towards the church. The small building attached to the church (that served as the priest's house in the show) appeared to now be a small store selling various merchandise, but it didn't look like it had been open for several months (or possibly years).

The village takes about six minutes to cover by foot at a leisurely pace. As I recognized many of the filming locations, and stopped to take photos, it took us closer to ten.

At the top of the hill is Avoca Handweavers. It has the distinction of being Ireland's oldest surviving business, the oldest working woollen mill in Ireland, and one of the world's oldest manufacturing companies.

There was just enough room in my suitcase for a small lap blanket for Paula. Plus, we needed a bit of a snack to balance out the pints.

No one was inside the small museum, where a video outlining the history of the mill was playing on an endless loop. We decided, since the credits were rolling, to wait for the short documentary to begin again.

The mill in Avoca village was originally set up as a cooperative in 1723. Local farmers could not only grind their corn, but also spin and weave wool for clothing for the local miners. In 1760, a fly shuttle loom, capable of weaving twenty meters of cloth a day, arrived and was soon put to use.

Three sisters inherited the mill in the 1920s, and were determined to find ways of injecting colour into the garments that up until then had been only brown and grey. They grew dye-producing plants and installed vats in local outhouses. Locals recall seeing Emily, Winifred and

Veronica walking around with twists of yarn between their fingers, constantly testing the brighter, more vibrant product that they were pioneering. Involved in all aspects of life in Avoca village, the sisters gave a great deal of time to their local community, teaching children the skills of embroidery and soft toy making. The business thrived through the 1920s and '30s as the Wynne sisters developed an international business selling rugs and wool fabric throughout Europe and America.

In the 1960s, however, the mill became neglected and fell into disrepair. Hand weaving was dying out, and the looms were largely silent.

In 1974, Donald Pratt, a solicitor engaged to handle the sale of the mill which now faced closure, decided to buy it himself. Along with his wife Hillary, he set about getting Avoca Handweavers back on its feet. He began by selling Irish designs from the trunk of his car, and slowly the business took hold. It wasn't long before the Pratts were exporting hand-woven rugs and throws all over the world.

In the 1990s, Donald and Hillary's children began their involvement in the business. Their daughter Amanda created the Avoca fashion label, as well as designing ceramics, candles and soaps. Simon, their eldest son, transformed the culinary end of the business from a small selection of jams and chutneys to a wide range of products and dining experiences across the country. Today, Avoca's famous woollen products account for just ten percent of the business while food and food-related products (like cookbooks) make up eighty percent.

New owners Aramark purchased Avoca Weavers for a reported fifty-one million euros in 2015, with plans to expand to the United Kingdom and possibly the United

States under the guidance of three of Donald and Hillary's children.

As the video ended, I remembered something about a tour of the facility but wasn't sure if it was meant to be self-guided or not.

"Should we go further in?" I asked Paula.

"What do you mean?"

"Well... I assume the tour is self-guided, since there's no one here."

"I don't think that's true," she replied.

"C'mon. We'll walk quietly."

The humming of the machines got louder and louder as we tiptoed further inside the mill. A little later we heard snippets of conversation from around the corner.

I stopped in my tracks. "There's a possibility that the tour is, in fact, not self-guided," I whispered.

Paula didn't look impressed. We snuck back before anyone noticed us.

Three professional-looking ladies greeted us warmly as we walked into the gift shop and café. Neither Paula nor I made any mention of our museum antics.

The full-sized hand-woven wool throws and blankets are beyond gorgeous. 'From sumptuous cashmere to Donegal wool, and soft lambswool to light and lofty mohair, an Avoca throw is a perfect addition to any home,' read the informative hangtag.

There was no way anyone could resist.

After searching through the various stacks with a little help, we found a small lap blanket featuring autumnal colours that Paula was happy with. There was just enough room in the suitcase.

. . .

We spent the night at a nearby B&B, and then poked about the monastic site of Glendalough the next morning. After driving to the airport and returning the rental car, we explored Dublin by foot for a day-and-a-half. We did all the touristy things one would expect: we queued up to see the Book of Kells at Trinity College; walked through Temple Bar (but didn't dare stop for a drink); photographed the statue of Molly Malone; paid a fortune to wander through the Guinness Storehouse; poked around Christchurch Cathedral; gazed in wonderment at the treasures within the archaeology branch of the National Museum, the National Gallery, and the Irish Museum of Modern Art; and then, rather unceremoniously, we boarded our plane and returned home.

Somewhere over Greenland, my mind was flooded with memories – interlaced with lines of poetry by Neruda, Rumi and Yeats. At first, there didn't seem to be any common thread. But as I slipped between reality and dreams, and looked out from thirty-five thousand feet to the world below, I began to make sense of it all.

Thought back to the path of small white stones that weave through the dewy grass, and the hints of greenery blending softly with subtle shades of blue and purple as night creeps into day. Thought back to the cold embrace of earthen structures and being lost in thought as I traced with my eyes the ancient Neolithic carvings.

"Something started in my soul," I whispered as I stared out at the abyss. "Fever or forgotten wings and I made my own way deciphering that fire."

Though Neruda was most likely describing a sort of literary ecstasy, I had no trouble relating the magic and mystery of the written word to the magic and mystery of Newgrange. How exactly I would decipher that fire inside me as time passed I did not know, but was curious to find out.

Thought back to the sweetness in the air, the music in the wind, and the desolate mountains flecked with moor grasses, myrtle, sedges and wildflowers. Thought back to the sea birds and Atlantic waves and sublime beauty of rare living things that find their home in the crisscrossing cracks between limestone pavements.

"The wound is the place where the light enters you," I whispered – remembering the oft-quoted line by Rumi. "How true that is."

Though we had puttered along from town to town, without any real sense of place, it still felt bittersweet every time we climbed into the rental car and drove away. I had become intoxicated and danced in a liminal state along the borders of two worlds. Bled from a slash to the soul, and yet a radiant warmth glowed from deep within – stitching me with threads of light.

Thought back to the heavy fog and old stone walls and winding rivers – the white sands and clear waters of Connemara. The pastoral patchwork and haunted lakes and freezing rain, and the sun's rays that warm nothing but the eyelids when one looks towards the heavens. The majestic yew and oak trees at Blarney, and the meeting of the Avonmore (*An Abhainn Mhór*) and Avonbeg (*Abhainn Beag*) rivers in Wicklow. The world slowly unfurling, and then falling quiet again at the close of the day.

The first stanza of Yeats' "The Lake Isle of Innisfree" came to mind as I looked down the aisle at the other passengers.

I will arise and go now, and go to Innisfree

And a small cabin build there, of clay and
wattles made;
Nine bean-rows will I have there, a hive for the
honey-bee
And live alone in the bee-loud glade.

Yeats speaks of Innisfree (*Inis Fraoigh*) in an idealistic way, describing the magical qualities of the different times of the day – where 'midnight's all a glimmer, and noon a purple glow' – and the peace he will achieve once he arrives. The poem taps into the soul's desire for harmony in natural surroundings, especially when 'stand[ing] on the roadway, or on the pavements grey'. The speaker is deep inside a daydream – a state of being I know all too well – and yearns to return to the 'lake water lapping with low sounds'.

Though we hadn't yet arrived home, I yearned to walk again through sacred corners of Ireland – wanting desperately to return to all those places where the spirits remain.

It shouldn't come as a surprise that Ireland drew me into a world of words. Nora Roberts once wrote that, "Ireland is a land of poets and legends, of dreamers and rebels. All of these have music woven through and around them. Tunes for dancing or for weeping, for battle or for love."

The country can boast one of the oldest forms of vernacular literature in the world. *Táin Bó Cúailnge* (or *The Cattle Raid of Cooley*), a story of a battle between Queen Medb and her husband written around the sixth century, is widely regarded as one of the first major epics in literature and storytelling. The mythic tradition has been a significant part of Irish literature for some time; tales of heroes and demigods and otherworldly events have been retold, reshaped and reused throughout the centuries.

Some might say it is the intervention of alcohol that has contributed to Irish literature (take James Joyce, Samuel Beckett or Brendan Behan as later examples), but one undeniable fact is that Ireland is steeped in a rich cultural (albeit chequered and turbulent) history that sets it apart from many others. The country and its people have been conquered and repressed and made to suffer at the hands of so many, and perhaps all these incursions ignited a culture and a literature as it struggled to fight back against suppression.

It can be argued then that the themes of nature and place have been surprisingly neglected in critical circles, despite the obvious engagement that authors and poets continue to have with both in their works. While cultural landscape is significant, so too is the physical landscape.

I heard of a young woman who, when crossing Ireland for the first time by train, wept for the entire journey. Overcome with the intense beauty of the countryside, she felt no other option but to take down the walls around her heart, drop her armour, and be open and vulnerable to all the visions that stir the soul.

Never thought that Ireland would have such an effect on me, but it did. And looking back on our time in the country over those eight days, I couldn't help but wonder how landscape, and the little interaction with the natural world, would continue to shape and inspire my own writing.

Back home, as the seasons changed from summer to fall, and then from fall to winter, my Irish bookshelf at the top of the stairs continued to grow. I researched, read travel memoirs, analyzed poetry, listened to music, attempted to learn the language, cooked stew and made soda bread. Still I found it difficult to summarize why I felt so connected to the land, history, myths, music, art, and the Irish people when someone asked why I was such a raging Hibernophile. The best thing, I decided, was to write it all down.

After shuffling through a crowd of people on the upper floor of Pike Place Market in Seattle, I bought a beautiful buffalo hide journal at a little kiosk. Later that day, as I sat overlooking the calm waters of the Pacific, I uncapped my fountain pen and wrote on the first page: 'There is a place I know called Ireland.'

CHAPTER 22

A PLEASANT HOUR ON THE WATER

In 1984, lighthouse keeper Paddy Ferriter watched from his post as a lone wild dolphin escorted the town's fishing boats to and from port. By August of that year, the dolphin was considered a permanent resident and, over time, became a playful, mischievous companion. Although it's not unique to find these social creatures living alone and befriending humans, Fungie was Ireland's first recorded occurrence.

Scientists and dolphin specialists are baffled as to why Fungie rarely ventures far from the mouth of the harbour. One story tells of a young female bottlenose dolphin that washed up on shore around the same time that Fungie arrived. Dolphins are thought to show great fidelity in relationships, and hopeless romantics hypothesize that Dingle's most famous resident stays to keep vigil.

Inspired by the ideas of English dolphin enthusiast Horace Dobbs, several sick people journeyed to West Kerry to be healed by Fungie in the early 1990s. Medical doctors and tourism websites were quick to add, however, that there have been no confirmed cases that a single person was cured of anything as a result of meeting Fungie. One website went as far as to post that they did 'not recommend swimming with dolphins as a substitute for professional therapy'. Whatever their reasons, streams of tourists still come to have their moment with this national treasure. Visitors today can either take an hour-long boat tour, or just take a selfie in front of the bronze statue.

The Dingle Boatmen's Association, 'comprising of seven passenger boats fully licensed by the Department of the Marine and manned by experienced and qualified crews', is responsible for the fleet that leave the harbour at regular intervals. Though the work may not be as romantic as life on the open ocean, the young crew make an honest day's pay, come home safe to their sweethearts, and are part of a successful business collective.

Still wasn't convinced, even with a pot of tea and a scone in my belly, that sixteen euros was worth a glimpse of the aging aquatic animal. And I wasn't sure if the boats were going out before tourist season officially began. But curiosity won out in the end.

A glass door next to a large poster of Fungie in all his frolicking glory was open. A young woman was texting on her phone behind a small desk.

"Excuse me."

"Oh, hello," she replied, putting down her phone. "Sorry about that. Can I help you?"

"Yes. I was hoping to head out today and see the dolphin."

"You can. Our next outing's not for forty-five minutes, though. But I can ring you through now, if you like, and then text you in about half an hour – to remind you."

"Actually, I don't have a phone on me. But you can ring me through, and I'll just go for a walk."

A little while later, I arrived to find a handful of tourists making their way to the pier. A young man in a thick sweater welcomed us aboard and I found a seat towards the back – wondering how rough the waters might be as I don't do well on small vessels. Pictured myself turning green and hanging over the side the entire time. Considered jumping back on the pier and asking for my money back, but refrained. 'Some adventures may require one to turn a little green, now and then,' I thought as the captain stood tall and cleared his throat.

"Welcome aboard," he announced. "We'll be off in just a minute here. Lovely day for it."

I took a few deep breaths of salty ocean air and calmed down.

"Fungie is being a bit standoffish today," he continued. "Had a little run-in with some other dolphins, y'see, that are passing through, but I'm sure he'll say hello. If everyone is safely aboard, we'll get ready to head out."

The wind picked up and cut through my layers of wool as the brilliant blues of ocean and sky reflected the amber sunshine. My nose froze and I curled my fingers into my new gloves before pressing them against my chest. Wrapped my scarf a little tighter around my neck.

There was a wide range of ages aboard. A retired couple snuggled in against each other, and a small boy sat on his mother's lap. A few couples in windbreakers held hands and looked out towards town. I was the only one travelling alone.

The young captain wore an air of confidence, and we were soon off to locate Fungie. A few other fishing boats were departing at the same time, all in radio contact. We puttered along and I felt oddly at peace, content to have forked over the equivalent of three pints for what was arguably the most touristy thing to do in West Kerry.

We cruised around the harbour for the next twenty minutes. The other boats kept in radio contact, but they too confirmed that the dolphin didn't want to be found. Another five or ten minutes went by, and I could tell the captain was getting concerned. A no-show meant full refunds. He adjusted his beat-up binoculars and continued to scan the waters.

Time ticked on. The captain radioed other boats, but no one had any firm location. The passengers huddled into each other, and I occasionally searched for the dolphin when I wasn't hugging myself to stay warm.

Half a dozen fishing boats, with nets coiled and hung to dry, were heading home across the harbour. It was the end of a long morning for those aboard, and I wondered if our captain ever plied the trade. It was not something I ever had romantic notions about. All of my fantasies take place on shore: living in a stone cottage with a fireplace, an aging wolfhound, and an antique writing desk – content to walk on solid ground and gaze out at the vast expanse.

We then made for open waters. It was a lot rougher than the harbour had been, and I took deep breaths to settle my stomach. But it wasn't working. Became more and more nauseous. Tried to keep an eye on the horizon and not look down at my cold fingers. Tried to think of comforting things.

"He doesn't usually head out of the harbour," said our captain, "but you never know. Just thought I'd have a look-about."

"Please hurry," I whispered.

For the next ten minutes we bobbed up and down, and rocked back and forth. I counted each slow minute.

There was still no sighting. The young captain checked his watch repeatedly. Picked up his binoculars and tried again. Suddenly, there was garbled excitement from over the radio. Our captain sat up, radioed back, and put the engine into gear.

A few minutes later, one woman pointed into the water. "I see him! I see him! Fungie's over there!"

He was barely breaking the surface of the water.

"There he is, folks," said the captain, with obvious relief. The dolphin didn't look very active, but it was nice to finally find the famed animal and conclude our tour. We followed Fungie around for a bit, and I wondered whether this was the same dolphin that had been frolicking in Dingle Bay since the mid-'80s.

The young captain seemed to read my mind. "You can tell that it's Fungie because there's a little nick on his fin," he said. "Bit of a tangle with a propeller about twenty years ago."

The dolphin surfaced near the boat and everyone (including myself) frantically snapped photos. Squinted against the light to see if I could spot the scarred fin, but decided it was best to let it go.

Once we had settled back into our seats, the captain turned the boat around and took us back. Happy to have met the little fellow, and it had been a pleasant hour on the water, but I was looking forward to being on solid ground again.

According to a local pamphlet, the Lighthouse Walk is 'ideal if you want to stretch your legs and take in some sea air. There are a number of interesting stopping points along the route, taking in flora and fauna, sprinkled with some local history.' Sounded just up my alley.

The trail, worn by the constant rhythm of gentle feet,

carried me along. Couples strolled ahead, hand-in-hand. Birds soared in the wind spirals. It was low tide and the seaweed that clung to the rocks glistened as the sun-kissed waters flooded the world in wondrous light. Small sailboats crisscrossed the harbour as a few tourists hugged the shore on rented stand-up paddleboards. A woman threw sticks for her Labrador on the beach. I found myself stopping often to fill my lungs with the briny breeze – content to be in the moment.

The entrance to Dingle Bay (*Bá an Daingin*) is distinguished by the ruins of a mysterious Victorian-looking tower called Hussey's Folly. Built in 1845, it was presumably erected by Land Agent R.M. Hussey to provide work for locals during the Famine. The building was later used as a customs watchtower, but now serves only as shade for those weary of the sun (on those rare days when too much sun is an issue). If nothing else, it adds some flair to the harbour and I took a moment to catch my breath in its shadow.

Half a dozen others were sitting on the steps and looking out towards the ocean. Whitewashed with red trim, the picturesque cottage adjoining the lighthouse tower has been unoccupied for over ten years but the automatic red light is still functional. Across the harbour is Eask Tower, built in 1847. Another famine relief project, it was built of solid stone and stands twelve meters.

The warmth of the sunshine parried the bitter wind that blew off the open ocean as the day's glorious crescendo washed over me. The lapping waters, the call of ocean birds, the puttering boats, the gentle applause of wind through the grasses, and the snippets of conversations seemed to reject any notion of melody, harmony or structure – and yet, despite the suspended patterns and displaced rhythms, a sense of joyous inspiration welled up inside of me.

Toyed again with the idea of buying a small house with a garden plot where I'd live out my final years in relative simplicity. My days would be punctuated with nothing more than gentle strolls through town and along the harbour. With my pen and notebook in hand, I'd jot down a few notes while having a cup of tea or downing a couple of pints or sitting by the fire as darkness takes over the world.

There was no doubt I was glorifying the charming little town, nestled comfortably in the bay, but I couldn't deny the overwhelming feeling that this was where I belonged. Fully aware that no place is perfect, and that daily frustrations exist everywhere, I wanted desperately to stay longer.

In no rush to return, I pushed aside my new gloves and found a local guidebook I had purchased a few days earlier. Hadn't yet taken the time to review the history so, with my time in Dingle quickly coming to close, found the bookmarked page and dove in.

CHAPTER 23

A STRONG AND VIBRANT CULTURE

Evidence of human occupation on the Dingle Peninsula spans six and a half thousand years, so it's safe to assume that the history of Dingle Town dates several millennia.

There is some mystery surrounding the proper name for the town – *Daingean Uí Chúis*, or O'Cush's Fortress. Some have speculated that it is a corruption of Hussey (or Huysse), a Flemish family that came to the area in the thirteenth century. The earliest reference to the town in Anglo-Norman is Dengen in 1252, but a document in 1290 refers to it as Dengynhuysse. Some scholars point to the *The Annals of the Four Masters*, compiled by four Franciscan friars between 1632 and 1636, which refer to a local chieftain named O Cuis (who ruled the area prior to the Norman invasion).

Though the town itself wasn't mentioned until 1252, it is thought that there was a settlement at present day Dingle sometime before 1216. When the Norman settlers arrived to the area in the thirteenth century, they developed the harbour into a substantial trading port. Butter, wool, hides, fish and meat were exported. Coal, salt, clothes and wine were imported. The town was laid out in a typical Norman pattern, with a long main street and lots of gardens and green space behind the houses.

The *Annals of Inisfallen* relay the Raid of Kerry in 1316 that, in turn, sparked off a war between the Normans and the Gaels throughout Ireland. It was probably after this raid that the town of Dingle was first walled, enclosing an area of six hectares.

By the fourteenth century, Dingle was a major centre of trade, particularly with Spain and France. Merchants' houses were built of Spanish design, and visitors to Dingle can still find small, decorated stones of Spanish influence set into the outside walls. English traders referred to Dengen as Dengle by the turn of the century.

The Spanish weren't just interested in trade. They combined with Irish rebel forces against the English in 1580 during the Desmond Wars (or the Desmond Rebellions). The earldom of Desmond was the greatest single lordship in Ireland but, despite the earl's reluctance to oppose the English, he was eventually forced to resist by military means in two campaigns: between 1569 and 1573, and again from 1579 to 1583. This rebellion was as much about religion as it was about land, and the wars almost destroyed Munster. Eventually this resulted in the Munster Plantation of the late 1580s, which saw extensive settlement of English colonists on the Desmond lands.

The Spanish intervention was tragically unsuccessful. The English massacred almost all the Spanish (and Papal Italian) forces. The Irish part of the rebellion was just as ruthlessly put down: the Earl of Ormond, known as the Black Earl, killed men, women and children, took livestock, and destroyed crops and houses across the peninsula. The

English army targeted churches as part of their efforts to break the spirit of the Irish, deliberately un-roofing them and burning their contents. (Once peace had returned, the Anglican Church maintained some of the old churches, but most were abandoned and left to ruin by the early eighteenth century. Of the nineteen medieval parish churches, only St James' Church in Dingle remains in use today. The only substantial remains are to be found at Stradbally (*An Sráidbhaile*) and Kilmalkedar.)

History goes well with a snack, I decided as a 'rumbly in my tumbly' broke the silence. Pulled out a bag of Keogh's crinkle cut crisps, washed it down with orange Fanta and – after wiping my greasy fingers on my pants – dove back in.

In 1585, Queen Elizabeth announced her intention of granting Dingle a charter, setting up a town corporation, and providing for the building of a wall to enclose the commercial quarter of the town. The charter was finally granted in 1607 and provided an administrative and electoral framework.

Dingle was yet again drawn into warfare between 1596 and 1603. What begun in Ulster with the rising of Uí Néill and Ó Dónaill against the English, soon spread to Munster. The local leader, William, Knight of Kerry, attempted to remain neutral during the early stages of the war, and refused the rebels admittance to his castle in Dingle in 1600. But his attempts to safeguard his position and property by maintaining a precarious balance between the English and rebellious Irish failed. When William publicly favoured the rebellion, the English army soon took the castles from the knight and suppressed the rebellion.

The English parliament then declared all Irish Catholic estates forfeited. This forced Irish Catholics of both English and Gaelic origin to form the Confederation of Kilkenny to defend their interests and to support King Charles I against his opponents in the civil war that was engulfing Ireland, England and Scotland.

Despite this upheaval, a certain amount of trade, farming and fishing continued. Dingle's foreign trade (both legal and illegal) consisted mainly of exports of butter and hides, and importation of wine, brandy, tea, tobacco and household goods. There was also a lucrative trade in raw wool and yarn.

Thankfully, there was an upturn in the economy in the mid-eighteenth century with the introduction of the linen industry. Tenant farmers were obliged under the Linen Act of 1666 to plant flax on a sixtieth part of all tilled land, and the Irish Linen Board subsidized the importation of high-quality flax seed from North America and its distribution at reduced rates in Ireland. In 1732, the Knight of Kerry imported superior quality seed on his own account at Dingle and Valentia. By 1751, there were twelve spinning schools in Kerry – one of which was in Dingle.

In 1792, a small band of Irish émigrés launched one of the most daring rescue plans in history: to free Queen Marie Antoinette from Temple Prison and bring her to safety in Dingle. James Louis Rice, a military intelligence officer of the Holy Roman Emperor Joseph II, masterminded the plan and the interior on the upper floor of Rice House was remodelled in the French style. The jailers had been bribed, and the plan was about to be put into action, but the ill-fated French queen decided instead to remain with her family.

I stuffed the remains of my snack away and stood up to stretch. Rubbed my legs warm as a young couple strolled past me to find their own chunk of stone. Then I returned to my book.

Major changes hit the textile industry in Ireland in the early nineteenth century, and Dingle's linen-based prosperity was over. Power spinning in cotton and linen resulted in a dramatic shift from domestic and rural industry to factory-based industry in cities and large towns. By the 1820s, the linen trade was all but gone from Dingle. The collapse came at a time when the population all over Ireland was rising rapidly – in Dingle it had reached nearly five thousand – and the decline of domestic industry was inducing chronic levels of unemployment and poverty. It was at this time that the majority of people living in the impoverished west of the country became almost exclusively dependent on the potato as a source of nourishment.

The people of Dingle suffered terribly during the Potato Famine of 1845-48. It is considered to be the worst tragedy in Ireland's history, and even today evidence of that tragedy can still be seen. Particularly prominent in the west and southwest of the country, famine walls and famine roads stretch along the rolling hills of Connemara, the Burren and the Dingle Peninsula. These walls and roads were merely to provide work and distraction, and they often led nowhere before stopping abruptly. The famine caused Ireland's population to drop from eight million to six million. One million died while another million emigrated under threat of starvation. The population of the country still hasn't recovered to pre-famine numbers.

Emigration, far from being a short-lived consequence, became a fact of life for succeeding generations. Many tenants, suffering from poverty and unable to pay rents, were evicted in the latter part of the nineteenth century. In the aftermath of the famine and mass emigration, and the stirrings of Fenian rebellion, the Roman Catholic Church established decisive allegiance and power.

Rebellion once again came in the form of the Land War (1879-90). The Irish National Land League was dedicated to bettering the position of tenant farmers and ultimately to a redistribution of land – especially from absentee landlords. Reforms in the law enabled tenants to buy their land with money loaned by the state and a new middle class took over from the landed aristocracy. This also brought about the rise of the nationalist movement.

Fifty years after the appalling tragedy of the famine, an astonishing revival took place. Landlordism had been defeated and a rediscovery of the strengths in Ireland's cultural tradition – its language, literature and sports – was fuelling a political movement for independence from Britain. The Dingle Peninsula, as a repository of the Irish language and culture, became a focus for the national movement and a stronghold of a new republicanism.

Dingle did not play a significant role in the Easter Rising in 1916, though volunteers did march into Tralee. In the subsequent War of Independence, the IRA carried out a number of relatively small-scale attacks on British forces and destroyed police barracks at Annascaul, Ballyferriter, Camp, Castlegregory and Cloghane (*Abhainn an Scáil, Baile an Fheirtéaraigh, An Com, Caisleán Ghriaire* and *An Clochán*), leaving only the Dingle barracks intact. In the Civil War (1919-21), Dingle remained overwhelmingly republican. The Dingle barracks were destroyed, as was the coast guard station. Towards the end of the conflict, Free State troops landed at the pier and took over the town.

The Irish Free State was the name initially given to the twenty-six of the thirty-two counties after the War of Independence. It was set up under the Anglo-Irish Treaty and signed by British and Irish representatives at the end of 1921. Peace and the Free State brought no new prosperity to

Dingle and, as in other parts of the country, large numbers of young people continued to emigrate. The area remained industrially underdeveloped, its economy and employment prospects almost exclusively centred on fishing and farming.

The Irish language was given prominence in the civil service (and in education in the Free State), and visitors came to the area west of Dingle to brush up where it was still in everyday use. Scholars came too, both from Ireland and abroad. But the real boom in tourism came in the wake of the filming of *Ryan's Daughter*. A large proportion of the massive budget for the film was spent on location in Dingle and the direct impact of this sudden injection of money into an impoverished area, which had not yet felt the benefits of the general improvement in the Irish economy, was considerable.

Despite some diversification in opportunities, the bulk of employment in Dingle remained in agriculture, fishing and tourism. While agriculture remained important to the local economy, the policies of the European Union left many farmers demoralized; as in other parts of Ireland, farmers had been trying to explore and develop agritourism and other alternatives. Dingle's attraction for the continental and American tourists increased in the 1970s and '80s to offset the decline in English tourists (which occurred as a consequence of the war in the North) and the presence of Fungie the dolphin brought about a boom in tourism in the late 1980s.

A substantial development of the harbour between 1989 and 1992 resulted in a dramatic increase in the number of tonnage of boats fishing out in Dingle. This increased employment both on water and on shore. However, the prices for catches were low, and many other problems made the fishing industry a lost opportunity for the port. Increased tourism benefitted proprietors of tourist-related businesses, but a large proportion of the jobs in the restaurants and hotels were only seasonal.

Dingle enjoyed new prosperity in the 1990s. New supermarkets, renovated public houses, freshly painted private homes and an increased number of guesthouses showed a level of activity and available income that compared well with other communities in Ireland. While the permanent population of the town declined to about fourteen hundred, those who worked and studied elsewhere returned regularly and frequently.

Today, there is a strong and vibrant culture in the town and surrounding area. Renewed enthusiasm for local traditions such as Wren's Day are evident. On St. Stephen's Day (December 26), crowds of people dress in motley clothing, wear masks or straw suits and take to the streets with accompanying musicians to celebrate a festival that long predates Christmas.

While the hilltop assemblies of Lughnasadh and the celebrations at holy wells are no more, the peninsula's various events and festivals make up for it. Those especially interested in boats and horses, or the Irish language and music, or walking, hiking and running will find no shortage of groups, gatherings or informative guidebooks.

Although County Kerry has featured in many films over the years, from *Ryan's Daughter* to *Far and Away* to scenes in *Harry Potter*, it was the release of two films in recent years that put the area on the movie map again – *The Lobster* (starring Colin Farrell and Rachel Weisz) and *Star Wars Episode VII: The Force Awakens*. Both ignited plans by Kerry County Council and Fáilte Ireland to promote the area as a tourist destination for fans and filmmakers alike. Recent figures show that the number of visitors (both domestic and overseas) to Kerry now sits at over a million-and-a-half.

WALKING BACK along the water's edge, I thought about the ever-unfolding history of this remarkable corner of the world. The ancient peoples and what inspired them when the sun did battle on early mornings. Those that arrived from far away and the stories they told as night fell. The wild Atlantic – how it gives and takes – and all the celebrations of life and light amongst the cold stone. Thought about the fog and mist, and frigid fingers and noses, and about the quilted greens of the countryside. The gods and goddesses and mythologies; the lives of great men and women; the manners, customs and pastimes across the centuries; the music and art and poetry; the little pebbles that disturb the stillness of the pond.

And then I was thirsty, and figured it was time to finally try the locally brewed beer: Crean's Irish Lager, from the Dingle Brewing Company. A seaman and explorer from Annascaul (half-an-hour east of Dingle), Tom Crean was a member of three major expeditions to Antarctica during what is known as the Heroic Age of Antarctic Exploration. During Captain Scott's 1911-13 Terre Nova Expedition, Crean walked fifty-six kilometres on his own across the Ross Ice Shelf to save the life of Edward Evans. This led to him receiving the Albert Medal. He then moved back to County Kerry in 1920 where he and his wife opened a pub called The South Pole Inn. He passed away in 1938. In July 2003, Crean was captured in a bronze statue. It depicts him holding a pair of hiking poles in one hand and two sled dog pups in the other.

That evening, I found a near-empty restaurant, dined on stew and soda bread, and then digested in my room while madly researching and writing in my journal. I was interested in learning more about *Tír na nÓg* – the supernatural realm of everlasting youth, health, abundance and joy. In the Irish myth cycles, it is the place where the *fae* live and heroes visit on quests. It is just outside the domain of humankind, off to the west, where there is no illness or death or time but only happiness and beauty. It can only be reached by way of magic.

The concept of the poet as seer, particularly as possessor of second sight, is related to and reinforced by the early Irish belief in the Otherworld. While the boundless knowledge that was to be found in *Tír na NÓg* was generally hidden from mortals, it was not wholly inaccessible to them. Attainable through contact with various Otherworld entities and locations, a class of men known as *filid* claimed to be able, by practicing certain rites, to acquire as much of this supernatural knowledge as was required for a particular purpose.

Illusion and transformation are themes found in Otherworld literature from the earliest period to the twentieth century. Because of its connection with knowledge, the Land of the Youth is a factor in the literature of inspiration in the ancient texts as well as medieval stories rife with characters that have visions, go into trances, are part of a prophesy, and so on. The *aisling* (or vision poem) developed during the late seventeenth and eighteenth centuries in Irish language poetry, in which the poet has a vision of an otherworldly woman – sometimes young and beautiful, and other times old and haggard. This female figure is generally referred to in the poems as a *spéirbhean* (heavenly woman). She laments the current state of the

Irish people and predicts an imminent revival of their fortunes.

These literary genres reinforce the view that the poet's second sight, including the ability to see into the future and have a clear vision of the norms by which humans live, is related to the poet's role as mediator between the human world and the Otherworld. Though I held little interest in combing through the old tales on this particular trip, I was certainly intrigued. Even wondering, had I lived in an earlier time, if I would be considered a *filí* and could see what others could not.

Other stories relay the island of Hy-Brasil. Legend has it that the mysterious land lies shrouded in mist, hidden from the eyes of mortals. One day, every seven years, the fog rolls back to reveal its distant splendour to anyone who might be looking.

But Hy-Brasil isn't just mentioned in fairy tales. It first appeared on a map made in 1325 by Italian cartographer Angelino Dulcert, and continued to be shown on maps until the 1860s. Meteorologists claim that Hy-Brasil is nothing more than a mirage, produced when layers of hot and cold air over the sea bend light rays that reflect banks of fog (or icebergs, or some such natural phenomenon) – thus creating the optical illusion of a misty island on the horizon – but explorers through the ages have shared a compulsion to find this enigmatic isle. In 1480, and again in 1481, expeditions set out from the port of Bristol and were apparently successful. In 1497, John Cabot (sent by King Henry VII to find North America) was said to have 'found the land previously visited by the men of Bristol'. Other explorers claimed to have seen the island and return with fantastical tales that include large black rabbits and a lone magician in a stone castle.

Some have speculated that Hy-Brasil is actually Baffin Island, off the coast of Northern Canada, or the Faroe Islands, or Porcupine Bank (a raised area of the seabed discovered two hundred kilometres west of Ireland, with its highest point only two hundred meters below sea level).

Mythology is full of ancient islands that have disappeared – the most famous being Atlantis – and while it might be impossible to prove that any of them existed, perhaps rumours stem from at least a grain of truth.

I like to think, as I wandered alone on the edge of the Atlantic, that there was always a bit of magic in the air – that perhaps I was invited to slip in and out of both realms, and was privy to that which is reserved for only a select few. Later, after walking down the hill and into town, nestling myself into a pub and throwing back a couple of pints while listening to traditional music and the cacophony of a dozen conversations, I decided that I would no longer doubt my otherworldly adventures or my conversation with the *cait sidhe*. I would accept it as truth, whether anyone else believed me or not.

On my way back up to the B&B, my mind whirling into little river eddies and then speeding across expanding galaxies, I felt a part of this world and the exquisite beauty found in everyday moments. Felt grounded and connected and content. And yet I also felt as if I were looking down from far above, watching time unfold over the centuries.

Thought back to my theory that the country is a land of contrasts, where history and myth seamlessly interlace with each other. And then it dawned on me that what made Ireland so appealing was not necessarily its duality, but the fuzziness or the blurring between the two realms. The hint that there is something beyond, just out of reach. Something that catches the light through the *féth fíada*, stirring the imagination and causing one to believe in something beyond that which can be easily explained.

Nothing ever is as it seems to be in Ireland. There is never a definitive truth. There is no one or the other – no black or white – but always a story or a song. Always a smirk or a wink. The country must be enormously frustrating for mathematicians. But perfect for someone like me.

CHAPTER 24

A BRUTAL, BLEAK EXISTENCE

The warmth of the sun's rays through the window on my face and the sound of lambs from next door woke me an hour before breakfast. Shimmied across the bed, sat on the edge, and looked out at the peaceful pastoral setting I had come to savour every morning at Dúinín House. No one seemed in a rush, nor was there much traffic on the street. An older gentleman passed by on his horse-drawn carriage.

It was my last full day on the Dingle Peninsula, and I wanted it to unfold organically and reveal little surprises as every other day had done. If the skies had opened and flooded the world with a miserable downpour, I might have taken a day off from exploring to sit in a pub and organize my notes. But with only a day left before driving east, I decided it best to putter around Slea Head Drive one final time.

Flipped through my guidebook on the dashboard of the rental car and found reference to a collection of *clochán* at Fahan. They are described as the most remarkable of any in all of Ireland. "You can't beat that," I said to the empty seat next to me.

A little while later, a faded sign on the side of an old stone building directed me to the 'prehistoric beehive huts'. While not entirely truthful, it did confirm I was in the right place.

An older gentleman was sitting in his hut at the foot of the path, listening to RTÉ on a small radio. The antennae reached almost to the ceiling. Paid him a couple euros and was about to continue towards the site with just a friendly nod, but I stopped to watch a few colourfully painted sheep munching away. I inquired as to their appearance.

"Ah, yah, that's for identifying them, y'know. They graze all the days, on the wide-open fields, shared by the farmers here round. When it comes time to claim them – the ownership and such – a customized sheep is easy to pick out."

Turned to look at the animals in various shades of pinks and blues.

"During mating season," he continued, "the rams'll be fitted with a bag of dye around its neck and chest. A bit of colour will show up on the ewe's upper back, y'know, and so then we know that the girls've been mounted. We can move the fellows around, then, to do their business."

I was getting better at following the thick West Kerry brogue, but still had to work at it.

"*Go raibh maith agat*," I said, trying out my Irish.

"*Tá fáilte romhat*," he answered with a smile.

The Fahan Beehive Huts, also known as Caher Conor (*Cathair na gConchuireach*), consists of five buildings – probably once single-family dwellings attached to each other with interconnecting doorways. Since stone huts of the same design have been built since Neolithic times, it's difficult to date the Fahan *clocháin*, but most agree that hermit Christian monks may have built some of the earliest (probably dating to the twelfth century, when Norman invaders forced farmers from the more prosperous areas to move to the marginal lands of the Dingle Peninsula). No mortar was used in their construction. The hillside at one time had over four hundred of the drystone, corbelled structures. Archeologists have been hard pressed to explain this extraordinary concentration. One theory is that those living in Fahan may have been working the land; another theory is that the beehive huts are associated with the local pilgrimage route. They may have provided accommodation for those arriving by sea, and would have served as an early form of bed and breakfast.

To my untrained eye, the thicker circular walls of the Fahan huts did seem an improvement from the earlier stonework at Dunbeg. It also helps to note that Caher Conor is kept in good condition with regular maintenance carried out by the Office of Public Works and, as they are located further up from the ocean cliffs, they are in no immediate danger of slipping away into the crashing waves.

While the complex wouldn't have allowed for a lot of privacy, I could understand why a group of people on the edge of nowhere would have felt it wise to build these huts within close proximity of each other. Whether monks, farmers or pilgrims, it would have been a brutal, bleak existence with less-than-ideal weather and food, but with the right amount of sheepskin blankets, wool sweaters and felted boots it would have at least been cozy. And there would have been a real sense of community. Laughter and love. And hope.

Beehive huts can be found in great number in County

Kerry. The most well-known examples are found at the monastic settlement on nearby Skellig Michael, recently used as a backdrop for *Episode VII* and *Episode VIII* of the Star Wars movies. A UNESCO World Heritage Site, this early Christian monastery (dated between the sixth and eighth centuries) clings to the steep cliffs of an isolated rocky island situated to the west of the Iveragh Peninsula. Wishing to emulate the sacrifice and withdrawal into a life of faith, early Irish monks found the remote islands a perfect place to settle. The monastic ideal was to demonstrate an intense devotion by such extreme acts of self-exile, and no Irish monastery was built in such a challenging location. If life at Caher Conor was tough, it was nothing compared to life at Skellig Michael (*Sceilg Mhichíl*).

There was one more significant archeological site that I was interested in checking out: The Gallarus Oratory.

A television bolted to a high corner of the small visitors' centre was loudly blasting a football game. The young man behind the counter was undisturbed by the little bell that announced my arrival. He didn't lower the volume.

"Just you, is it?"

"It is," I answered.

"Ah, grand." All this while he kept his eyes fixed towards the screen. One of the benefits of working before the tourist season officially begins is that you get to watch the game without being disturbed too often.

A fine display of framed photographs and hangings adorn the walls but I didn't linger long. Walked out the back door, along the crushed stone walkway, past lush green lawns and a low stone fence, and then stood in awe at the site itself.

Called 'a most perfect early stone building' and the 'most distinctive single monument of the Dingle Peninsula', the Gallarus Oratory (*Séipéilín Ghallarais*) represents the height of drystone corbelling. It is thought, for this reason, to be later than most oratories (or small chapels). Still, its date has been the subject of much argument – as is often the case in Ireland. Most oratories were built in the seventh and eighth centuries, but the refinement of its construction and its arched east window suggest that Gallarus was built much later. The name is open to several interpretations as well, but one possibility is that it signifies a 'house for foreigners', referring to the people who came from outside the area to take part in the pilgrimage.

The shape of the oratory is similar to that of an upturned boat. It has a door in the west wall that is wider at the base than the top, and a small window in the east wall. The flat-headed or lintelled doorway most likely contained a wooden door or a curtain hung over the entrance, as a line of stones above the doorway suggests.

Though I could understand how someone might form rough walls of stone to create barriers against animals or protection against raiding tribes, I could not begin to fathom how someone could create a stone hut where everything fit so perfectly together to create such sharp lines while preventing any rainwater from getting in.

Light patterned the rough walls inside. Through the back window shone the colours of Ireland against a foreground of grey, and I pressed my hands to the stone that had been smoothed by all those before me. Thought about the pilgrims that gathered here – in this 'core of old dark' – and their short prayers as they looked down at their feet, or towards the mountain, or at the fading light of day. Wondered if they too felt some sense of connection: either to the earth, or each other, or a higher power. Did they breathe in the sweetness in the air and think of home? Did they hear music in the wind and smile at the memory of a song or a lullaby? Did they gaze out towards the sea from the doorway, and wonder when they would look into the eyes of their children again?

Gallarus Oratory possesses an austere simplicity and reminds casual visitors of those long ago who created a sacred space from what was buried in the soil. There is a sense that every stone was taken with tender care, and that every element still possesses the heartbeat of the country. Like so many other secluded sites across the peninsula, Gallarus continues to shelter the weary traveller from both the physical and emotional hardships of life.

Looking again out the back window, I thought about all those that gathered to construct the oratory. And if I listened closely, I could hear them breathing – could hear them inhale and exhale, as the ocean ebbs and flows. Could hear them strain as they stacked one stone on top of another. Could see my reflection in their eyes like the waters of quiet coves – all the colours of memories long ago and dreams of what may one day be.

And I felt at peace. Didn't feel isolated or lonely or afraid. Instead, I felt comforted – and knew that those long ago had felt the same. They too had felt a sense of community at the edge of the known world, and that the light from within would conquer whatever darkness shadowed the land.

Since our earliest history, we have drawn inspiration from ancient archeological sites. Because these places require our imagination to fill in what we don't (and may never) know, they have always been associated with the occult and with dreams. They are places an observer can get lost – where time slips away. Ancient Hebrew poets found inspiration in the ruins of Sumer, Assyria and Babylon. One of the primary literary tropes for pre-Islamic Arabic poets was known as *wuquf 'ala al-atlal* (stopping by the ruins). In their poems, ancient sites are spectral and ephemeral things. In the words of sixth-century poet Tarafa, they 'appear and fade, like the trace of a tattoo on the back of a hand.'

Like many others, ancient sites make me feel connected to cultural memory. They fill me with an evocative melancholy and allow for moments of stillness in an otherwise busy life. While modern-day ruins reflect traumatic and horrific memories, the ruins of the ancient past are still places where time stands still, where the ghostly presence of history can be felt, and where one can lose one's self in contemplative silence.

Places like Gallarus Oratory allow us to step away from a version of history that is distorted to suit present moral sensibilities and political agendas. It reminds us that we are all participating in a shared story, and are not merely a constellation of individuals travelling different orbital paths.

While I have found some level of solace and comfort and inspiration in the endless expanse of desert in southern Arabia or among tall cedars that tower in the coastal rainforests of Vancouver Island, it is the evidence of those that lived long ago that continues to excite me, affect me and propel me forward. It is not just because they prompt a melancholic meditation on the fragility and folly of civilization, or because of a near-permanence that is so missing in our rapidly assembled and continuously rebuilt landscape, but because ruins are only partial information – the remnants of a much larger, more layered and complex living entity. It is within this partial knowledge that creative interpretation and fantastical imaginings ignite.

. . .

THOUGH SLEA HEAD Drive is dangerously narrow, and the sharp blind corners would make a believer of staunch atheists, I drove on without worry and hummed along to the radio. When the road finally widened, I spied a hand-painted sign that read: CAFÉ. Another sign further along read: HOME BAKING. It seemed silly to pass on home-baked goods and a lovely cup of tea.

The two-story stone house appears inviting and well-kept from the outside. The trim painted white, and the sunroom – painted white with red trim – looks like a peaceful place to watch the Atlantic storms approach from the west. There are a couple outdoor sets of wooden tables and chairs, and a bench under the main window.

The top half of the Dutch door was open to let in fresh air. The only thing missing was people. "Hello," I said, announcing myself.

It was dark inside, but my eyes soon adjusted. The small living room, with an old couch in pink paisley along one wall, is sparsely decorated. There are a couple sets of small tables and chairs to accommodate visitors, but the focal point of the room is the fireplace. It takes up an entire wall. The brickwork is stained with age and soot. A motley collection of cast iron fireplace tools and a set of bellows hang beside it. There was a small fire burning – enough the cut the damp – and a couple thin cushions on either side.

"You've very welcome," said an elderly woman wearing a hand-sewn apron. She seemed the quintessential grandmother and was hunched over with age as she moved slowly across the room.

"Here is a menu for you. Take your time. I'll be back in a bit, so."

Wasn't sure how much time I needed. There were only two food options and two drink options. For food there was either scones and jam, or homemade pie. For drinks there was either tea or coffee. Suspected the coffee was instant.

"Have you decided?" she asked about five minutes later.

"I'll have some tea, please... and homemade pie."

"Ah, yes. Forgot to mention I'm out of pie today."

"Okay. Guess I'll have scones and jam, then."

"Good choice," she said and disappeared back into the kitchen.

Listened to the gentle crackling of the fire and settled into my chair. There were little tokens of the church lined up to one side of the windowsill. There was also an old issue of *National Geographic* and a couple books missing their dust jackets.

The clouds retreated across the sky as the waves crashed and the winds blew. Though they had battled most of the morning, the sun had ultimately defeated the fog and was now lighting the front of the room in golden hues. A young couple in rain jackets pulled up and sat down at one of the outdoor sets. The man had a large camera, which he carefully placed next to his chair. Together they flipped through a guidebook.

"Are you having a grand day out?" the elderly woman asked as she placed the tray on my table.

"I am, thank you."

Thought she might continue the conversation – comment on the weather, perhaps – but instead she disappeared into the kitchen and I was left to my own devices.

The elderly woman and a man likely to be her husband were quibbling in the kitchen about something I couldn't make out. Maybe she was running out of cream and was giving him a hard time for not refilling the fridge. Or maybe she was cursing her decision not to make pie, and somehow he was to blame.

Didn't stay to find out. After warming my hands by the dying fire, I paid with coins from my pocket and headed out.

Nearby Coumeenoole Beach (*Com Dhíneol*) also featured in *Ryan's Daughter*, and a commemorative rock stands on the edge of the shoreline engraved with the name of the movie. There were also a number of cars in the parking lot. (Actually it was only three, but it seemed like a lot after having the peninsula largely to myself for the past week.) A man sold Nutella crêpes from a small food truck.

A wide staircase of paving stones led me to where a mountain stream carves up the tight bay. Dark shadows give the beach a claustrophobic feel, but the water shimmered with light as it filtered through the cold sand. Young families walked around in tight circles, making trails of footprints with their bare feet, and the sounds of children at play echoed off the rocky cliffs.

As I untied my shoes, and sank my toes into the sand, I thought about the couple opening their house as a café. Though the elderly woman and her husband were preoccupied in the kitchen and weren't interested in a chat, I appreciated that there was no performance. They didn't dance a jig or play a tune on the fiddle. Weren't selling t-shirts or snow globes. There was no attempt to sell Ireland. They were merely providing a service to those needing a break in their day.

The idea was such a foreign concept back home. Not sure if it's an issue of fear – of strangers or food prep regulations or having enough insurance – or if we've merely lost our desire to meet new people, but I hope in time we will open our doors again and invite strangers to sit by the fire. Maybe we'll run out of pie, but that will be okay.

Some may argue that rural Ireland is no longer the quaint place it once was, and that the entire country has become grossly modernized. But, despite modern conveniences and the widespread use of televisions and computers, the Irish are still unafraid of quiet moments for reflection.

Unlike many of us living across the pond, they know that failing to spend time walking along the water's edge, climbing mountains, sitting on stone fences, strolling among the ruins, or taking tea by the dying embers of a small fire may forever quiet the secrets told in soft whispers. They know that failing to spend time focusing on haunting melodies, the gentle ebb and flow of the tide that mirrors our breath, the seabirds that ride the thermals, or the wildflowers that carpet the clifftops may forever quiet the voices that give us permission to laugh at nothing or weep slow, dirty tears. What would it take, I wonder, for that to happen again here? Must something monumental occur to remind us that we are best when we are connected to something beyond ourselves?

Thought I might indulge in a quick pint – just to tide me over. Sidling up to the bar and resting my elbows where so many had done before, I could understand why pubs are still the social hubs of any Irish community. There is something glorious about slipping into the dark in the middle of the day and escaping the hubbub of the streets.

Dick Mack's was not so busy that I needed to shout my order. Savoured my pint, lost myself in the wall of whiskeys, and then looked around to find three older men sitting shoulder to shoulder. They seemed quietly content to sip their drinks and enjoy each one another's company with their caps askew and tweed jackets draped over thin frames.

The barman, with a small towel over one shoulder, watched the world go by. He occasionally made eye contact with the men, and they answered back with a nod.

"Excuse me," I said as the barman walked towards me. "Wonder if I might ask you a question?"

"If it pleases you," he answered.

"I've been trying to figure something out," I began. "A lot of tourists come over to see where their great-grandparents lived, and they want to find their ancestral home or maybe dig around the archives. It seems to be the thing to do these days. But there are many others who come to Ireland because they feel some strange attraction to the land or the people or the culture – maybe it's the music or art or poetry or whatever. Maybe the drink."

"It could very well be the drink..."

"Yeah, maybe," I said with a smirk. "But besides that, do you have any insight as to what makes this country so attractive to so many people?"

"That's a fair question," replied the barman as he took a deep breath and stretched the kinks from his neck and back. "Not sure I'm the one to give you the best answer. But, since you're asking, I'd have to say it's because nothing much happens around here with too much worry. Look around you, and you see life unfolding without anyone getting trampled – like they might in some big American city. And no one's in a rush, y'know. No one here is forgotten and, if anyone needs a helping hand, someone'll come forward. We look out for each other. Dublin might be different, but I don't think so."

"You make a good point about the pace of life. I get the

sense that Ireland – rural Ireland, especially – unwinds at a pace more conducive to contemplation."

The barman laughed. "It sounds like you're on to something, there."

The table of older men needed another round, so our conversation came to an end.

While savouring my pint, I realized that for the most part I had focused on those who had lived long ago. On the communities that once were, without reflecting much on those that still exist. But of course there is still a sense of community in rural (and even urban) areas of the country. The people are just as welcoming and caring than ever before. Perhaps it's not always easy to see that while tearing across the country in the comfort of a rental car, or when wandering alone, but it is there. (And always will be.)

Centuries of turmoil, conquest and famine – and subsequent immigration – have certainly taken their toll on the Irish. But it has left them with a deliciously dark sense of humour and a welcoming attitude towards strangers.

Paid for my drink, and wandered without direction down back alleys as the shadows stretched across the streets. As the town emptied and the shop doors were locked for the night, I disappeared inside my head once again. In a roundabout kind of way, my thoughts turned to the Wicklow woods in the east of the country. Of St. Kevin and his monastic settlement. Paula and I had spent most of a day hiking around Glendalough without saying much to each other as we cherished the quiet and were reminded how much we both appreciate the absence of noise.

CHAPTER 25

A CRUCIAL INGREDIENT TO CREATIVITY

I've been escorted out of dance clubs more than once. After falling asleep in a back room somewhere, sprawled out on a filthy couch, I've been repeatedly woken up by security and shown the front door. The burly, heavily tattooed men all assumed I had consumed large amounts of alcohol, but this was rarely the case. I had usually fallen asleep because I was exhausted from writing papers and studying for exams. But what ultimately drained the life out of me were the annoying young people paying outrageous prices for mediocre cocktails in tight quarters as terrible music boomed through towering speakers. For years, I felt compelled to take part in these late-night frivolities. Other university students seemed to be enjoying themselves, and I often wondered why I couldn't just relax and have a good time.

Almost twenty years have passed since my failed attempts to boogie-woogie with the hip kids, but I'm no better at pretending to have a good time in crowded rooms. I avoid house parties, go for afternoon coffee half-an-hour before the bookstore closes, and shop for groceries after dinner when I'm less likely to have to make small talk with a dozen people whose names I forget. Some may label me as shy or selectively social or even pretentious (and they may be right), but I prefer the term 'introverted'.

Teaching is a highly social profession, so it would follow that all teachers must be extroverts. But that's not true. While I enjoy lunching with other teachers and chatting with parents, I am desperate for a cup of tea and a sleeping cat in a sunbeam by four o'clock.

I experience mixed emotions when dealing with extroverts. Sometimes I'm jealous at how easily this half of the population can seamlessly move from one meaningless conversation to another. It is said that extroverts are socially active, are likely to move ahead in their professional lives, and express their feelings easily as compared to introverts. They're often gregarious, full of life and charismatic. And yet I possess little patience for those that feel the need establish dominance when shaking my hand or punching me in the arm like some half-wit orangutan. Certainly not interested in someone bellowing in the back alley after several drinks when I'm trying to focus on my writing.

It's a common perception that extroverts make great first impressions, love being a part of a team, can network easily, and are confident risk takers that speak their mind. Between the open-plan offices and team brainstorming sessions, the workplace is increasingly an extrovert's playground. But the world needs introverts to create and to lead. Introverts are prudent, learn by listening, leverage their quiet nature, demonstrate humility, manage uncertainty, and are comfortable working alone.

To promote learning in the classroom, teachers encourage their students to engage in discussions by asking and answering questions. Many include class participation as part of the overall grade. New curriculum standards favour student-centred, activity-based group projects, and those who argue to work on their own are seen as problem cases. Though an introvert myself, I often forget what it must be like for many of my students who would prefer a quiet place to organize their thoughts rather than having to bring attention to themselves and consistently prove they understand the material with their hands in the air.

When I was a student, I found it difficult to connect with extroverted teachers – especially when they focused all their attention on those who played sports, won trophies, and strutted around in shiny blue basketball shorts. Often wondered why the poets, painters and photographers were not acknowledged in the same way as their athletic counterparts during the morning announcements.

Solitude is a crucial ingredient to creativity, and I always appreciate my time alone in the woods to work out any issues I may be having. But solitude is not celebrated today. Tales of pilgrimage have made way for tales of action, and we continue to invest in those that bark the loudest. How easily we forget that introverts can also successfully ignore the status quo and push for change; the difference is that they have no need for the spotlight and have far less ego. Perhaps the lesson to be learned is that in business, school and politics, the most effective thing can be a whisper in a world that only shouts.

Though I wear the title of introvert proudly, I'm not so sure about defining myself so easily. There were times in my life when I enjoyed the company of others. When I had a group of close friends.

In the three years between my first trip and my solo

excursion, I often wondered about a sense of belonging. Would it be possible to cast off my introverted tendencies if I journeyed to Ireland on my own? Could I engage in long conversations with locals while resting my elbows on worn oak bars? Could I become more confident and outgoing just by willpower alone? Or was this too much to ask? Would I instead wander alone up mountains and along the coastline with nothing but sheep as company?

I knew it wasn't going to be easy to push aside such a significant aspect of my personality. Flying across the Atlantic would do little to change my very nature. But there was a large part of me that wished it was so.

Had I known that one day I would meet a cat (or something that took the form of a cat) at an archeological site in danger of falling into the sea, and she would remind me about my inner authenticity and quote Shakespeare as we looked out towards the promontory, I may not have worried quite so much.

And I wondered if something similar had happened to St. Kevin.

BORN IN 498 TO NOBILITY, it is said that an angel appeared as he was about to be baptized and told his parents that the child should be called Kevin (thus becoming the first person in history to carry the name). Kevin is the Anglicized form of *Caoimhín*, derived from the older Irish *Cóemgein* and composed of the Old Irish elements *cóem* (kind, gentle, handsome) and *gein* (birth). It might be argued, however, that Kevin had a difficult time living up to his name – at least in his relationships with other people.

Apparently, his childhood was marked by a horrible temper and dislike of those around him – although he loved animals – and at the age of seven his parents sent him to a monastery in Cornwall. While there, Kevin kneeled inside a small hut in the wilderness on the first day of Lent. With his arms outstretched in prayer, a blackbird landed in his palm and proceeded to construct a nest. Kevin remained perfectly still, and was fed berries and nuts by the bird. By the end of Lent, the last blackbird hatchlings had flown from the nest and Kevin returned to the monastery.

This only cemented his appreciation of the natural world and, after being ordained to the priesthood, Kevin spent seven years as a hermit in the mountains surrounding Glendalough (*Gleann Dá Loch*). He went barefoot, wore skins, ate random greenery, learned to play the harp in a nearby cave, and spent his time in prayer. It was a lonely life, but a lonely life seemed to suit Kevin.

Blessed with good looks, Kevin unconsciously won the affections of a beautiful maiden named Kathleen who is said to have had 'eyes of the most unholy blue'. Ignoring the fact that he was bound by sacred vows, the bold Kathleen followed Kevin into the woods. Kevin wasn't interested in having anything to do with Kathleen, and to prove it he threw himself into a bed of nettles. He then gathered a handful of burning weeds and scourged the maiden before claiming, "The fire without extinguished the fire within." Great debate rages as to whether Kevin then bravely ran away or attacked fair Kathleen further. Needless to say, the relationship didn't work out.

After seven years in his cave, a farmer named Dima discovered the skin-clad hermit in his hideout when he followed one of his cows that had continually wandered off. It was found that the cow had come to lick the saint's clothes and feet, only to return at evening to produce astonishing amounts of milk. Kevin decided to teach the farmer about Christ and the Gospel, and eventually Dima begged him to come out of isolation and teach his family as well. After a day of prayer, Kevin saw it was God's will that he return to society. He soon began to attract followers. Seeing the need of a central place from which to sermonize, he decided to establish a monastery further up the glen. It was at this new site that Kevin and his monks started to erect the first rough churches, cells and round tower that would make the settlement a centre of pilgrimage.

The charismatic St. Kevin attracted numerous visitors to the area. As word of his holiness spread, Glendalough became the parent of several other monastic foundations and, having firmly established his community, he then retired into solitude for four years. He only returned at the pleading request of his monks. So numerous were his followers that Glendalough became a veritable city in the wild woods of eastern Ireland.

Widely noted though he was, St. Kevin was always a hermit and a pilgrim at heart, and disliked being tied down. He died in 618 (at the age of a hundred twenty) of natural causes. After Kevin's passing, the monastery continued to thrive – expanding into a diocese of over fifty thousand acres that covered most of County Wicklow and parts of Dublin and Kildare. As well as the monastic component, it also had a role in providing pastoral care and scholarship to the wider community.

The history of the monastery after Kevin's death is sketchy but records show Vikings ransacked it on a number of occasions in the ninth and tenth centuries. Despite these attacks, Glendalough thrived as one of Ireland's great ecclesiastical foundations and schools of learning until the Normans destroyed the monastery in 1214 and the dioceses of Glendalough and Dublin were united. Though English forces destroyed the settlement in 1398, Glendalough continued to attract pilgrims on the saint's feast day (June 3) and St. Kevin's Church served as the local parish church. The explosion in interest in the ancient world and the emergence of tourism from the early nineteenth century onwards led to renewed interest in the history and heritage of Glendalough. Today, the area boasts a visitors' centre as well as wooded trails and walkways. Speckled with age, many of the gravestones and tall crosses now fall into each other like flowers that follow the rising sun.

The present remains of the monastic site tell only a small part of the story. It once included workshops, areas for manuscript writing and copying, guesthouses, an infirmary, farm buildings, and dwellings for both the monks and a large lay population. A thirty-meter high round tower still remains, as does the Cathedral of St. Peter and St. Paul, with its tenth-century nave.

Glendalough's trademark is St. Kevin's Kitchen at the southern edge of the monastic site. This compact structure, with a miniature round tower-like belfry, protruding sacristy and steep stone roof, is considered a masterpiece of its time. It was never an actual kitchen, instead getting its name because its belfry resembles a kitchen chimney. The oldest parts of the building date from the eleventh century.

Wicklow is the epitome of the rugged, romantic countryside, and both Paula and I could easily understand why Glendalough continues to be a favourite for those that travel across Ireland. The substantial remains of the important monastic settlement are certainly impressive, but an added draw is the splendid setting: two dark and mysterious lakes tucked into a long, glacial valley fringed in forest. It is, despite its immense popularity, a deeply tranquil and spiritual place. Tourists and travellers alike have little difficulty in understanding why those solitude-seeking monks came here in the first place.

The area is a popular place for day-trippers down from Dublin, and we passed a few as they approached from the opposite direction. But they too acknowledged the need for silence and merely nodded rather than saying anything unnecessary.

The Green Road walk is advertised as an easy stroll along the valley floor to the lower lake, with majestic oaks that dominate the woodland and a boardwalk to explore the wetland and its inhabitants. While the wild Atlantic coast conjures up images of crashing surf over jagged rocks, rugged mountains and landscapes of changing hues, Glendalough promises to still the mind, inspire the heart, and fill the soul with its dark forests, lush greenery, cascading streams and calm lakes.

It was as the upper lake came into view that we were reminded that sometimes the sounds of silence are the most essential aspects of a life worth living.

Those that write about Glendalough beyond the monastic ruins tend to keep their descriptions brief, for its beauty transcends words. I too found it difficult to compose anything meaningful as the voices in my head were struck silent. Dark, shadowy trees rose from the soft earth and the sun drew out the bronze and golden hues buried deep in the dank soil. Blanket bog, spongy heath, deciduous woods, coniferous plantations, cliffs, lakes and rivers provide habitat for the birds that call out to each other. While strolling past the myriad of verdant greens, we could understand when Kevin decided to spend much of his life here.

After photographing the Poulanass Waterfall – where the waters carve its way as broken beams of light reflect the blanket of greenery that covers the sleeping earth like a soft thin sheet – we tried to locate (from a safe distance) the small cave in which Kevin spent his life as a hermit. What is now known as Kevin's Bed may have been a Bronze Age tomb and is difficult to access, and therefore not encouraged for the random tourist with a trail map folded in their back pocket.

Kevin later built a circular hut of which only a few stones now remain. After we both stood in silence – lost in our own thoughts on the impermanence of life – we headed back.

On the way, we sat at a weathered picnic bench next to a take-away stand where a decent selection of greasy goodness awaits the hungry traveller. Ordered the curry chips and tea.

Later that evening, after stopping to watch the Avonmore and Avonbeg rivers combine to form the River Avoca, and sitting under the same tree that Thomas Moore had when he composed his famous poem, we found a local fish 'n' chips place for dinner. It was an anticlimactic ending to a full day of adventuring, but we didn't mind.

CHAPTER 26

A PLACE OF OTHERNESS

As early afternoon became late afternoon, I took one final drive around the end of the peninsula and passed many of the sites from earlier in the week. Approaching Ventry, an open sign next to a large stone house – painted yellow with purple trim – piqued my curiosity. Thought it was another converted teahouse, and was about to drive by, when I noticed a sign advertising the Celtic & Prehistory Museum. Imagined it to be nothing more than a small collection of trinkets lined up along someone's fireplace mantle, but my guidebook recommended a visit. Parked the car, adjusted my cap, and walked inside.

Not only does the museum house Ireland's only intact wooly mammoth skull (with its tusks still attached), it also contains a large nest of dinosaur eggs, a complete baby dinosaur skeleton, and a cave bear skeleton. Also on display are tools, weapons and other artifacts from the Jurassic, Stone Age, Bronze Age, Celtic and Viking eras. The guidebook also mentioned a little gift shop featuring fossils, crafts, jewelry, antiques and other unusual gifts.

What the guidebook didn't mention was the family of four clogging the foyer. Abrasive American speech patterns echoed all around me as the children raced around without any regard for others. They headed towards the darker rooms that house the Celtic and Viking displays, so I disappeared towards the prehistory exhibits. There was no one at the front desk to take my money. Figured I would pay the entry fee when someone returned to their post.

The Romanian cave bear skeleton gave me pause and, with its large black, circular tusks that would have aided in battle or assisted in foraging the hard ground, the wooly mammoth skull (pulled out of a fishing net in 1999) is an impressive piece.

The Stone Age hand axes used for butchering, skinning and digging are fascinating, as are the early farm tools and goddess figurines from the Early Bronze Age. Reflected on what I had seen at Brú na Bóinne and marvelled at the early spiral art of the early Hallstatt and La Tène cultures. Several pieces incorporated or celebrated the number three – either three knobs or three heads or three arms – much in the same way that there were three spirals featured in the Neolithic art at Newgrange.

There are circular Saxon and Viking artifacts that celebrated the sky and the sun, as well as several animal totems of owls, boars and stags. Unlike the massive collections in many museums, the small rooms here are manageable. Though many of the pieces are less to do with Ireland as a country, and more to do with the people that would later influence Irish culture, I was glad to have stopped and looked around.

At the gift shop, I caught up with the loud American family who seemed to be spending more time deciding what to purchase than they had in the museum itself.

"Look at this, Shirley. Over here," the husband thundered. "There's authentic Celtic coins for sale. A whole basket of them. How can I pass on something like that? That is a unique thing. You don't see that every day."

"No, you certainly do not," agreed the equally loud wife as the children continued to run around the displays. Suspect I hadn't seen the owner because he was hiding. Wanted desperately to join him.

It was only later that I realized that the American family was a blessing in disguise. They reminded me what a typical tourist does in Ireland: relying on GPS or sat-nav, and swinging their selfie sticks in small spaces; eating in chain restaurants and complaining about paying a couple euros to see "a bunch of old rocks"; or parading through gift shops and looking for tokens of a country without any real sense of its history or culture.

While sifting through the same coins that the husband had fawned over minutes before, I hoped that somehow – through my solo adventures – I had shifted from tourist to traveller. Though hardly a brave explorer, in any sense of the word, I wondered if by subjecting myself to some mild form of adventure and becoming lost on several occasions I was able to at least scratch the surface of a country whose history teaches resilience, traditional language provides wit and wisdom, struggles give strength, and culture provides independence of mind.

Hoped that by scouring through dog-eared texts, scratching notes in a flurry of fingers, sitting on cold stones until my butt went numb, and conversing with whatever animal or spirit shared my path, I had shown my 'willingness to be part of the Irish Nation'.

Hoped that I would later be able to capture my experiences on the page. The best thing about travel writing is the travelling, and the worst thing is the writing, but I looked forward to unravelling the magic and mystery of the country while losing myself in the world of words – revisiting the wild shores, mist-covered mountains and warm pubs.

After finding the owner of the museum soon after the American family left, and paying him the entrance fee, I headed back into Dingle.

A few minutes later, it dawned on me that I'd be leaving the following morning. A wave of melancholy caused my vision to blur. Perhaps it was the haunting melody of oceanic blue that caused me to turn inwards. While looking out towards the ever-changing Irish Sea, I thought of my wife and the first moment I lay eyes on her.

She had stepped out of a floatplane and onto the small dock of the First Nations fishing village where I was teaching. Over the next couple days, we walked along the water's edge and around the community. We had dinner together, and then talked about everything and nothing as night fell. Couldn't put into words what I felt, but knew it was the beginning of something special – something that would change my life for the better and never let go.

Maybe I'm a hopeless romantic, or maybe it's something else, but Ireland will forever be a part of me in the same way that Paula will forever be a part of me. Whatever I end up doing in this life, I will always have a place in this world that feels like home – a place to embrace the quiet, watch the turning of the tide, and listen to the spirits; where I can walk into the fog and drift from one world into the next without really knowing where I am or how much time has passed; where I can stroll into a pub to knock down a pint or two by the fire, and then stumble into bed somewhere (up a hill, probably) with traditional music playing in my ears.

Some readers might remind me that there's a massive difference between visiting a place for a week or two and living there long enough to experience all aspects of the culture (including the darker days of winter), but I couldn't deny the connection I felt. Couldn't deny the overwhelming sense of peace and contentment that washed over me every morning as I watched the fog dissipate, and every evening when the world became flooded in colour.

Before Dingle Town closed up, I had one final scoop of ice cream and chatted with the young man who so enthusiastically detailed the making of small-batch frozen treats. Touched base with Mazz at the record shop to let her know that I had survived the horse ride. Popped into the bookstore and picked out a thin volume of poetry. Bought a couple pins for my backpack and a t-shirt at Strand House. Sat on a bench outside Paudie's Bar and a corgi came waddling along to join me. Together we looked out as the sun fell further into the harbour.

Later that night, spent some time at O'Sullivan's and, rather than having to scream, "I'll! Have! A pint! Of Guinness!" over the noise of the pub, I merely nodded to the man behind the bar and was presented with my drink. An hour-and-a-half later, the music still playing in my ears, walked back up the hill one last time, fighting gravity and looking up at the stars that were laid out like a warm blanket. Turned around to catch one final glimpse of the lights of *Daingean Uí Chúis* – a place of stories and laughter, of music and fireplaces and well-poured pints. Passed farmhouses and rolling fields until I finally fumbled with the key in the lock, making more noise than I should, and then tiptoed down the hall and into my room. Didn't so much fall asleep but pass out with a smile on my face.

After my final breakfast at Dúinín House, I sat in my room and looked out the window at the slow rhythm of rural Ireland. Mindlessly packed one thing at a time into my suitcase, trying to delay the inevitable as the morning light illuminated the patchwork green of nearby rolling hills through thin clouds. A gentle wind blew off the mountains and towards town. Checked the bathroom in case I had forgotten anything, then the wall sockets for power cords and around the bed for laundry.

Though I had made the most of each day – punctuating horse rides and dolphin tours with quiet walks in the mist; balancing record stores, bookstores and ice cream shops with pilgrimage trails and archeological sites; engaging in friendly conversation and tossing back pints while listening to traditional music; warming my frozen nose and fingers after escaping the Atlantic winds – I also felt as if I had only experienced a small fraction of what the Dingle Peninsula has to offer.

Saudade is a Portuguese expression that is almost untranslatable. It's been described as the 'presence of absence' – a melancholic longing or deep yearning for something (or someone). It is the awareness of absence, especially for that which will never be experienced again. A profoundly bittersweet nostalgia that puts one in a deep emotional state of sadness. A form of homesickness.

I never fully comprehended the meaning of *saudade* until I closed my suitcase and piled my belongings at the door. While excited to see my family and share my experiences, I was not looking forward to once again feeling like a stranger in a familiar land.

Spending time in Ireland is like disappearing into literature. The reader discovers that their longings are universal longings, that they are not alone and isolated, and that they belong. During my time in West Kerry, I had become accustomed to a sense of belonging – of being enveloped by a history and mythology that spoke to my soul – and now I had to leave. Felt open and vulnerable and connected, but also guided and comforted by that which cannot easily be explained. Wasn't sure if I would ever feel that way again. Already I yearned to return into what Thoreau called the 'dew-cloth, dream drapery'.

A few minutes later, I said my goodbyes to Pat and Anne, threw my suitcase into the trunk, strapped myself into the rental car, and hit the open road.

"You're flustered and you're hungry," I told myself after spending the night outside Avoca. "Pull over, eat your weird sandwich of indeterminate flavour, and you'll be able to focus again."

"Fine," I replied while reaching over to the passenger seat. "I will."

The lady of the house had offered to prepare a snack since I'd be heading out before breakfast. Wasn't sure if it had been at the bottom of the banister all night but grabbed it anyway, just in case.

Had left early so I'd have plenty of time to top up the tank before returning the rental car and checking in at the airport. Unfortunately, there didn't seem to be a convenient gas station directly off the highway, so I pulled into a suburban town on the outskirts of Dublin. Got lost, of course.

Luckily, the sandwich did the trick. Ate it in three bites, took several deep breaths, and was able to think straight. It still took me close to an hour to weave in and out through the busier neighbourhoods – and it's possible I made a few illegal U-turns – but arrived at the car rental office with lots of time to spare. Half-an-hour later, a helpful airline employee printed my ticket and weighed my checked baggage. It was 0.1 kilograms under the limit. (Wool sweaters are heavy.)

Sitting in the waiting area, all I could think about was everything there wasn't time for. So many places to explore and experiences to be had – still so many strange animals to talk to, and haunting whispers from the world beyond, and glorious sunsets and cozy pubs scattered across the country. One day I will return to visit Skellig Michael and Inis Mór, and spend a night or two on the Great Blasket Island while listening to nothing but the wild Atlantic as the seabirds ride the trade winds and the grey seals come to shore.

Perhaps one day I will take part in Wren's Day celebrations (or at least watch from the side-lines). Cup in my hand the exquisite fuchsia flowers (known throughout the peninsula as *Deora Dé* – or tears of God) as I hike the Saints' Path in its entirety. Attend countless free lectures and workshops, or assist in archeological digs, or take summer classes in the Irish language and get beyond just *dia dhuit* (hello) and *slán go fóill* (bye for now).

Irish poet Nuala Ní Dhomhnaill once wrote that 'Irish is a language of enormous elasticity and emotional sensitivity; of quick and hilarious banter and a welter of references both historical and mythological; it is an instrument of imaginative depth and scope, which has been tempered by the community for generations until it can pick and sing out every hint of emotional modulation that can occur between people. Many international scholars rhapsodize that this speech of ragged peasants seems always on the point of bursting into poetry.'

Not so sure about the 'ragged peasants' comment, but she does make a strong argument for learning the endangered language. So does UNESCO. They estimate that, if nothing is done, half of the nearly seven thousand languages spoken today will disappear by the end of the century. Will Irish (*Gaeilge*) be one of them?

Later, while sitting at my desk in the comforts of home, I was able to begin the long process of reflection. One dark and stormy night, as something ominous weighed heavily over the valley, I flipped through my journal – pages of short phrases, poetic ramblings and rough sketches. Nothing made much sense or had any structure.

Safe from the thunderous rain and howling winds, I sipped a bit of whiskey, nibbled on a bit of cheese, and looked over at the cats. Molly slept on the windowsill and Bella on a folded blanket next to me, and waited patiently for some soft thoughts to solidify while ambling through the landscape of my mind.

Ireland isn't so much a place of prose but of poetry. Robert Frost once remarked, 'Every poem is a momentary stay against the confusion of the world.' So too are those places that ignite an all-consuming fire. Those places that feel like home, and yet maintain a certain amount of mystery and magic in every moment.

Naturally, I am not the only one that has fled to Ireland to find poetic refuge. Thomas Cahill tells the story of how Europe evolved from the classical age of Rome to the medieval era in his book *How the Irish Saved Civilization*. Without Ireland, the author argues, the transition could not have taken place. Not only did Irish monks and scribes maintain the very record of Western civilization – copying manuscripts of Greek and Latin writers, both pagan and Christian, while libraries and learning on the continent were forever lost – they brought their uniquely Irish worldview to the task. When the seeds of culture were replanted on the European continent, it was from Ireland that they were germinated.

We may never know whether Ireland became the land of saints and scholars because of Patrick's evangelization, or because of its openness and interest in competing ideas, or because of its remote location, but it certainly became an asylum for those with a burning desire to capture Truth and Beauty in the written word.

"One of the things that I think poetry does," said American poet Ellen Bass, "is help us to see our personal experience as part of the human experience, and this is especially needed in times of personal crisis."

Writing about my adventures and misadventures, I constantly stole quiet moments to stand in front of my growing poetry collection and read from those that had been captivated by the spectrum of silence before me.

Former Poet Laureate Billy Collins once wrote, 'A poem is an interruption of silence, whereas prose is a continuation of noise.' It was through the act of reading poetry and occasionally writing it, that I finally understood what aspect of Ireland had the biggest impact on me. It wasn't the way history and myth seamlessly interlace with each other – though I certainly appreciated that. Wasn't even the blurring between the two realms that allowed me to be vulnerable and open. What had ultimately guided me and comforted me during my time in Ireland was silence.

Many of us are constantly bombarded by artificial noise. It has become the accepted norm and, therefore silence – once we are finally given the opportunity to be within it – can be frightening. We're afraid of silence because we equate it with insignificance. We want to be seen and heard, and to make ourselves relevant. But in our quest to be noticed, and thought well of by others, we often drown out our inner voice. Even small doses of meditation can force us to confront ourselves, and sometimes what we find staring back is nothing but emptiness.

The assumption for many is that the quiet is out there, just beyond our reach. Make it to the end of the day or the week or summer break or retirement. Margaritas and warm sandy beaches. But the peace we seek is not out there somewhere. It's here, now, in this moment – within all of us. Silence helps bring us back to a place of rest and clarity within. We can see and hear things we otherwise wouldn't, and our desires become few and simple. If we are lucky, we find our inner voice of contentment and realize we're already everything we need to be.

I attended a conference in Vancouver recently with almost a thousand other teachers. After signing in, I sat alone with my bad coffee and fake bacon and stared off into the empty abyss. Perfectly content to work out some ideas in my head over breakfast, allowing the morning to unfold at a rate conducive to self-reflection. But other teachers with far too much enthusiasm thought I was lonely or shy and skipped over to sit next to me for some peppy small talk in the windowless room. Didn't bother to tell them that I had no burning desire to fill my immediate space with senseless chatter and was perfectly comfortable with silence. Maybe I should have.

Though Ireland is often associated with pints of black stuff and nights of drunken debauchery – where streams of whiskey are flowing, and locals are endowed with the gift of the gab, and there's mighty *craic* to be had at any time of the day or night – there is another aspect of the country kept secret from those that spread cultural stereotypes. Ireland may be a nation synonymous with drinking, yet drunken hooliganism is not as prevalent as it is in other parts of the Western world. While pubs host lively conversation and traditional music, the Irish still respect the quiet of the night. No one feels the need to draw attention to themselves – hooting and hollering, and revving truck engines like silly peacocks on parade.

Those that have an intimate knowledge of silence understand that our deepest human relationships with it will cause us to not only understand our true self, but also put us in tune with any higher power that may exist. For the religious, silence offers a way to ponder and listen for the divine. Early (and modern-day) Christians, for example, commonly chose silence because of a belief in a god who speaks. Silence, for them, was often a retreat from worldliness and the inauthentic.

American poet Adrienne Rich once wrote, 'The impulse to create begins – often terribly and fearfully – in a tunnel of silence.'

I didn't journey to Ireland to search out the divine or have any sort of revelation. Never imagined I would come to understand the 'presence of absence' or take the first few steps towards a connected consciousness. Certainly didn't come to see myself reflected in the void. But through my travels, and my willingness to be comforted by the silence, I learned to be open and vulnerable. Learned to confront my issue with intimacy, and slip into a sense of shared universal existence. Learned to listen and to write.

It was Ireland that helped me to understand the exquisite power of silence. While there were certainly moments of joy (and even clarity) in the crowded pubs, it felt as if I were given permission to spend my days unapologetically alone, and not feel like some sort of solitary oddity. Didn't need to be a social person to fit in. There was no need to push myself too far outside my comfort zone.

There were clues all along, but I was either rushing from one place to another (often with my head in a guidebook) or trying to get un-lost and un-trampled.

While attempting to unravel the mystery of my connection to the history and mythology, I gave little thought about whether there was any kind of unseen power that was guiding me along. Never gave pause as to what force had taken my hand so that I might find my way again.

It was silence that allowed me to sit with the orange tabby cat as the first beams of sun slowly washed the world in an amber glow and reflected off the outer wall of Newgrange. Silence that allowed me to stand transfixed by the ancient carvings and reflect on my internal chamber. Silence that allowed me feel the distance between heaven and earth collapse when I stood inside the five-thousand-year-old passage tomb to hear the whispers of the ancient people that prayed for light to defeat darkness and bring the world back into balance.

Silence that guided me when Paula and I explored archeological sites, monastic settlements, and cemeteries. It was there as I ruminated on all those that had stopped to place their hands on the cold stone, feel the earth move, and understand the impermanence of life. It was there at

Clonmacnoise, when I acknowledged my need for a sacred space. It was there in the hills of Connemara, and at the Cliffs of Moher, and in the Burren. It was there as we explored the grounds at Blarney and huddled for warmth at the Rock of Cashel.

Silence was there at Glendalough. While there may have been the trickling of streams, the lapping of lakes, the calling of birds, and the whistling of winds, there was also an absence – a delicious absence of us. And it was within this absence that everything became a source of light.

It was during my solo adventures, however, that silence lifted me and carried me: whether huddled in the corners of Kilmalkedar or standing alone at the small stone houses on the edge of the world. At the top of Mt. Brandon, where I connected to the natural elements. The one warm line of all those that had come before me and all those that would follow. Of that which is no longer – the beauty of what isn't there and the space between – while standing inside the circular enclosure at Kilcolman. Witnessing the battle of a thousand hues of blue at Inch Beach. Enveloped in the absence of colour while walking to the schoolhouse. Slipping unseen between the two realms. Staring out at the inky blackness of the Atlantic at the pier at Dunquin, and investigating the ruins of Rahinnane Castle, and when reflecting on the passing of time at Fahan and the Gallarus Oratory.

Conversing with the *cait sidhe* – discussing my inner authenticity, my resistance and doubt, and the golden threads that connect all of us to everything and everyone.

It was there when I stumbled up the hill and into bed at Dúinín House, the stars shining above me. When all seemed possible.

The juxtaposition of Irish culture draws more than ten

million visitors a year to its rugged shores. They come for the pubs, castles and ancient sites. The pony rides, dolphin sightings and high-caloric breakfasts. They come to drive narrow winding roads, kiss stones, and walk among forty shades of green. Don't blame them. Did all those things. And loved it.

But ultimately what I found so captivating was the intensity of silence that permeates Ireland. It is not so much an absence of sound, but the presence of something that is *not* sound. A place of otherness.

Now, when asked why I have such a strong connection to the country, I answer succinctly. "It is the silence. Only this and nothing more."

It's not true, of course, but I like confusing people and walking away. Perhaps that's the Irish in me.

AFTERWORD

It's been eight years since my solo adventure. Eight years since my awkward journey from small-town Canada to small-town Ireland. Landing in the country with sour-smelling jeans. Falling awkwardly into the driver's seat. Knocking back day-old bread with lukewarm tea. Getting lost and lost again. With a coiled map book. A posted detour. A random encounter with local wildlife. And then waking up as gentle sunlight poured in through the windows of Dúinín House.

If I could transport myself – Star Trek style – and beam into Dingle right now, I'd find the town much like I remember it: the pubs, the bookstore, the record shop, the ice cream place, the fishing boats, and all the tourist tat. I'd still get misplaced and turned around, but eventually I'd stumble upon the archeological sites, the quiet beaches and the narrow paths that weave from one world, into the other, and then back again.

Gosh, what I wouldn't give for just a day on the peninsula. I'd wake up early, tiptoe down the hallway, drive down the road in a rental car, and sit on cold stone at

Kilmalkedar before breakfast. Devour a plate of fried meat and freshly baked bread, and then explore to my heart's content.

Would I ride an elderly pony to the top of Ballymacadoyle Hill again? Or go looking for the *cait sidhe* at Dunbeg Fort so we could continue where we left off all those years ago? Heck, yeah. Wouldn't you?

I'd climb Mount Brandon, but maybe pack a bit more food. And then walk along Inch Beach after purchasing another sweater and scarf. Stroll to the lighthouse and the pier at Dunquin. Maybe visit the Celtic & Prehistory Museum. Buy the coin. Just because. And then I'd check out the sandwich boards in front of the pubs, and hopefully see Méabh's name scrawled across in chalk. A pint or two. Who am I kidding? Half a dozen. Stumble up the hill under a blanket of stars.

All that and so much more. Finally visit the Blasket Islands. Probably get seasick, but that's okay. Browse the books at An Café Liteartha. Find some expensive tome on Ogham stones or the history of the Saints' Path. Sample the offerings at the Dingle Distillery. The fluttering of caramelized apple, raisins and vanilla.

But, of course, no town stays the same. Change is inevitable. Some of the teashops and pubs have either closed their doors or have expanded. The Cúl Gáirdín Café Gallery is no more. Gone are the totem poles and tikki heads. O'Sullivan's Courthouse Pub now hosts the occasional evening of Texas barbecue: briskets, smoked sausages, pulled pork, and homemade salsas. Not against the idea. Better that than fish 'n' chips.

In other news, it turns out that there is now a decent cappuccino to be had. Apparently, Bean in Dingle is the place to go.

Sadly, Fungie no longer frolics in the waters of Dingle Bay. In October 2020, there was growing concern for his welfare after he had gone missing for several days. By mid-month, marine experts declared that he had either moved on to new waters, or simply passed away. Reported sightings by the general public after that were dismissed as 'well-intentioned, but incorrect'.

Eight years on, my fingerless gloves the colour of seaweed are still holding strong. They've been stitched up a few times and now sport bits of grey, green and blue. After saving my pocket money, I ordered a beautiful pendant from Brian de Staic's jewelry shop. The alphabet stone at Kilmalkedar in sterling silver. Wearing it right now.

But of course, frayed wool and a bit of silver aren't the only changes that have occurred in my life. My children are now grown-ups and are no longer interested in snow globes featuring mildly offensive preposterous-looking leprechauns. One has left home; the other will soon follow. Those of you that have read the afterword to my previous book, *Frankincense Land: A Canadian Family in the Sultanate of Oman*, will know that Paula and I are no longer together. We currently live only a kilometre apart, but some days that seems like a far greater distance. I can no longer rely on her amazing sense of direction or her ability to find a sick bag in the blink of an eye. But I'm so grateful for those amazing days we shared in Ireland. And I'm so grateful for our entire life together. All the adventures and misadventures. So much love and beauty and laughter.

The events in my first travel memoir take place in my twenties. The events of this one take place in my thirties. Now, at the age of forty-five – in the company of Cherie and our ridiculous cats – I see the world and my place in it differently than before. The magic I found in Ireland allowed me to find the magic at home. Sitting at the base of cedar trees or placing my hand on the trunk of yew trees. Asking the universe for guidance as I traipse through the coastal and interior rainforests. A small offering of tobacco or a piece of quartz or sunflower seeds for the squirrels. Sacred reciprocity for all those seen and unseen. Finding peace and forgiveness. But that is another story and shall be told another time.

About the Author

The author of *Frankincense Land: A Canadian Family in the Sultanate of Oman* and two volumes of *Life, in a Nutshell,* Chris Brauer lives with his girlfriend in southeastern British Columbia – on the traditional unceded territory of the yaqan nuʔkiy. He splits his time between teaching elementary school and writing random musings on social media. Chris enjoys wearing wool sweaters, listening to jazz, travelling to far and distant lands, and arguing with his cats.

Manufactured by Amazon.ca
Bolton, ON

33024745R00175